CASES AND MAPS

CASES AND MAPS

A Christian Introduction to Philosophy

MARK COPPENGER

Illustrations by
CHAD NUSS and HARRISON WATTERS

WIPF & STOCK · Eugene, Oregon

CASES AND MAPS
A Christian Introduction to Philosophy

Copyright © 2019 Mark Coppenger. All rights reserved. Except for brief quotations in critical publications or reviews, no part of this book may be reproduced in any manner without prior written permission from the publisher. Write: Permissions, Wipf and Stock Publishers, 199 W. 8th Ave., Suite 3, Eugene, OR 97401.

Scripture quotations, unless otherwise noted, are from the New King James Version,® copyright © 1982 by Thomas Nelson. Used by permission. All rights reserved.

Wipf & Stock
An Imprint of Wipf and Stock Publishers
199 W. 8th Ave., Suite 3
Eugene, OR 97401

www.wipfandstock.com

PAPERBACK ISBN: 978-1-5326-5544-9
HARDCOVER ISBN: 978-1-5326-5545-6
EBOOK ISBN: 978-1-5326-5546-3

Manufactured in the U.S.A.   OCTOBER 21, 2019

Contents

Preface | vii
Acknowledgements | xi
Introduction | xv

Cases | 1

    The Trial of Socrates (*perils of philosophy*) | 3
    Robertson v. Oelschlaeger (*domain of philosophy*) | 7
    Aronow v. U.S. (*meaning; political philosophy*) | 13
    Brancusi v. U.S. (*definition of art*) | 18
    The Case of Armin Meiwes (*civil liberties*) | 22
    Gleitman v. Cosgrove (*sanctity of life*) | 26
    Katko v. Briney (*action*) | 30
    Kitzmiller v. Dover Area School District (*intelligent design*) | 35
    McGuinn v. Clarke (*personal identity*) | 41
    Naruto v. Slater (*animal rights; friendship*) | 46
    Owen v. Crumbaugh (*rationality*) | 51
    People v. Elmer (*time*) | 55
    People v. Nathan F. Leopold Jr. and Richard Loeb (*justice*) | 60
    People of the State of California v. Orenthal James Simpson (*proof*) | 65
    Ranieri v. Ranieri (*speech acts*) | 70
    Repouille v. U.S. (*character*) | 76
    Robbie v. City of Miami (*problem of evil*) | 81
    State v. One "Jack and Jill" Pinball Machine (*value*) | 86
    U.S. v. Causby (*space*) | 91
    Whistler v. Ruskin (*aesthetic quality*) | 95
    White-Smith Music Publishing Company v. Apollo Company (*ontology*) | 99
    Worcester v. State of Georgia (*law; property rights*) | 102

Maps | 107

    The Assad/Nusra/ISIS/Kurd Map (*truth; postmodernism*) | 109
    Auto Assembly Line (*existentialism*) | 113
    The 1:1 Scale Map (*universals*) | 117
    Backstage (*personhood*) | 121
    The Cineplex (*pre-established harmony*) | 126
    Eastern Kentucky Coal Mine (*epistemology*) | 130
    Four Corners (*causation*) | 133
    The Land of Crest (*philosophical fictions*) | 137
    The London Tube (*pragmatism*) | 140
    Madrid's Art Museums (*the arts*) | 145
    Mount Peck (*naming*) | 149
    New London Channel (*Golden Mean*) | 154
    Outsized Texas (*Categorical Imperative*) | 158
    The Oxbow River (*dialectic*) | 162
    Palestine (*logical positivism*) | 166
    Pineal Gland (*dualism*) | 170
    Prester John (*logic*) | 174
    The Progressive Treasure Map (*faith*) | 179
    The Strip Map (*phenomenal/noumenal distinction*) | 182
    Strongpoint Defense (*paradigms*) | 186
    The T and O Map (*medievalism*) | 190
    The Upside-Down World Map (*morals*) | 194
    Weather Map Copies (*foundationalism*) | 198

Index of Names | 203
Index of Scripture | 207

Preface

As we were turning out onto the highway for a family trip when I was in junior high school, the conversation turned somehow to Marxist philosophy and "dialectical materialism." These weren't typical topics, but my father did teach philosophy at Ouachita Baptist College (now University), and I may have asked him about what he'd been covering that week. He wasn't a philosopher by training. He had a seminary degree, and, with the G.I. Bill (earned as a naval chaplain in the South Pacific in WWII), he'd gotten a doctorate in church history from the University of Edinburgh. As was often the case in Christian colleges, the administration turned to the religion department for help with philosophy, and my dad was drafted. Along the way, he did supplementary work in philosophy at George Washington University and the University of Colorado, and so, along with Greek, New Testament, church history, and such, he took on a variety of philosophical courses. And it was in this context that the conversation made some sense.

In this brief exchange, I also picked up something about a *Communist Manifesto* and the *bourgeoisie* and his lack of enthusiasm for this ideological perspective. But I was intrigued by the vocabulary and the big things in play. Perhaps it was at this point that the hook was set, the time from which I was drawn to the study of philosophy—on through college, graduate school, and teaching assignments in both college and seminary.

I headed off to Vanderbilt for the PhD, where I majored in epistemology. But I took courses all over the place, little knowing that I would teach a version of many of them down the line, including aesthetics, symbolic logic, philosophy of science, Plato, and ethical theory. As my degree neared completion, one of my profs (John Lachs, whom I had for German idealism) asked me to join him in a Vanderbilt-based program in community education, with a focus on human rights, funded by the National Endowment

Preface

for the Humanities, and so, over two years in that work, I absorbed a lot of normative ethics.

One of the best (yet, at that moment, most frustrating) class sessions was my very first. Richard Ketchum was teaching Plato, and I'd bought my big Princeton/Bollingen volume of the ancient's collected works. I assumed that I would fill my notebook with pages of explication, preparing me to talk about Plato in courses throughout my life. But Professor Ketchum spent an entire class period on a couple of paragraphs in the *Theaetetus*, wrestling with us over the question of whether Plato had gotten things right. I did the math, and it became clear to me that, at this rate, we'd not get through the *Theaetetus*, much less the other dialogues. Besides, how in the world could I use the notes, such as they were? We'd try one idea and then another; back up and clarify and then shoot down the clarification; pose counterexamples and then toss out reformulations—all herky-jerky, with no firm resolution. What sort of future lecture could I get out of that!

Then it hit me that we were there to *do* philosophy, not admire or disparage it from a safe distance. And even though Plato was long dead, we were supposed to treat him as present to us in the classroom as an interlocutor to be taken seriously. And the same sort of experience repeated itself in many of my courses. I think, for instance, of Clement Dore, from whom I took epistemology in my first semester (and who became my dissertation advisor). We were each to prepare a paper for classroom presentation, and I took on a chapter in Alvin Plantinga's *God and Other Minds*, one of our texts. I sawed and hammered and painted the best I could and then brought my little bird house to class for scrutiny. At the end of my presentation, Professor Dore granted a little, but didn't find a key premise plausible, so that was that.

I went back to my apartment and straight to bed without eating. I was a failure and had been exposed as a philosophical fraud. But then, at around eight, an older graduate student, John Robert Baker, called to make sure I wasn't discouraged. He told me he'd had a similar jolt when reading his first graduate paper, and he was somewhat dashed back then. But he discovered that this happened to everybody, and such was the rough and tumble of philosophy. He assured me that I did just fine, and, thanking him, I got up and fixed supper. In the parlance of Bob Dylan in the day, he comforted me with the message, "I would not feel so all alone; everybody must get stoned" (and not in the drug sense).

Preface

I suppose it's something of an acquired taste, but that taste I surely acquired, and, in this book, I'm happy to commend the tasting to others. In this book, you won't find anything near a full meal of this or that dish, but rather a buffet or tapas, with a little of this and a little of that. And then come the discussion questions, which should help put you in the soup.

Of course, it's both commonplace and sane for parents to fear their children's first exposure to philosophy at the college level, for there is much that is ungodly and anti-godly in play there (a topic we address in the first case, the one with Socrates), but there is a great heritage and current fellowship of believers wading into the fray without flinching and with warranted aplomb. I trust that the cases will underscore the dialogical and disputational character of philosophy and that the maps will enforce the notion that philosophies are supposed to alert you to the terrain and point the way to places you might go, for better or worse, depending upon the sense of the philosopher.

Acknowledgements

I'm especially grateful for the work of my illustrators, Chad Nuss and Harrison Watters, both of them students at Southern Baptist Theological Seminary, where I teach. They bring different styles to their work, and both approaches serve this book well. Chad did the bulk of them—thirty out of forty-five—and Harrison pitched in fifteen as we got closer to publication (for Robertson, Aronow, Katko, Naruto, Leopold and Loeb, Ranieri, Robbie, Jack and Jill, Backstage, Madrid, Mount Peck, New London, Pineal Gland, Prester John, and Weather Map).

Here's a look at these men, through self-portraits and small bio sketches:

Acknowledgements

Chad Nuss, illustrator

Mr. Nuss earned an undergraduate degree in illustration and design from the Ontario College of Art and Design in Toronto, Ontario, and an MDiv from Southern Baptist Theological Seminary, where has done further study on the use of comic books in evangelism. He is also writing and drawing a science fiction graphic novel called *The Silence*, which uses the comic book genre to address philosophical, worldview, and religious issues. Mr. Nuss regularly posts new artwork, illustrations, and comic book pages on his website: www.thesilencecomics.com.

ACKNOWLEDGEMENTS

Harrison Watters, illustrator

Harrison Watters is studying politics, philosophy, and economics at Boyce College in Louisville, Kentucky, with the goal of doing Christian culture-shaping of some sort in the future. For now, he does illustration work through his homegrown business, StoryMaking Studio, and works as a podcast technician for oGoLead, a leadership training company founded by former Yum! Brands CEO David Novak. You can access the range of his work at https://harrisonwatters.myportfolio.com.

I also want to thank my colleague Ted Cabal and recent SBTS PhDs, Chris Bolt, Eric Williamson, Tawa Anderson, and Paul Wilkinson for helpful comments as I neared submission of the manuscript. Thanks are also due to my son-in-law, Jeremy Broggi, who did some legal research for me. And, as always, Sharon, my wife of forty-eight years, was my sounding board and encourager.

Introduction

It is commonly thought that philosophy is a hopelessly abstract and even useless discipline (one whose majors can count on careers as cab drivers and baristas, though, of course, we're grateful for both). Well, certainly, degrees in philosophy don't translate as immediately into job opportunities as do degrees in secondary education, criminal justice, or hospitality management. But, as we would say, sincerely, to prospective majors at Wheaton (where I taught full-time from 1975 to 1981 and where I taught as an adjunct in the early 2000s while a pastor in Evanston), philosophy would prepare them well to pick up on a range of vocational interests, from law to medicine to business to the military to the ministry. The ability to address big questions; to tackle difficult texts and craft clear, critical summaries; and to doggedly scrutinize arguments for either value or disappointment: these were the things that would stand them in good stead wherever they went to work. (All true, but with the caveat that ideological sophistry, often purveyed in philosophy departments, can make you a bigger fool than you were when you entered . . . but more on that later.)

About halfway through my Wheaton professorship, I came to a new understanding of the extensive pertinence of philosophy to every corner of culture and public policy. It had been clear in ethics, where we wrangled with the morality of such pressing matters as the recently concluded Vietnam War and the recently legalized practice of abortion. But as I prepared to teach a course in bioethics, I discovered the riches of a law library. While finding my way around one nearby, learning how to find important and engaging cases on euthanasia, medical records privacy, informed consent to surgery, and such, I discovered that everything we covered in our other courses was in play in the courts. And so the idea of opening discussions with cases came to mind; hence, the first twenty-two chapters of this book.

I should add that it's frustrating to leave out so many good cases, and a new one entices me every week. For instance, a few days ago, I rewatched

Introduction

The Exorcism of Emily Rose, based on the German trial of a priest convicted of diagnosing a young woman's fatal malady as spiritual rather physical. (Her name was Anneliese Michel in real life.) There was talk about whether the state should recognize the possibility that demons (not epileptic seizures) were the source of her torment, an issue ripe for both philosophical and theological discussion. My first impulse was to contact one of my illustrators for a drawing and to get to work on another piece with discussion questions. But time is up. Still, I'd encourage the reader to put on philosophical glasses when reading through the news, for the angles I highlight in this book are everywhere.

Similarly, I've been frustrated by the fact that I've left out so many philosophers and schools of thought and concepts. The content of the courses I've taken and taught come back to haunt me as I bring this work to a close. Where is the piece on Pythagoras, Rousseau, Bergson, Merleau-Ponty, Whitehead, Adorno, or Quine? Where are treatments of hylozoism, neo-Platonism, the *via negativa*, the Gettier problem, the Kalam argument? Alas, again, this would need to be material for a longer book.

And, yes, I'm aware of the volumes and schools of Eastern philosophy not covered in this book. Indeed, this is a work devoted to Western philosophy, the philosophy that derives from the work of Socrates, with his analytical treatment of the overarching themes of life. While acknowledging the traditions stemming from the work of Gautama Buddha, Confucius, and Lao Tzu, let me simply observe that their way of doing philosophy was more aphoristic, allegorical, and ethereal than what Westerners, particularly of the British and American traditions, employ to sort things out, and that a map/casebook from that perspective must await another writer and illustrator.

The other strong influence came as a surprise, the result of my being drafted to work in the Southern Baptist Convention's communications shop back in the early 1990s. There, as I oversaw print and video productions, I relied heavily on artists and graphic designers for magazine and poster layouts, illustrations, storyboard sketches, and logos. Though I'd taught aesthetics for a number of years and had worked with a host of art professors and their students, I'd not contracted for their efforts. But when it was my job to do so, I was struck by how professional and gifted they were, how gracious, patient, and accommodating they could be toward one so clumsy as I was. And, in this vein, I've been delighted with the work of Chad and Harrison. They've set the text off dramatically.

Cases

Though consideration of these twenty-two cases will not bring you transfer credit to a law school, it could conceivably prompt you to pursue a JD, freshly appreciative of the rich philosophical nature of what the courts engage. More likely, it will give you greater appreciation for the life-importance of philosophy. And I hope the discussion questions will drive you further in this direction, not just to stir your imagination, but also to help you home in on settled answers to questions for which you already have working answers, for good or ill. You may not have wrestled with the issues, but your behavior shows that you've been working with conclusions all along. For instance, if you're agnostic, you'll likely act as an atheist would—not confessing Christ, not going to church, not evangelizing, etc. Your life reveals your conviction that you don't believe God exists, or at least not in any form that should impact your life.

This is not to say that I hope fascination with discussion you find below will drive you to the profession of philosophy or even admiration for that profession. Indeed, it may lead you to have less respect for much of what passes for professional philosophy. As I look toward an upcoming meeting of the American Philosophical Association (Pacific Division), in Vancouver, I'm intrigued, even gratified by some of the titles; I smile at others, and cringe at yet others. Besides, who knows where these scholars are going with their presentations? For starters, many titles are so jargon laden, so bent toward backroom scholastic arcana, that they would likely make no sense if I listed them. Some seem conventionally comprehensible—"Self-Awareness and Self-Doubt"; "Honor as Virtue"; and one I chair, "Towards a Theory of Self-Undeception." The Society of Christian Philosophers offers a promising paper, "Divine Forgiveness and Reconciliation." Several sound fun—"The Good, the Bad and the Ugly"; "Digestion (Pepsis) and Moral Education in Epictetus"; "There's Nothing in the Rule Book That Says a Dog Can't Play Basketball: Two Ways the Laws of Nature Might Govern." Others are obviously edgy and/or mystifying—"Democracy without Voting"; "The Phenomenology of Ritual Resistance: Colin Kaepernick as Confucian Sage"; "Platonic Feminism and the Politics of Disappearing Ink"; "Himpathy and Intersectionality: Toward a Feminist Prison Abolitionism"; "A Taekwondo Muddle" (for, yes, the Society for the Study of Philosophy and the Martial Arts); "Microaggressions, Torts, and the Right to Apology"; "Confronting the Incomprehensible in the Ongoing Dispossessive Logics of Colonialism"; "Excavating Stand Your Ground"; and "Don't Know, Don't Care." One, for the Society for the Philosophy of Sex and Love, is just plain nasty (I'll spare you the title). It's quite a buffet, or perhaps a dog's breakfast. At any rate, I plan to be stretched, informed, and occasionally edified, but I can't say that I expect to gain as much wisdom (life-important truth) as I would from a good sermon series (though philosophy is purportedly "the love of wisdom"). The problem is that so much of the thinking and arguing that goes on is sub-Christian or anti-Christian, with corresponding fall-offs in insight. Nevertheless, I'm grateful both for the Christians who are in there pitching on these matters and for the common grace and shared humanity that enables non-believers to say some good and true things in this context.

Back to the cases, I should add that the practice of law is not as exciting on a daily basis as some of the wrangling you find here. Yes, there's drudgery in the profession. No, you're not always dealing with cannibals, world-famous artists, rock groups, Indian tribes, precocious monkeys, ex-NFL stars, or séances, but even in the mundane, there are big issues afoot, and that's where philosophy pitches in.

The Trial of Socrates
Athens, 399 B.C.

Three of Plato's dialogues—*Apology* (defense), *Crito* (a refused offer of escape from custody), and *Phaedo* (reflections on immortality)—are devoted to the conviction and execution of Socrates. The charge was twofold: atheism and corrupting the youth of Athens. His defense was that he invoked the gods and that there were no youth to come forward with a complaint. The jury, consisting of the mass gathering of citizens, didn't buy it, and he was sentenced to death, which was effected by his drinking the prescribed hemlock.

The Bible seems equally unimpressed with philosophy. Indeed, the only direct comment on the enterprise is a warning in Colossians 2:8, where Paul says, "Beware lest anyone cheat you through philosophy and empty deceit . . ." Granted, this same apostle reasoned with Epicureans and Stoics on Mars Hill in Acts 17, even quoting the philosophically trained Greek poet Aratus to make a point. Some invited him to come back for more conversation, but he moved on down to Corinth, determined to focus on his message of the crucified Christ and not upon some broad theistic apologetics.

Of course, Christian philosophers have stepped forth in the succeeding millennia and have drawn on secular thinkers—Thomas Aquinas most notably in his appropriation of Aristotle, and Augustine in his broadly Platonic framework. But the relationship has always been fraught with tensions and even outright warfare.

Back to Socrates. Was he guilty? Well, for one thing, if he'd done a thorough job of corrupting the minds of his students, then they wouldn't have known they'd been corrupted. (What if someone asked a member of Hitler Youth if Hitler had corrupted him? Or consider a disciple of the

1960s drug enthusiast Timothy Leary. What if he'd been wrecked by Leary's counsel to "Turn on. Tune in. Drop out"? Chances are they would have both said things were just fine and that their leader had taken them to a higher level.)

As for his atheism, he did, indeed, speak respectfully of such gods as Pan and Asclepius, but he was quite content to ask impiously (in *Euthyphro*) whether the gods were the source of morality or whether they could even agree on what it was. A contemporary version of that response might fall along the lines of admitting there was a "higher power" but discarding particular doctrines.

For Christians, it often boils down to the question of whether parents might be pleased that their child, just off to college, has enrolled in a philosophy course. After all, there are countless stories of freshmen being "liberated" by secular professors from the notions they absorbed in Sunday school and home.

So, what is it about philosophy that's so dangerous? Well, it deals with "the big questions" (e.g., "What is man?"; "What's the big story?"; "Who's worth listening to on these matters?"), and many are the answers which are either indifferent or hostile to Christianity. But must a philosopher come out with answers antithetical to the faith? Not at all. Many world-famous and influential philosophers have professed faith in Christ and worked within a biblical framework, from Pascal to Leibniz to Berkeley to Plantinga (and, of course, the aforementioned Aquinas and Augustine).

Still, since the seventeenth century, "modern"/secular philosophers have pretty much ruled the roost, including the likes of Hume, Kant, Mill, Nietzsche, Russell, Ayer, Derrida, and Dennett. And since philosophy departments, professional journals, and academic societies are self-perpetuating, they "fill the airwaves" with more or less dismissive talk regarding traditional Christianity. So, the believing freshman at most schools is likely to walk into territory not particularly friendly to his spiritual upbringing when acknowledged at all.

That being said, a fair number of well-trained Christian philosophers have surfaced in the last several decades and formed both the Society of Christian Philosophers and the Evangelical Philosophical Society, with journals of their own. Some big names have joined in, including tenured professors at Notre Dame, Michigan, Wisconsin, UCLA, Brown, and Chicago. And they've published books with Oxford, Cambridge, Harvard, Yale, and a range of other secularly influential presses. So, Christian philosophers aren't lepers, though they do, indeed, work in a discipline where many of their counterparts are quite guilty of the charges leveled against Socrates: they are, indeed, atheists, and they do, indeed, corrupt the youth.

What, then, are Christians doing in the field? Is the point to fight the good fight, engaging in apologetics at every hand? Well, there is that, but there's much more. As American pragmatist William James put it, philosophy is "an uncommonly stubborn attempt to think clearly." And there's a lot to think clearly and stubbornly about that's not covered explicitly in the Bible. For instance, what are we to make of democracy? Is it the best system? There's no verse addressing it directly, so there's room to think and talk things over with other people who don't mind the give and take of pointed discourse. Thus, we have "political philosophy."

What about abstract art? Is it kosher? Should one invest in it or hang it in one's home? Again, no verse settles the matter decisively, so we jump into the field of aesthetics. And what shall we make of the testimony of "experts"? What makes them experts in the first place, and how much weight should we give them when sizing up their medical, diplomatic, economic, and climatic declarations? Welcome to epistemology. And so on.

Ah, but shouldn't we be talking only to Christians on these matters, consulting people who share our worldview? Why consort with people who don't operate with the proper intellectual context? Well, these "outsiders" are made in the image of God, they come equipped with a measure of reason and conscience, and they can get a lot of things right. All truth is God's truth, and we shouldn't turn up our nose at any of it, no matter where it comes from. Besides, they often make more sense than fellow believers, who are themselves often divided on many of these issues. So let's all pitch in together and try to figure things out.

Sometimes I tell my students that a philosophy paper should not only accord with the counsel of Scripture but should also be cast in terms that could gain purchase with someone who didn't accept the Bible as either authoritative or helpful. They shouldn't rely on chapter and verse to settle their point out in the public square. Nothing wrong with chapter and verse; indeed, we rely upon it for life and light. And it's quite legitimate to cite it in societal discourse. But on matters where the Bible is not decisively on point or where the audience couldn't care less about our scripture, we have recourse to other arguments.

Cases

Discussion Questions:

1. What is your general impression when you hear the word "philosophy"? Is it positive? Negative? Why?

2. Have you ever met a professional philosopher or professor of philosophy? Did he or she strike you as so in love with wisdom (from the meaning of the term) that they would pursue it with every good resource and tool at hand?

3. Are you familiar with Christian philosophers who work in the realm of apologetics, defending the faith against gainsayers? Do you know any of their arguments?

4. What did the Epicureans and Stoics Paul encountered on Mars Hill believe and teach? Was it totally out of synch with Christianity or was there overlap?

5. Should Christian colleges and seminaries have philosophy departments? Why or why not?

6. Rene Descartes, a professing Christian, said that we needed to start from scratch in doing philosophy. Doubt everything you can, even the existence of God, until you get to bedrock certainty (in his case, that he existed as a thinker), and then build up from there.

    Another professing Christian philosopher, Alvin Plantinga, said we can start with belief in God as bedrock; that it is "properly basic." Who makes more sense?

Robertson v. Oelschlaeger

U.S. Supreme Court 137
U.S. 436 (1890)

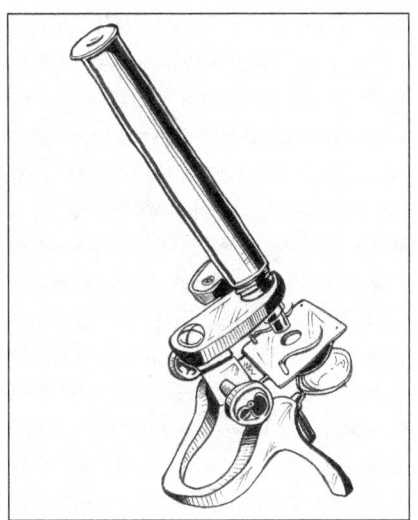

In 1844, a Mr. Oelschlaeger was importing a variety of instruments when a collector for the port of New York imposed a 45-percent duty on the goods. Oelschlaeger objected that the official had misclassified the material as unspecified manufactured products made of metal, when, in reality, these were, in the words of the law, "philosophical apparatus and instruments," and thus required only a 35-percent tariff.

The court decided that some of the instruments qualified as philosophical and others did not; the former devoted principally to "observations and experiment" in seeking "discoveries in nature" for "developing and exhibiting natural forces"; the latter were "implements for mechanical or professional use," which were "usually employed in the trades and professions for performing the operations incidental thereto." For instance, the judge held that a "large compound microscope" and an "astronomical telescope on tripod" were philosophical. But a "jeweler's magnifying glass" and an "ophthalmoscope" were not. He left six for the jury to decide, and they counted a "double-barreled field glass" (binoculars) philosophical, and an "opera glass" not. The Supreme Court differed with the judge in his calling a stereopticon philosophical (when it was really a device for amusement), but they basically agreed with his approach, so Oelschlaeger paid two rates, depending upon the item.

It's interesting to see the way they used the word "philosophical" in the late nineteenth century, for the concept has evolved through the millennia.

CASES

Today, it sounds odd to call a microscope an instrument of philosophy. So what is philosophy anyway?

It goes back to the Greeks, to the people who coined and employed the term (men like Herodotus, Thucydides, and Plato), a word built from "love" and "wisdom," thus denoting a "lover of wisdom." It enjoyed broad currency in New Testament days, showing up, for instance, as *philosophias* in Colossians 2:8. So who wouldn't want to get on board with loving wisdom? Well, Paul had his reservations, expressed in that passage—not with wisdom itself, but in how the world went about pursuing and presenting it, without reference to or respect for Scripture. This isn't to say that everything philosophers did was bad. Paul didn't ban philosophical talk from the fellowship of believers. But he did say they needed to be very careful about it.

So what were these philosophers up to? In the beginning (in the persons of Thales, Anaximenes, Anaximander, Parmenides, Heraclitus, Empedocles, Epicurus, Pythagoras, etc.), they engaged in what we call "cosmology," the study of the fundamental nature of the "cosmos," the natural universe. In a culture of sheepherding, soldiering, homemaking, and such, it was no small thing for a man to step back and spend time on the question, "What's it all about?" And so they came up with a variety of guesses, from water to flux to unchanging being to the Boundless (whatever that was). By the way, some say this last-named guess marked the true beginning of philosophy, in that it had the required level of abstraction.

These were the pre-Socratics, the forerunners to the philosopher who, so to speak, "moved the game inside," where he addressed human topics such as friendship, knowledge, justice, and courage. But, like the others, he was pressing for the ultimate answers, the standards by which we may evaluate the hum and buzz of human activity, and the stage on which such activity occurs. Amalgamate all this (from Thales to Plato and then to Aristotle, who did some important taxonomical work, specifying categories of study), and you have philosophy as inquiry into the big stuff heretofore beyond one's reach.

To make a very long story short, people became increasingly confident that a lot of things were not beyond their reach. Science kicked in, and physics, chemistry, and biology became their own realms, with a host of subspecialties and combinations coming into play, e.g., biochemistry and genetics. When you came to the point you could run controlled experiments and crank out mathematical formulae to translate science into technology (e.g., taking Bernoulli's principle about the relationship between flow and pressure and applying it to airplane wings for lift and race-car spoilers for track grip), philosophy could bid *adieu* to the day-to-day work of that discipline and move on to new frontiers. (Not surprisingly, the social *sciences* are still in the birthing process, in that applying math to human behavior can easily leave a lot to be desired or presume to say too much about what's important.)

On this model, the very expression "philosophical apparatus" seems an oxymoron. If you can use an apparatus to do your work, it's no longer philosophy, but rather science. But the terminology in the Robertson case seems to fit with the practice we see at university graduation exercises, where scholars receive PhDs (doctorates in *philosophy*) in mathematics, physics, chemistry, and biology (subjects that used to be spoken of as forms of "natural philosophy").

So are these degrees anachronisms, charming vestiges from the day when mortarboards were actually used to carry mortar up ladders as students helped to build or repair their schools? Not really, for there is a philosophical aspect to these various subjects when well taught, namely, the disputed, theoretical frontiers of their thought. PhDs are not just practitioners of this or that science (or other disciplines, such as literary criticism, American history, or art appreciation). They are supposed to be people who can bring critical tools to bear on the very methods and value of literary criticism, American history, and art appreciation, asking whether what they're doing makes sense, is well done, or even matters. They're equipped to theorize about their theories, to work at the boundaries of their vocations, to philosophize, if you will—hence the PhD. Furthermore, they're supposed to be able to join in the integrative work of the academy as a whole, joining their colleagues in big-picture thinking about the rightful place of their disciplines in the life of mankind, and how their scholarship both feeds and feeds on what others are doing, for good or ill—synoptic, synthetic, comprehensive thinking.

Professional degrees, such as the Doctor of Medicine (MD), Doctor of Jurisprudence (JD), and Doctor of Ministry (DMin), are meant to equip practitioners to do their jobs well. Their aim is not to force students to step back and ask tough questions about whether what they'll be up to is sensible and worthy. (That doesn't mean they can't and won't do this, or, on the other hand, that PhDs will do this; rather, it has to do with the basic parameters of the degree program.)

CASES

When PhDs "rise above" their particular work on Meiji Dynasty tapestries, nationalistic themes in the poetry of Walt Whitman, payday purchasing patterns on military bases, hurricane predictions for Bermuda, and such, and fly at the level of theoretical dispute (e.g., among "Whig," "Great Man," and "From Below" historians) philosophers will "meet them in the air," ready to pitch in through the philosophy of science, philosophy of the arts, philosophy of mathematics, philosophy of history, philosophy of man, and so on. And it's not as though we philosophers are filling in until science can snatch those topics from our grasp, for you can't settle the biggest biggies with a test tube, an expedition, or a focus group.

So how do you settle them? Well, in one sense, you don't, since there will never be full consensus on, for instance, the nature and value of religion, democracy, museums, leisure, unions, cloning, and universities. But some answers are demonstrably better than others, and, besides, you can't remain indifferent or neutral. Issue by issue, you'll have a position, or one will have you (to paraphrase G. K. Chesterton).

If philosophers, as philosophers, don't do their principal work with spectrometers, archaeological digs, or polls, then what do they employ? For what it's worth, I give my students ten questions they can use to jump into most any philosophical topic, ways to tease out insight and to distance themselves from muddle. I call them "Elements of Dialogue," a tip of the hat to the dialogical masters, Socrates and Plato, who set the methodological table for us:

1. Can you give an example? (illustration)
2. What's at stake? What difference does it make? (application)
3. Where are you going with this? (destination)
4. But wouldn't that mean . . . ? (implication)
5. What exactly do you mean by . . . ? (clarification)
6. So it is kind of like . . . ? (analogy; comparison)
7. But what about . . . ? (counterexample)
8. Wouldn't it be better to look at it this way? (alternative paradigm)
9. So you're saying . . . ? (summarization)
10. But how does this square with . . . ? (cohesion)

As harsh as it might sound, the chief tool philosophers use is the *reductio ad absurdum* ("reduction to absurdity"), whereby someone ventures a guess or proposal and then we get to work on seeing if can stand up to scrutiny or, instead, generates absurdities (or, in formal logic, contradictions). If the latter, back to the drawing board, and it starts all over again. Ideally, answers get less and less crazy as we go along.

What shall we make George W. Bush's 1999 answer to a question raised in an Iowa presidential debate—that Jesus was his favorite philosopher? He caught a lot of heat for that, but was it deserved? Well, certainly Jesus has a firm grasp of the answers to the biggest questions, and he loves wisdom more than anyone else. Furthermore, his wisdom trumps any worldly wisdom that might be thrown up against his. But, unlike ordinary human philosophers, Jesus doesn't have to wrestle with questions, to puzzle out answers. He knows everything. (The *Oxford English Dictionary* says a philosopher is "one who devotes himself to the search of fundamental truth," and Jesus, being omniscient, is not a searcher.) Yes, as a boy, there was a time when Jesus needed to "grown in wisdom," as it says in Luke 2:52, but that was part of his submitting to the limitations of the incarnation; when he was in the manger in Bethlehem, he wasn't doing calculus in his head or figuring how to best relate to the Sanhedrin several decades later.

Furthermore, he doesn't address in Scripture every little puzzle in the world, at least not directly or explicitly. He offers broad principles, but he doesn't get down in the weeds with academic philosophers on such questions as whether conceptual art is really art, whether monarchies are better than oligarchies, or whether time is a substance.

Though some Christians are inclined to think of philosophy as essentially apologetics when it's worth anything at all, they miss the point that philosophy is an activity devoted to all sorts of big, conceptual problems which are neither settled by the Bible nor threatening to Christianity. Jesus remains on his throne whether or not we decide to go with a realistic or an abstract sculpture for our city park. But if I'm on the board commissioning the work, and if we have a budget of $300,000 to get it done, I'd surely like someone to think through this with me before I vote. And if I'm on the library commission fielding complaints that the librarians have put Chris Hitchens along with C. S. Lewis (or vice versa) on the shelves, I need help in sorting out the purpose of public libraries in the first place, and I don't see a biblical proof text to settle the matter.

Cases

We need to do some philosophizing on such issues, and, alas, we don't have a mechanical "philosophical apparatus" to get it done. But we do have our wits and our interlocutors. So game on, careful not to become what the aforementioned *OED* calls "philosophasters"—"shallow or pseudo-philosophers; smatterers or pretenders in philosophy."

Discussion Questions:

1. Is psychology more nearly a science or a philosophy of human nature?
2. Have you ever discovered you were unreflectively captive to an idea until someone set you free from it by pointed questioning and argument? Was this a good thing? Or did they lead you away from something good, which you hadn't thought much about, but which was still right?
3. Some areas of philosophical study end in "logy" (from the Greek *logos*, meaning "word," "concept," "essence," or "ruling principle"). So we have ontology (the "science of being"), epistemology (the "study of knowledge," how we gain and justify belief), deontology (the "principles of duty"), and axiology (the "study of value"). In John chapter 1, Jesus himself is called the *Logos*. What connection might there between the Logos and these various "ologies"?
4. We have cabinet offices with grand names. Do you think the heads and employees of the Departments of Justice, Education, Defense, Homeland Security, Health and Human Services, and Labor have a good grasp of the first principles of justice, education, and so on?
5. If you had a million-dollar grant and uninterrupted years to study and pursue some question in philosophy, what would it be?

Aronow v. U.S.

U.S. Court of Appeals
Ninth Circuit 432 F.2d
242 (1970)

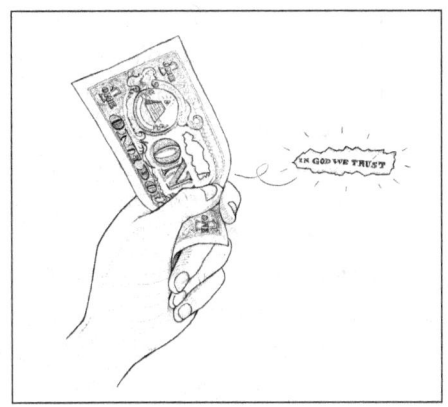

STEFAN Ray Aronow brought suit claiming that the law which called "In God we trust" the "national motto" and required that it be inscribed "on all United States currency and coins" violated the Establishment Clause of the First Amendment. In response, the court observed,

> It is not easy to discern any religious significance attendant the payment of a bill with coin or currency on which has been imprinted "In God we Trust" or the study of a government publication or document bearing that slogan. In fact, such secular uses of the motto was viewed as sacrilegious and irreverent by President Theodore Roosevelt. Yet, Congress has directed such uses. While "ceremonial" and "patriotic" may not be particularly apt words to describe the category of the national motto, it is excluded from First Amendment significance because the motto has no theological or ritualistic impact. As stated by the Congressional report, it has "spiritual and psychological value" and "inspirational quality."

In other words, they judged the motto to be virtually content free, a piece of blather, a greeting card wish. No harm, no foul.

Of course, this plays nicely into Soren Kierkegaard's critique of the empty Danish religion of his day. When, in 1854, a departed bishop was eulogized as a "truth witness," Kierkegaard lumped him in with those who robbed the faith of its meaning: "Truly, there is something that is more against Christianity and the essence of Christianity than any heresy, any schism, more against it than all heresies and schisms together, and it is this:

to play at Christianity..." And things didn't seem to be getting better when, in 2005, a Danish Lutheran Pastor named Grosboell declared there was "no heavenly God." He was reinstated as pastor by the state church authorities in response to the pleas of his parishioners. Apparently, the requirement that their ministers should honor the Apostles' Creed, the Augsburg Confession, and Luther's Small Catechism had "no theological impact."

Of course, this case also deals with political philosophy, with the reasonable framing of constitutions (and, indeed, the very existence of constitutions) and not just matters of personal consecration. In that vein, what shall we make of the U.S. First Amendment, which, among other things, proscribes "the establishment of religion" and ensures "the free exercise" thereof? Advocates argue that "a free church in a free state" is the ideal and that when church and state are not properly separated, both are weakened. The church becomes something of a house pet rather than an incisive prophet, and the state loses an independent voice to keep it honest.

This is not to say that state church voices are always anodyne. English pastor and Oxford professor John Keble shook things up mightily when, in 1833, in a ceremonial sermon for the annual opening of the nation's courts, he preached "The National Apostasy," with words such as these:

> Whatever be the cause, in this country of late years, (though we are lavish in professions of piety) there has been observable a growing disinclination, on the part of those bound by VOLUNTARY OATHS, to whatever reminds them of their obligation; a growing disposition to explain it all away. We know what, some years ago, would have been thought of such uneasiness, if betrayed by persons officially sworn, in private, legal, or commercial life. If there be any subjects or occasions, now, on which men are inclined to judge of it more lightly, it concerns them deeply to be quite sure, that they are not indulging or encouraging a profane dislike of God's awful Presence; a general tendency, as a people, to leave Him out of all their thoughts.

So "state-sponsored" preachers can show some redemptive edge (though his nineteenth-century language is not particularly piercing to our ears).

Of course, church-and-state disputes are not just a family matter within Christendom, a tussle among American Baptists, British Anglicans, and Danish Lutherans. Indeed, atheists (such as the notorious Madalyn Murray O'Hair), Jews (Steven Engel of *Engel v. Vitale*), and those of other faiths have brought suit against one form civic piety or another (e.g., a WWI memorial "Peace Cross" in Bladensburg, Maryland).

Of course, talk of proper government ranges far beyond jousting over this or that coin inscription, classroom prayer, or the White House Christmas tree. In Saudi Arabia, the Muslim homeland, Islamic sharia law reigns, with evangelism forbidden and apostasy a capital crime. On the other end of the spectrum, Western atheists such a Thomas Hobbes and Jean-Jacques Rousseau have proposed "godless" systems, the former prescribing an absolute monarch for the state "Leviathan," the latter championing a "social contract" among natural rights holders.

Government designers have been at it from ancient days, from Aristotle's discussion, in *Politics*, of monarchy, oligarchy, and democracy, to John Locke's *Two Treatises of Government*, which emphasized "the consent of the governed." And, yes, we have the oft-assigned classic *The Republic*, by Plato, which British philosopher Karl Popper ranks as a totalitarian abomination along with the system designed by Karl Marx, communism. In *The Open Society and Its Enemies*, he argues that there is nothing more dangerous than a utopian scheme, one that says we can achieve a "heaven on earth" if we will just institute the right policies (never mind that we might well need to "break some eggs to make an omelet").

Though Popper wasn't commending a faith-based state, we should note that one of the biggest antidotes to the sort of tyranny he sketches is recognition of the biblical notion of the Fall, described in Genesis 3. Armed with the conviction that men are not essentially good, but rather sinful and dangerous, the Americans in particular (yes, many with seriously Calvinistic convictions) imposed a "separation of powers" to help keep everybody honest. No one could be trusted with massive authority, so a host of checks and balances were put in place to protect "God-given rights," based on the Ten Commandments (e.g., the right to life from "Don't murder" and the right to property from "Don't steal"). Thus we have such "constitutional firebreaks" as term limits, vetoes, veto overrides, the electoral college, a free press, judicial review, impeachment, competing branches, and a bicameral legislature.

Speaking of Popper, he also raised a matter germane to the Aronow case, the issue of "falsifiability." He said that respectable claims had to face at least the possibility (if not the actuality) of disconfirmation. If nothing could conceivably count against a proposition, if it could handily dismiss any imaginable counterevidence, then it was an empty claim. Some suggest that Darwinism has this problem; others that declarations of God's

CASES

goodness are uncannily resistant to gainsaying. (We consider these criticisms in our treatment of the Kitzmiller and Robbie cases.)

So what shall we say of the statement, "In God we trust"? Can we think of anything that might come to pass which would cause us to observe, "Well, I guess we don't really trust in God"? Does our defense spending show that we rely on arms instead of him for deliverance? Or does it show that we believe the stewardship of our freedoms under God requires prudent action, even as we pray for help? Does granting liberty to pornographers mean we've lost faith in and broken trust with God's canons of righteousness, or does it mean that we don't need law to enforce moral rectitude, but rather that we rely upon the Holy Spirit and our God-given powers of persuasion to bring our citizens around to the right path?

Are we really saying something substantive by this motto? Well, Stefan Aronow thought so, enough to fight it in court. He had the sense that it helped create and maintain a sense of accountability, one that could somehow channel behavior in directions that might prove objectionable to those of his mindset. Perhaps it would stigmatize atheists, making it harder for them to rise in society. Perhaps it could lead us to quote the Bible in making out our case for certain public policies. And besides, whose version of God might prevail should demographics shift? Would Allah displace Yahweh as the standard? What about Krishna? If the latter, would we be opening the door to a caste system? If the former, would we start talking about jihad when considering war?

We're told that one's entire genetic code is written into every cell. So too in philosophy. In looking at something as small as the inscription on a dime, we get into just about everything, from to polity, to anthropology, to lexicology, to integrity, and beyond.

DISCUSSION QUESTIONS:

1. Are you pleased that "In God we trust" holds this place in American polity? Why or why not?
2. Some in the U.S. Congress are pushing to remove ". . . so help me God" from the end of oaths of office. Is this a good cause?
3. Are anti-blasphemy laws a good idea?
4. Some disparage "civil religion" as a cheap substitute for and diversion from the real thing. Others say that, nevertheless, it's better than no

religion and that it has a salutary effect on a nation. Which way do you tend?

5. The story is told that the Harvard philosophy department wanted a quote from the Greek sophist Protagoras inscribed on their new building, Emerson Hall, dedicated in 1905. It read, "Man is the measure of all things." President Eliot intervened, and instead words from Psalm 8 were cut in stone: "What is man that thou art mindful of him?" What would you say to the proposal that our national motto be changed to Protagoras's declaration?

Brancusi v. U.S.

54 Treas. Dec. 428 (Cust. Ct., 1928)

Constantin Brancusi 1876-1957 | *Bird in Space*, 1923

In the 1920s, Paris-based Romanian sculptor Constantine Brancusi sent a piece of sculpture named *Bird in Space* to America for display. He expected it to enter tariff-free as a work of art, but customs officials said it didn't qualify. Rather, they classified it as a metal tool, along with kitchen and hospital supplies. The problem was the government's working definition of sculpture—"reproductions by carving or casting, imitations of natural objects, chiefly the human form." It didn't look like bird, so they assessed him a 40-percent import charge, in effect saying, "That isn't art!" Drawing on the testimony of expert witnesses from the art world, the judge ruled that the state's definition was out of date, and that it needed to be adjusted to accommodate abstract art, whether or not people liked it.

The issue fell nicely into the ancient philosophical "What is it?" form, brought to high art itself by Socrates and his student Plato. As noted above in the Robertson case, the first philosophers (the "pre-Socratics") focused on big-box cosmology (suggesting that the universe was essentially water, the Boundless, flux, etc.), but then Socrates brought discourse down to the concerns of human life in a series of dialogues, e.g., knowledge (*Theaetetus*), justice (*Republic*), courage (*Laches*), friendship (*Lysis*), love (*Symposium*). (Plato wrote them up, and a lot of scholarship has gone into saying how much was real Socrates and how much was Plato putting words in his mentor's mouth.)

So sweeping and exemplary was this collection of exchanges that twentieth-century philosopher Alfred North Whitehead said, in *Process and Reality*, that the "European philosophical tradition" was best typified as "a series of footnotes to Plato." Basically, Socrates would prompt an interlocutor (victim) to offer a definition of a great theme, such as piety/righteousness in *Euthyphro*. Sure enough, the student would give it a shot, e.g., "What the gods endorse." Then Socrates would raise a troublesome question—"But what if they disagree among themselves?"—and they would be off to the dialogical races. We've been doing the same thing for millennia as we've grappled with the same issues and others.

Many have asked, "So why should we bother if famous minds haven't settled things?" And the traditional and correct answer is that you'll be unavoidably using an implicit definition of one sort of another, and it's not a bad idea to get clear on what exactly it is you're assuming, and then think it over. It has practical implications, as Brancusi discovered.

Turns out, Socrates and Plato's view of art was pretty close to that of the U.S. authorities. They spoke of it in terms of *mimesis*, "imitation," and therefore didn't much appreciate the artistic enterprise. Believing in the existence of fixed ideals, they counted earthly horses, beds, and such as more or less faithful copies of the transcendent models. Now, if someone ventured to draw a horse or bed, he'd be making a copy of a copy, resulting in something third-rate. (Think of the degradation of quality when you keep copying successively old copies on a Xerox machine.)

CASES

Of course, this definition, *mimesis*, works better for sculpture and painting than music and architecture, but it's not aged well as a definition for any of them. Indeed, through the centuries, a good many definitions have vied for respect, e.g., Tolstoy's insistence that real art faithfully conveyed the artist's emotions and built wholesome community, or Clive Bell and Roger Fry's declaration that "significant form" was the point to painting. But artists, being a creative and often transgressive breed, have continually pushed the boundaries.

One famous/infamous example was a porcelain urinal appropriated from a discard pile by Marcel Duchamp. He wrote "R. Mutt" on it and entered it in a competition. The organizers weren't impressed, but the world has tipped its hat to his conceit, featuring this "readymade" in many art history books. And that's just the start. Now we're asked accept a pile of Jolly Rancher candies dumped into a corner along with the invitation to take one, unwrap and eat it, in memory of someone who died from AIDS. Or to cooperate with handwritten instructions to imagine the sands of an hourglass completing their fall in a minute or two; so you stand there letting the conceptual sand fall in your mind. (I draw these examples from visits to the generally admirable Art Institute of Chicago.)

To accommodate one curiosity/perversity/novelty after another, some have abandoned the Socratic/Platonic project of discerning the essence of the thing. They say it's a fool's game, for there's no property in the thing itself that serves to qualify it. So, under the influence of Ludwig Wittgenstein, channeled by Morris Weitz, they've moved to a sociological definition, calling art an "open concept," whose ever-changing boundaries are determined by the "Artworld" (a term coined by Arthur Danto), i.e., the "club" of artists, professors, curators, critics, and publishers who make the calls (hence, George Dickie's "institutional theory of art").

I still think the old project is worth the trouble, and, at this point, here's my working definition: *Art is that aspect of personal activity undertaken to enthrall the beholder, whether or not it intends to or succeeds in transmitting truth, prompting goodness, exhibiting skill, or manufacturing things.* That takes a lot of explaining (and there is little space for it here), but, for starters, the first part excludes colorful rust patterns and spider webs, since neither oxidizing iron molecules nor spiders are persons. (The only sense in which they are art is as works of the supreme person, God. And, of course, they may well have aesthetic value.) As for "enthrall," I mean something more than merely "instruct" or "mesmerize." As a medical student, I may be *enthralled* by the skillful incisions of a teaching surgeon in an operating theater, or I may be *mesmerized* by the ringing in my ears that I notice only when I lay my head on the pillow. But these are instances of fascination due to professional development and concern for one's health. I mean something more disinterested (as opposed to uninterested), a perspective detached, if only briefly, from practical concerns. Maybe "charm" is a better word. And, again, this definition leaves open the question of whether the art is well done, decent, or edifying. It leaves room for the existence of bad art (where the intended charm didn't materialize) and purposely offensive art (where the shock or insult was well executed and engaging).

Yes, it can make conceptual room for the Jolly Ranchers and imaginary hour glasses, but it doesn't have to praise them. And it doesn't have to wait for certification from the elites, stuck in limbo until acknowledged in their journals, galleries, and syllabi. There can be art in the staging of tractor pulls as well as in the composition of symphonies.

Discussion Questions:

1. If you were drafting customs law, how would you define works of art if you wanted to give them a financial break?
2. The Artworld sees itself as the arbiter of what counts as art. How good a job is it doing?
3. Is golf an art form? Is brain surgery? Is tweeting?
4. Which definition of art seems to be implicit in the judgments and choices of the public at large?
5. Does the government have any business taxing citizens to fund a National Endowment for the Arts, which makes grants in the millions of dollars to a range of artists? If so, what criteria should it use?

The Case of Armin Meiwes
German Constitutional Court, Karlsruhe (2006)

Armin Meiwes | Bernd-Jurgen Brandes

Two German men, Armin Meiwes, a computer specialist, and Bernd-Jürgen Brandes, a computer engineer, met in March of 2001 for the purpose of cannibalism. Both men frequented a website devoted to those keen on the notion of humans consuming humans, a site on which Meiwes posted an appeal for a willing victim. Brandes volunteered, and the subsequent home video of the event showed his assent to both mutilation and homicide. Both men attempted to consume a portion of Brandes's flesh, and after Brandes had bled to death, Meiwes cut him up for cold storage. Over the next several months, Meiwes ate forty-four pounds of this human meat.

The next year, Meiwes was again on the Internet hunting for a volunteer, and his appeal referenced the Brandes deed. When their deadly transaction and encounter came to light, Meiwes was arrested and convicted of manslaughter in a Frankfurt district court and sentenced to eight years in prison. But there was widespread dissatisfaction with this decision, and the

German supreme court conducted a retrial, where Meiwes (nicknamed the "Rotenburg Cannibal") was given life in prison.

This seems a fitting resolution to the affair, given the heinous nature of the crime, but those of the libertarian persuasion are not so sure the court got it right. Indeed, they're reluctant to applaud the lower court's assessment of a lesser sentence, or of any sentence at all, for the act in question was performed by "consenting adults," and thus was a "victimless crime."

John Stuart Mill's work *On Liberty* serves as the classic rationale for this perspective. He divides human acts into two types—those affecting oneself and those impacting others. He argues that we should grant people the freedom to do the former, while reserving the right to intervene when they do the latter. By this standard, our self-harm is none of your business; harm to others most certainly is.

For example, if I wish to shadow box in my back yard, I'm free to do so, but not in a rush-hour subway car, where my punches would land on fellow commuters. And while I should be free to report that there's a fire raging in faraway California, I must not cry "Fire!" in a crowded theater, a declaration which could provoke a deadly stampede. Free speech is essential, but it's not absolute in Mill's system.

Translated to the current political arena, libertarians object to laws requiring motorcyclists to wear helmets and to authorities who arrest heroin dealers. Of course, matters are often not so clear cut. The rider who dashes his head against a curb or the addict who sleeps away his days in the shadows of "Needle Park" become our problem in many ways, costing society in terms of lost productivity, heartbroken/broken families, medical and disability expenses, carelessly discarded needles, etc. Indeed, no man is an island. And even if he stays functional, the damaging ripples from his choices are all too familiar. For instance, while one man keeps his sports wagering to a manageable minimum, the very institution of gambling on games sets players and coaches up for compromise, whether on account of greed for bribes or fear from threats.

Of course, there are rocks on both sides. If we set out to keep the culture clean from bad ideas and treat its citizens as children needing the firm hand of the "nanny state," then we forfeit the genius of Western society and move toward the totalitarian agendas of Islam and communism. Rather, we have chosen the free exchange of ideas (including those of Islam, Scientology, atheism, and Satanism) as well as protections for unpopular, ridiculous, and even repellant behaviors (including gorging to the point of gross obesity, tattooing smiley faces on one's forehead, or bequeathing one's entire estate to establish a cat hotel).

It's Mill's conviction that, as crazy as things might get, the clash of rival notions is more productive of cultural well-being and progress than the way of suppression. And the ubiquitous backwardness of nations who fear and despise freedom is testimony to the value of his thesis. Furthermore, there are biblical arguments for liberty, including Paul's statement in 1 Corinthians 5:11 that we "seek to *persuade* men" (and not *coerce* them), and the parable of the wheat and tares in Matthew 13:24–30, which cautions against zealotry in weeding out troublemakers this side of the Judgment.

So back to Messrs. Meiwes and Brandes. These men were fools in the full biblical sense of mental and moral degeneracy. But they didn't force other Germans to take part in their revolting enterprise. Why not just leave them alone to "work out their damnation" while Christians set about to "work out their salvation," as in Philippians 2:12?

Surely, though, as Theodore Dalrymple has written, those who prescribe freedom for Armin Meiwes reduce hard-core libertarianism to absurdity. And, strangely enough, Mill himself has provided a qualifier that, however unwittingly, underwrites the cannibal's sentence. For in the first chapter of *On Liberty*, he writes that his framework doesn't apply to children or to "those backward states of society in which the race itself may be considered as in its nonage [period of immaturity of youth]." For "despotism is a legitimate mode of government in dealing with barbarians." Indeed, "liberty, as a principle, has no application to any state of things anterior to the time when mankind have become capable of being improved by free and equal discussion."

He surely had in mind illiterate and savage natives in far-off climes— suitable subjects for British colonial paternalism—when he wrote this in Victorian days, but as Meiwes and Brandes have demonstrated, you don't have to leave Western Europe to find headhunters and cannibals. We appear to be coming full circle, from civilization back to barbarism, and Mill's dream of the nation as a lively debating society dims when the participants descend so far into sociopathy that they've shown themselves rationally and ethically incapable of handling liberty.

So yes, the burden of proof should be upon the one who would infringe upon the liberties of others, but it is not an unbearable burden when the harm to others and, indeed, to the most basic standards of humanity is egregious.

Discussion Questions:

1. If we speak of "consenting adults," at what age should we assume that adulthood begins? In some nations, a girl may be married with parental consent at age fourteen. In some religious traditions, the line drops to twelve and even nine. The onset of puberty seems to be the deciding factor. Is that a morally workable criterion?

2. In 2003, Swedish pastor Aake Green was convicted for "agitation against an ethnic group" for preaching a sermon saying that homosexuality was illicit, though God in Christ could deliver gays from their behavior. He was sentenced to a month in jail for what the prosecutor deemed "hate speech." Two years later, upon appeal, the Supreme Court of Sweden dismissed the indictment. But censorious speech codes are a growing phenomenon in the West. Did the Swedish Supreme Court get it right in the Green case?

3. The Sedition Act of 1798 made it illegal to "write, print, utter, or publish . . . any false, scandalous and malicious writing" against the government. Facing fierce opposition in the states, it was allowed to expire in the early days of Thomas Jefferson's administration, which began in 1800. Later, in the war year of 1918, Congress passed the Espionage Act, which forbade (with punishment of up to twenty years in prison) "disloyal, profane, scurrilous, or abusive language" which subjected the United State flag, military, and government to contempt. Is there ever justification for such curbs on what might be called "treasonous" speech?

4. A variety of religious (or quasi-religious) groups are outlawed or treated harshly in countries around the world, e.g. Falun Gong in China, Scientology in France, Jehovah's Witness in Russia, Christianity in Saudi Arabia. When, if ever, is it appropriate for a government to oppress, suppress, or outlaw a religious group?

5. Does the legalization of recreational marijuana make good public policy sense?

6. Are some things outlawed which shouldn't be outlawed? Are there some things legal which shouldn't be legal?

7. In "'On Liberty' Reconsidered," Thomas Sowell argues that J. S. Mill was simply using grand words to advantage "progressive" elites, insulating them from criticism and interference, requiring respect from the masses, but giving none in return. Could Sowell have a point?

Gleitman v. Cosgrove

Supreme Court of New Jersey
227 A.2d 689 (1967)

When Dr. Robert Cosgrove Jr. told Sandra Gleitman she was two months' pregnant, she told him that a month earlier she had contracted German measles. The doctor assured her that this wouldn't matter, and reassured her along the same lines three months later when she asked again (at the prompting of army doctors at Fort Gordon, where her husband was stationed). And so the pregnancy proceeded. Sad to say, the child, Jeffrey, suffered from defects in sight, hearing, and speech, necessitating several operations and attendance at a special school for blind and deaf children. The parents sued—she over the effects on her emotional state, and he, Irwin, for the costs of caring for the damaged child.

At trial, an expert medical witness for the Gleitmans said there was indeed demonstrable risk of defects when German measles were involved, and that common practice was to inform parents of the danger, giving them the option to abort the child. So then the case became a matter of he said, she said or who said, where said.

To complicate matters, there was a third plaintiff, the child, Jeffrey, suing for his own birth defects. The problem with this was that Dr. Cosgrove could have done nothing to help him, for the measles had already worked their damage by the time he found that she was with child. In typical medical malpractice suits, the alleged victims would name either a "sin of commission" (sawing off the wrong leg) or "sin of omission" (failure to remove all surgical sponges from a cavity before "closing up") leading to further or greater affliction or impairment. But the charge was not that the doctor failed to administer some sort of corrective medicine or to refer Sandra to a specialist in fetal surgery. No, the only "cure" for Jeffrey's maladies was death by abortion.

Judge Proctor was not impressed by Jeffrey's plea, which was formulated by his attorney:

> The infant plaintiff is therefore required to say not that he should have been born without defects but that he should not have been born at all . . . In other words, he claims that the conduct of defendants prevented his mother from obtaining an abortion which would have terminated his existence, and that his very life is "wrongful" . . . The normal measure of damages in tort action is compensatory. Damages are measured by comparing the condition plaintiff would be been in, had the defendants not been negligent, with plaintiff's impaired condition as a result of the negligence. The infant plaintiff would have us measure the difference between his life with defects against the utter void of nonexistence, but it is impossible to make such a determination. The Court cannot weigh the value of life with impairments against the nonexistence of life itself.

He continued, with a word on parenting:

> A considerable problem is raised by the claim of injury to the parents. In order to determine their compensatory damages, a court would have to evaluate the denial to them of the intangible, unmeasurable, and complex human benefits of motherhood and fatherhood and weigh these against the alleged emotional and money injuries . . . It is basic to the human condition to seek life and hold on to it however heavily burdened. If Jeffrey could have been asked as to whether his life should be snuffed out before his full term of gestation could run its course, our felt intuition

> of human nature tells us he would almost surely choose life with defects as against no life at all. "For the living there is hope, but for the dead there is none." Theocritus.

Note that he rendered his opinion six years before *Roe v. Wade* became the law of the land. This 1973 ruling swept away state laws on the matter, greenlighting a culture of widespread aborting, with sixty million performed since the decision was handed down (penned by Justice Harry Blackmun). In that context, Judge Proctor's words are particularly refreshing:

> The right to life is inalienable in our society. A court cannot say what defects should prevent an embryo from being allowed life such that denial of the opportunity to terminate the existence of a defective child in embryo can support a cause for action. Examples of famous persons who have had great achievement despite physical defects come readily to mind, and many of us can think of examples close to home. A child need not be perfect to have a worthwhile life. . . . Eugenic considerations are not controlling. We are not talking here about the breeding of prize cattle . . . Though we sympathize with the unfortunate situation in which these parents find themselves, we firmly believe the right of their child to live is greater than and precludes their right not to endure emotional and financial injury.

His statement that the "right to life is inalienable in our society" echoes Thomas Jefferson's expression in the Declaration of Independence, his citation of the "self-evident" truths "that all men are created equal, that they are endowed by their Creator with certain unalienable Rights, that among these are Life, Liberty, and the pursuit of Happiness." Jefferson was a deist, and his copy of the Bible was a cut-and-paste affair, where he took out troublesome supernatural and soteriological passages, leaving it a book of moral counsel. So though Christians and Jews tied the life-right to humans being made in the "image of God," he found enough from the "light of nature" to draw the line against murder. Immanuel Kant, another non-Christian, argued that "rational nature" lay at the heart of ethics, and that treating a person (an exemplar of "rational nature") simply as a tool for one's projects or gratification was illegitimate. He would have resonated with Judge Proctor's dismissal of the "prize cattle" approach and also his impatience with the Gleitmans' ruling interest in emotional and financial convenience.

Well, we've come a long way from Judge Proctor's ruling, and the carnage has been horrific.

Discussion Questions:

1. What shall we make of suicides by those who don't believe in the afterlife? Do they put in question the judge's statement that humans are wired to choose life despite difficulties, even when faced with "the void of nonexistence"? Do our efforts to stop suicides when we are able (say, by diverting the attention of a bridge or ledge jumper so that others might sneak up and grab him or deploy a net or air bag below) resonate with the judge's opinion that a person in his right mind will prefer life, so we're giving the despondent time to clear his head?

2. The emotional-impact plea is something of a puzzle. For one thing, we can't typically deploy it to avoid military draft, skip taxes for a year, or excuse perjury. As stressful or dangerous as obeying the law might be, anxiety provides us no trump card to escape responsibility. Why should it be different in this instance? Life can be tough. So at what point do we say that the level of mental distress, either current or projected, is so considerable as to warrant the elimination of a helpless and innocent human being?

3. The Westminster Catechism declares that "the chief end of man is to glorify God and enjoy him forever." What if one argued that the Gleitmans would bring glory to God by their selfless care for Jeffrey and that they would find true blessedness in this approach to the matter? If they rejected this perspective, what would you suppose their notion of the point to life might be?

4. The judge points to people who lived fruitful and fulfilling lives despite their daunting congenital disabilities. Examples range from Helen Keller to Jim Abbott (who played Major League Baseball despite being born without a right hand). What other examples come to mind, whether the handicap came at birth or developed during a lifetime? And what about parents who have cherished their experience with a physically or mentally damaged child?

5. Is it fair to say society is too litigious? Or should we be glad that the vast majority of lawsuits, including the Gleitmans', serve to keep potential offenders honest and to protect the innocent?

Katko v. Briney

Supreme Court of Iowa
183 N.W.2d 657 (1971)

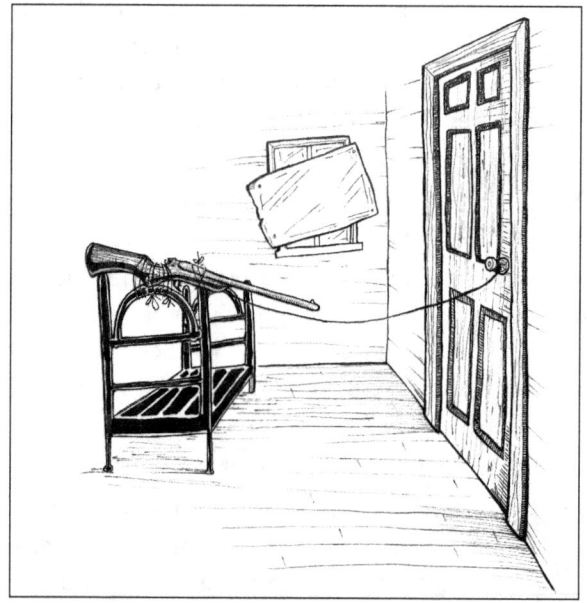

Bertha Briney had inherited a farmhouse in Iowa, though she and her husband, Edward, had never moved into it. Over the years it had fallen into disrepair, and several break-ins had occurred. Edward had put up "No Trespassing" signs around the place, but to no avail. Finally, he rigged a booby trap, a "spring gun," to go off when an intruder opened a bedroom door. And sure enough, Marvin Katko, who had broken in before, tripped the device and took a point-blank shot to the legs. He sued for damages, and the Iowa court ruled that what Briney had done was out of bounds.

If he'd been inside when the burglary was in progress, he might have been excused, but the unmanned device was illegitimate.

Wait! Briney didn't shoot the man, did he? After all, he'd done what he could to avoid shooting anyone by posting warnings. Wouldn't it be just as reasonable to say that Katko shot himself? And even though Marvin didn't mean to do it, he was certainly the one who pulled the trigger. So who did the deed?

I use this case to introduce "action theory," the study of the proper way to say that someone did something. It might sound like a straightforward matter, but even the following anecdote, often used for inspiration, shows that descriptions count: When three workmen were asked, separately, "What are you doing?," the first responded, "Laying stone"; the second, "Building a wall"; the third, "Building a cathedral." They were all doing the same thing, but the scope of their understandings differed.

To push things a bit, let me play off another familiar tale, a proverb which has taken a number of forms through the centuries:

> For want of a nail the shoe was lost.
> For want of a shoe the horse was lost.
> For want of a horse the rider was lost.
> For want of a rider the message was lost.
> For want of a message the battle was lost.
> For want of a battle the kingdom was lost.
> And all for the want of a horseshoe nail.

So we might raise the question, who brought down the kingdom? Was it the blacksmith who neglected to place that last nail in its crucial place? Or was it his assistant who dawdled on his errand to get a fresh batch of nails, and who arrived just moments too late since the rider had to rush off? And if we can blame the fall of the kingdom on a lazy assistant, how could any of us avoid blame for at least one catastrophe? (One thinks of the "butterfly effect.")

As you might imagine, this concern has shown up constantly in tort law, the civil law of wrongs. In a famous and influential 1928 case, *Palsgraf v. Long Island Railroad*, a conductor helped a latecomer onto the train, accidentally dislodging the passenger's package. Unfortunately, it contained fireworks, which went off under the train, and the explosive concussion and ensuing panic caused a big railway scale to topple over on a pregnant woman, who miscarried. She sued the railroad, which (in the days before "strict liability") escaped penalty since the outcome of the conductor's innocent act was unforeseen.

The law also has to deal with cases where someone attempts to do something criminal but it's logically impossible. For instance, a fellow rigs a false side in his suitcase so he can smuggle lace doilies from Belgium back into America. He hopes to avoid a tariff on such items, not knowing that, while he was in Europe, the tariff had been repealed. When the customs official discovers the lace in the hidden compartment, he knows the man tried to break the law but that there was no longer such law to break. Should he be charged with "attempted theft" in the sense that shooting a corpse, thought to be alive, would be "attempted murder"?

"Intention" plays a big role in discussions of human action. (Of course, birds do things too, like migrate, but most see a big difference between swallows and Guatemalans making their way to San Juan Capistrano.) Yes, I sneeze, and it may be reported as something I did, but it wasn't intentional. So does it make sense to describe the sneeze as an *action*? And how far may an intention extend in describing an action? If you intend a tweet to ruin an authority figure (call him Nigel), and it does, is it fair to say of you, "He brought down Nigel"? How much credit or blame is due one, especially when the prospects were incredibly remote despite the depth of one's intentions?

And what are intentions anyway? Are they part of a causal chain, like falling dominoes, with your ambition to unseat a celebrity driving you to feverishly key in 280 momentous characters? But what if you're just horsing around, tossing out something outlandish, meant as a joke? If the consequences of those were the same, would we still describe them both with "He destroyed Nigel's career"? (Incidentally, G. E. M. Anscombe, whom we meet in the "newspaper weather map" piece, wrote extensively and influentially on the matter of intentions.)

Back to Edward Briney's intentions. He said he didn't mean to hurt anyone. How might that be? The window with the gun was covered with tin, so intruders couldn't see what was coming. And there was no sign announcing the presence of a loaded firearm. So his claim seems empty—unless, that is, we read it very generously to say that he didn't mean to hurt *just anybody who might come along* (e.g., surely not a young woman fleeing a rapist and seeking refuge in the old house), and that he hoped the device would never be triggered. But he clearly meant to injure any thief who might venture therein, for, as he testified, he "was mad and tired of being tormented."

His wife, Bertha, moderated his plan a bit by persuading him to lower the barrel so as to hit the invader's knees rather than his belly. And that raises the question of group action. May we give her joint credit for maiming Katko, since the couple collaborated? Or, rather, should we say that Bertha and not Edward saved Marvin's life?

Rich material for philosophical sorting, a topic heavy with implications for praise and blame, reward and punishment.

Discussion Questions:

1. When I was a pastor in Evanston, Illinois, I prepared a handout linking prominent street names to the city's Christian heritage, signs honoring, for instance, such Methodist luminaries as John Wesley and Francis Asbury, and Women's Christian Temperance Union founder Frances Willard. The project took me to the Northwestern University archives, where I read through the files on the various presidents, beginning with devout Christians, but leading to secular administrations. I'm always intrigued by turning points in this context, and I think the shift occurred under President Marcy, himself a street namesake. If this is the case, would it be fair to say that Marcy set the university on a new path and thus "fathered" its secularization?

2. In a 1977 Massachusetts case, *Commonwealth v. Golston*, we learn of a man who selected a citizen at random on a city sidewalk and hit him in the head with a baseball bat. The damage was devastating, and the victim was put on life support. When it was clear that he was "brain dead," the hospital "pulled the plug," and Golston was charged with murder. At trial, his team argued that the man was still alive when they were separated, and that the party who changed the victim's status from living to dead was the medical staffer who turned off the respirator. So who did the killing deed?

3. Thomas Aquinas introduced the "principle of double effect" to provide moral cover for the unavoidable collateral damage that comes from doing a justifiable deed. For instance, today, if life-saving chemo or radiation treatment for a cancer-stricken pregnant woman results in the death of the child in her womb, it is more appropriate to say

that the doctors saved her life (with unfortunate consequences for the baby) than that the doctors killed the baby. This issue comes up in a quandary posed by British philosopher Philippa Foot in 1967. She asks us to consider a runaway trolley bearing down on five men at work on the rails. If our subject pulls the switch, diverting the train to a side track, she saves five lives, but a single man at work on this other section is killed. Should she pull the switch? If so, what does she say to the child who confronts her, tearfully, with, "You killed my daddy!"?

4. Is standing on the shore watching a man drown when you could have extended a cane pole for him to grasp an act or a failure to act?

5. As the saying goes, "Sticks and stones will break my bones, but words will never hurt me." Is this true? Is battery typically more harmful than calumny?

Kitzmiller v. Dover Area School District

U.S. District Court for the
Middle District of Pennsylvania
400 F. Supp. 2d 707 (2005)

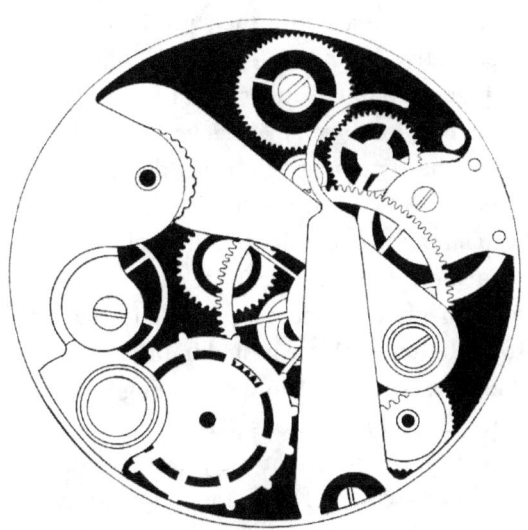

Not thrilled that the state of Pennsylvania required the teaching and testing of students' grasp of Darwin's theory of evolution, the Dover, Pennsylvania, school board passed a measure requiring ninth-grade biology teachers to read a statement saying that Intelligent Design was an alternative account of the origin of life, and to let the students know that the ID book *Of Pandas and People* was available to them. With the help of the American Civil Liberties Union and Americans United for Separation of Church and

State, eleven parents, including the eponymous Tammy Kitzmiller, sued for removal of this statement. The Thomas More Law Center took up the cause of the plaintiffs. The trial featured a range of disputing experts.

In the end, Judge John E. Jones sided with the ACLU, saying that the ID movement was really an agent of fundamentalist creationists, who wanted to use it as a "wedge" to get Bible indoctrination into the public schools. Besides, he argued, it wasn't science at all, and so it had no place in the science classroom.

He held that true science shunned reference to the supernatural, that it insisted on empirically verifiable or falsifiable statements, and that "methodological naturalism" was the valid way to speak of origins. To open the door to ID would be to supplant science with the "establishment of religion" in violation of the First Amendment.

In due course, Judge Jones was honored by the American Humanist Association with their religious liberty award, and by the Geological Society of America, which gave him their presidential medal. Not so impressed were conservative commentators Bill O'Reilly, Ann Coulter, Phyllis Schlafly, and distinguished philosopher Alvin Plantinga.

In a piece for *Evolution News & Science Today* (evolutionnews.org), Plantinga said that the statement "God has designed 800-pound rabbits that live in Cleveland" was "clearly testable, clearly falsifiable and indeed clearly false." So reference to God doesn't disqualify a statement from empirical validity. Furthermore, statements of particular design are no more immediately confirmable or disposable than the claim that "There is at least one electron." Rather, both are nested in broader conceptual schemes, which rise or fall as a package of understanding (or misunderstanding). And in this connection, ID is a serious player.

Plantinga went on to argue that the judge had succumbed to (or arrogated to himself the privilege of) arbitrary stipulation:

> Suppose I claim all Democrats belong in jail. One might ask: Could I advance the discussion by just defining the word "Democrat" to mean "convicted felon"? If you defined "Republican" to mean "unmitigated scoundrel," should Republicans everywhere hang their heads in shame? So this definition of "science" the judge appeals to is incorrect as a matter of fact because that is not how the word is ordinarily used. But even if the word "science" were ordinarily used in such a way that its definition included methodological naturalism, that still wouldn't come close to settling the issue. The

question is whether ID is science. That is not a merely verbal question about how a certain word is ordinarily used.

Of course, Jones had all the encouragement he needed to do this from the plaintiff's "experts." Indeed, this is a conceit widely held by materialistic scientists, as we see from this rare candid statement by Harvard evolutionist Richard Lewontin. The prof let this slip in a *New York Review of Books* book review back in 1997, and Berkeley law professor Phillip Johnson brought it to light that same year in a *First Things* article, "The Unraveling of Scientific Materialism":

> We take the side of science in spite of the patent absurdity of some of its constructs, in spite of its failure to fulfill many of its extravagant promises of health and life, in spite of the tolerance of the scientific community for unsubstantiated just-so stories, because we have a prior commitment, a commitment to materialism. It is not that the methods and institutions of science somehow compel us to accept a material explanation of the phenomenal world, but, on the contrary, that we are forced by our a priori adherence to material causes to create an apparatus of investigation and a set of concepts that produce material explanations, no matter how counter-intuitive, no matter how mystifying to the uninitiated. Moreover, that materialism is absolute, for we cannot allow a Divine Foot in the door. The eminent Kant scholar Lewis Beck used to say that anyone who could believe in God could believe in anything. To appeal to an omnipotent deity is to allow that at any moment the regularities of nature may be ruptured, that miracles may happen.

And we couldn't let that happen, could we. So the game is rigged, and Judge Jones was in on the game, perhaps unwittingly, but certainly self-congratulatorily.

To show the arrogance of this understanding of science, I pose a forensic medicine case, one involving a dead jogger in Central Park. Though there are no signs of foul play, and though it's assumed to be an instance of heart failure, one detective has his doubts—and he's right. An extremely clever assassin had insinuated a tiny, pin-prick, hard-to-detect-poison device into the runner's left shoe, and a microscopic hole under the second toe ultimately revealed the lethal entry point. Though his colleagues laughed at him for his conspiracy theory, he persisted, insisting that another party was involved. And in doing so, he didn't cease to be scientific.

CASES

That's what the ID people are saying, in effect—that somebody was involved in engineering the circumstances before us. And, by the way, we'll meet him one day. In fact, his existence makes the most sense of what we see before us, and the agnostic position seems to be the one requiring the most strain to maintain.

Of course, Judge Jones and Kitzmiller and the ACLU will disavow any interest in addressing the existence of God and his sovereignty. They're just standing up for the integrity of science. Never mind that revolutionary scientists from Newton to Leeuwenhoek to Mendel freely associated their work and findings with divine "intelligent design." Many scientists have now moved beyond that to the "high country" of naturalistic insulation/isolation. (One wonders if they'd say "Shut up" to a brain surgeon who found no tumor the day after the MRI had announced a golf-ball-sized malignancy and then exclaimed, "It's a miracle. They said they were praying for one, but I didn't think it was possible." Would he have to turn in his scientific credentials on grounds of epistemological treason?)

One last thing: Judge Jones prides himself on uncovering an ID strategy of advancing biblical creationism by means of a "wedge" strategy. But so what? What business does he have judging the motives of the parties? Why couldn't he just as well fault the plaintiffs for their ulterior interest in undermining belief in the Creator God? "Oh yes, they may dress up their atheism in fine talk of science and all that, but we know what they're up to." How would that fly? Not far. But that's the sort of irrelevancy he entertains to the contrary. A sorry spectacle.

DISCUSSION QUESTIONS:

1. Phillip Johnson distinguishes science that works with repeatable testing (e.g., concerning the impact of second-hand smoke on the lungs of non-smokers or the load-bearing qualities of various alloys) from that which admits of no reruns to confirm or disconfirm the hypothesis (e.g., the origin of the universe or the reason for sparrow bones in an ancient grave). He argues that it's illegitimate to presume that the reliability of the former (in biomedical research and metallurgy) carries over into the reliability of the latter (in cosmology and archaeology). Is he right?

2. David Hume argued that even if nature suggested design, it wouldn't prove the existence of the God of the Christians, for the world is

demonstrably flawed and our experience of it could just as well point to the first stumbling effort of a baby god or the last acts of a dying god. What do you make of this?

3. In *Witness*, his account of leaving communism, Whittaker Chambers wrote:

> It was shortly before we moved to Alger Hiss's apartment in Washington. My daughter was in her high chair. I was watching her eat. She was the most miraculous thing that had ever happened in my life. I liked to watch her even when she smeared porridge on her face or dropped it meditatively on the floor. My eye came to rest on the delicate convolutions of her ear—those intricate, perfect ears.
>
> The thought passed through my mind: "No, those ears were not created by any chance coming together of atoms in nature (the Communist view). They could have been created only by immense design."
>
> The thought was involuntary and unwanted. I crowded it out of my mind. But I never wholly forgot it or the occasion. I had to crowd it out of my mind. If I had completed it, I should have had to say: "Design presupposes God." I did not then know that, at that moment, the finger of God was first laid upon my forehead.

He'd been a savvy writer for *Time* and was involved in intricate spy plots. Had he now gone soft in the head?

4. Which takes more faith: to believe in an intelligent designer or to believe it was all the result of natural forces?

5. Hebrews 11:2 says, "By faith we understand that the universe was formed at God's command, so that what is seen was not made out of what was visible." If it's a matter of faith, was Judge Jones right in saying it had no place in a science classroom?

6. Some Christians have espoused a Darwinian account of origins, but they say God used some sort of guided natural selection as his method—theistic evolution. Why might God work in this way? Is it a plausible option or, rather, a stretch?

7. A number of other astute writers have argued for Intelligent Design, e.g., Michael Behe, with his insistence on "irreducible complexity," and William Dembski, with his case for the statistical unlikelihood

of the materialist account. Are you familiar with these thinkers and their notions? Or with others in this vein?

8. For purposes of calibration, instruments need an external standard to check their accuracy, e.g., atomic clocks to determine whether the time we read on our smartphones is the right one. But what about calibration for instruments purporting to determine the age of geological samples? What independent device tells us that the carbon-14 method is up to the job? Can we appeal to potassium-argon dating? If so, what give us confidence that it's a reliable indicator of the age of the Earth's rocks, pegged at around 4.5 billion years? About the best we can do is to consult the rings in old trees, the most ancient at around 5,000 years. That should be the extent of our calibrating confidence. But doesn't that force an astounding leap of extrapolation: "If it's reliable for 1/900,000th of the way back in time, it must work the rest of the way. It's been uniform so far. No reason to think otherwise of the distant past."

Well, for one thing, the biblical account describes one-time cosmic events, miracles, upheavals, fast-forwards, slow-downs, etc. Are believers to take seriously the scientist (and his acolytes) who say these things couldn't have happened, or at least couldn't be spoken of "scientifically," when the basis for their sweeping declaration is beneath miniscule? Wouldn't it rather be right to say that we're all "faithing it" a bit in this arena?

McGuinn v. Clarke

United States District Court for
the Middle District of Florida
Docket # 8:89-CV-DV-00518 (1989)

BEGINNING with five members in 1964, the rock group The Byrds went through a host of permutations over the next thirty-six years, with eleven different men serving with the band in its first ten years. Only Jim McGuinn was there throughout the changes, and he himself evolved spiritually to the point that he changed his name to Roger under the tutelage of a religious advisor of the Subud faith, a form of mysticism founded in Indonesia in the 1920s. (Happy to say, McGuinn became a Christian in 1977.) Some who left the group (David Crosby in 1967, Gram Parsons in 1968) went on to careers with other bands (in the former case, with Crosby, Stills, Nash and Young; in the latter, with the Flying Burrito Brothers). Finally, after several iterations, the group disbanded in 1973.

But then, in the late 1980s, Michael Clarke, who had left in 1967, attempted to appropriate the Byrds' name for his own band, which included another original member, Gene Clark. At this provocation, Roger McGuinn joined with David Crosby and Chris Hillman, yet another original member, who left in 1968, in a preemptive/retaliatory reunion tour in 1989, and in a suit claiming false advertising, unfair competition, and deceptive trade practices.

So, we may ask, who were the real Byrds in 1989? The Clark/Clarke version, which had two of the original members, or the reconstituted McGuinn version, with three? Did three beat two? Or did the fact that the version with three had simply ceased to exist for over a decade matter? Could they really claim to be the *real* thing in perpetuity when they weren't a thing at all for years?

On top of this we may ask whether McGuinn was the same McGuinn who started with the band, or had his soul transformation, ultimately to Christianity, made him a different person, meaning that, at a deeper level, there were no more than two founders present in the "McGuinn" band in 1989?

In this vein, philosophers have wrangled for ages over the essential properties of a thing. The Greeks puzzled over the case of a ship which had been restored one plank at time. Aristotle said it was the same ship if the "formal cause" (the design) was identical. But what of two exact replicas? And a simpler case involves the notion of "grandfather's ax," which, through the years, had seen the head and handle replaced at different times. Then there's the matter of the seventy-year-old man who has an entirely different set of cells, replacements for those in his twenty-year-old version. Is physical continuity the key?

A big arena for this discussion concerns the nature of personal identity—what makes you *you*? Classical and medieval philosophers spoke of each man having a soul (the medievalists informed by biblical attestations), but the eighteenth-century Scottish philosopher David Hume said he couldn't discover his own soul through introspection. As he wrote in *A Treatise of Human Nature*:

> For my part, when I enter most intimately into what I call myself, I always stumble on some particular perception or other, of heat or cold, light or shade, love or hatred, pain or pleasure. I never can catch myself at any time without a perception, and never can observe anything but the perception.

So he gave us a "bundle theory" of the soul—a rope, if you will, of experiences with no single fiber or strand running the length of the line. This stood in opposition to the conviction that the soul was like an electrical wire, with an unbroken thread of metal running though it all.

This raised the further question of what it was that made my experiences *mine* and not somebody else's, and the major Humean critic, the German Immanuel Kant, answered by postulating what he called the "transcendental unity of apperception," the necessary ground for the ownership and organization of experiences. The soul's not a thing seen, but rather the means by which our seeing is possible or orderly.

Earlier, in Britain, seventeenth-century philosopher John Locke had said that memory was, so to speak, the principle of ownership. Remembrance ties things together for the individual. Even though I'm only currently aware of my present headache, the headache I remember having a week ago is mine by virtue of its place on the "hard drive" of my consciousness. So we're not created anew in each instant. We have a story, which makes each chapter an instance of us.

Of course, the question naturally arises, "How about amnesia?" If the person can't tie his current existence to the past, how can he be the same person? And what of his eternal destiny if he dies before sorting out his faith, having forgotten through amnesia or dementia that he made a commitment to Christ in his "former life"? In what sense is he still a disciple? (A Christian would trust that God does the sorting and saving, and he keeps track of his own, even when they can't keep track of themselves.)

It works the other direction, too. When a person is saved, he becomes, according to the Bible, a "new creation." He is "born again." How then, is he the same person? Well, certainly, we say, colloquially, that "he's a completely different man," but we also say, colloquially, that "he used to be wild," implying that it was the same person back then, but with a different character. (I think it's reasonable to say that Bob is still Bob, but with a different perspective and temperament. The "entirely new person" talk is hyperbole, but with a good point.)

Materialists, of course, tie personal identity to the physical body, but a thought experiment can challenge that conceit. Playing off illustrations in the philosophical literature, I ask my seminary students to imagine that a classmate slumps over dead and that, in the midst of our fruitless efforts at resuscitation, one of us gets a call from someone claiming to be that very person who died before our eyes. He expresses his astonishment that he's standing in front of Buckingham Palace in a red uniform and bearskin hat, but he insists that he'd just arrived in that body and that he was in class only a few minutes earlier.

CASES

Baffled, we gather our wits as best we can and start asking questions: "Who was sitting on the back row and asked about whether we should double-space or single-space the term paper?" "Bob Falkenberry." "Okay, who was sick today and had to miss class?" "Rupert Davis." "Try this: Dr. Coppenger told a joke about what?" "The Jeff Foxworthy one where he says that you may be a redneck if the last words of a close relative were 'Hey, y'all, watch this.'" "Well, yes."

And so on it goes, checking out at every turn. Would it be so crazy to say the palace guard was the same person, yet in a different body? And might this not also be the case if all the memory checks turned out positive, but now the fellow cursed like a sailor and said he had no use for Christ? Couldn't we say he'd changed bodies and also had a transformation in spirit and conviction, but that he was still our acquaintance?

This sort of thing keeps philosophers busy. But it also should intrigue the man on the street, or in the pew. What is your essence, both as a human and as an individual? And how much of what you currently are—body, conscience, convictions, dispositions, memories, associations, appearance—could drop away without your ceasing to be the same person?

DISCUSSION QUESTIONS:

1. Some have claimed that departed Christians fall into "soul sleep" when they die, existing in a state of unconsciousness until Judgment Day. Indeed, they are so oblivious to what's happened and is happening that the very next experience they have after death is the presence of Christ at the end of history on Earth. And not only is their awareness on hold; their physical bodies are gone (whether rotted in the grave, consumed in a fiery wreck, or eaten by fish after a fatal spill overboard). So, in what sense could you be anywhere?

2. The Bible speaks of demon possession (in one case with a "legion" of occupying minions); psychology speaks of Dissociative Identity Disorder, the appearance of multiple personalities. So how do we sort out the real person from the pretenders, from the parasites?

3. Texas Governor George Bush refused to stay the execution of convicted murderer Karla Faye Tucker. Many prominent voices, including those of Christian leaders, urged him to reconsider since she had become a vibrant Christian in prison. She wasn't, so to speak, the

same person who had brutally dispatched a man and a woman with a pickax? What do you make of their plea?

4. Hebrews 4:12 says that "the word of God is alive and active. Sharper than any double-edged sword, it penetrates even to dividing soul and spirit, joints and marrow; it judges the thoughts and attitudes of the heart" (NIV). How are we to think about this? Is there a difference between soul and spirit? If so, which, if either, is more essential to our personhood?

5. Eastern religions teach reincarnation according to karma, with, for instance, a thief in peril of returning as a rat in his next life. But if the rat has no recollection of the thief's thieving (or of his previous human life at all), in what sense can we say it's the same person?

6. Several companies offer DNA and archival studies to determine ancestry, and the ads for these services feature customer testimonials where the people say how pleased they were to learn more about who they were. To what extent, if any, does knowledge of your forefathers' and foremothers' ethnicity and circumstances help you get a better fix on your personal identity?

Naruto v. Slater

U.S. Court of Appeals,
Ninth Circuit (April 23, 2018)

This case was brought on behalf of a seven-year-old crested macaque on the Indonesian island of Sulawesi "by and through his Next Friends, People for the Ethical Treatment of Animals, Inc." The plaintiffs claimed that the monkey, Naruto, suffered from copyright infringement, but the court ruled that animals couldn't have copyrights. The controversy began when David Slater left his camera unattended, and the monkey took some selfies, which Slater later published.

This was the same PETA that ran an ad one holiday season featuring the feathered occupants of a turkey farm on one side and Holocaust dorm residents on the other, with the wording "Holocaust on a Plate," equating the slaughter of Thanksgiving and Christmas birds with the slaughter of Jews. But surely there is a morally relevant difference.

I was little relieved to hear a panelist at an American Philosophical Association breakout session suggesting that it would take 10,000 German shepherds to equal one person in value. That is to say, if we had a shipload of 10,001 German shepherds and a dingy with one man on it, we would ensure the survival of the former over the latter if we had to choose.

Of course, the Christian would object that man is created in the image of God, and animals are not—and this makes all the difference. (Christians are not alone in this special esteem for humanity. For instance, Immanuel Kant said that rational nature was an end in itself, and that entities that lacked it could be treated as means—as in a meal, a zoo exhibit, or an organ donation, e.g., of a pig's heart valve—without their consent.)

To be sure, Christians have been in on the crusade against animal cruelty. In England, pastor Arthur Broome's 1822 book, *The Duty of Mercy and the Sin of Cruelty to Brute Animals*, helped lead to the founding of the SPCA in 1824. In America, Alexander Majors, one of the founders of the Pony Express, had a rule for his wagon freight company (whose holdings were so extensive it was said that should the company's wagons and oxen be lined up, they would extend fifty miles). It simply read, "Man and beast must rest on the Sabboth."

It's one thing to stave off cruelty to animals and rescue them from torment, but quite another to grant them human rights. For one thing, the biggest transgressors would be animals themselves. Just watch *Animal Planet* or *Nat Geo Wild*, and you'll soon see some vicious predation, as with crocodiles of the Serengeti grasping a wildebeest by the neck and dragging it under water in a death roll. If we're going to treat them like humans, then we'd have to position closed-circuit cameras at river crossings so we could identify the murderous beasts and bring them to justice. (English philosopher Roger Scruton has argued that if we grant them human rights, we should also insist that they answer to human duties, a standard they cannot meet.)

Perhaps you've heard that some radical environmentalists have gone back to the writings of seventeenth-century philosopher Baruch Spinoza for support in extending rights to non-sentient beings, including trees and rocks. Arguing that there was only one substance, Spinoza forged a pantheism that rendered rivers as divine as children. This should have struck Spinoza as a reduction to absurdity of his rationalistic metaphysics, but he was content with the absurdity, as are a host of our contemporaries.

Australian philosophy Peter Singer popularized the term "speciesism" in his 1975 book, *Animal Liberation*, arguing that granting unique value to human persons *per se* was immoral. He has puzzled over why we experiment with chimps, "yet would never think of doing the same to a retarded human being at a much lower mental level" and (as reported in the *New York Times*) "would allow parents and doctors to kill newborns with drastic disabilities (like the absence of higher brain function, an incompletely formed spine called spina bifida or even hemophilia) instead of just letting nature take its course and allowing the infants to die." (On a personal note, it was a joy to see one of my preaching students, a life-long victim of spina bifida, and confined to a wheel chair, graduate with the MDiv from SBTS.)

An interesting aspect of the case is the claim that PETA enjoys "next friend" status, which the court denied on account of the organization's failure to have a "significant relationship" with this particular animal. Not surprisingly, philosophers have dug deep into the notion of friendship, beginning well back in the persons of Plato (whose portrayal of Socrates in the *Lysis* dialogue shows dogged pursuit of the essence of this phenomenon) and Cicero (who takes up the matter in *De Amicitia*). Both discussions are steeped in talk of virtue, of whether true friendship requires the parties to be morally upright, a criterion that scarcely applies to a macaque. (Incidentally, the court faulted PETA for *using* the macaque for their own fundraising, since the settlement they wrangled from Slater went into their own coffers.)

Still, the animal rights enthusiasts proceed apace, as in Charles Siebert's *The Wachula Woods Accord: Toward a New Understanding of Animals*, where he speaks of Roger, an engaging twenty-eight-year-old veteran of the Ringling Brothers Circus, a creature he ventures to suggest is something of a "humanzee." In an interview with the *Animal Inventory* blog, Charles (not Roger) champions "a new collective interspecies empathy, as opposed to the ongoing parochial factionalism rooted in old rival religions and the false notion of human exclusivity."

In a 2018 *Wall Street Journal* article, Amanda Foreman noted that the Egyptians had a cat god named Bastet, "who was a goddess of violence as well as fertility," and that "in 1484, Pope Innocent VIII fanned the flames of anti-cat prejudice with his papal bull on witchcraft, *Summis Desiderates Affectibus*, which stated that the cat was 'the devil's favorite animal and idol of all witches.'" So attributing moral gravitas (whether positive or negative) to animals has a long history. Fortunately, we have the Bible to dispel the notion. They're wonderful creations and gifts of God, proper objects of our stewardship and kind dominion (Genesis 1:28), and yes, even of our consumption (Genesis 9:3).

Strange it is that "progressives" are taking us back to a day (ancient Egypt) and, in effect, to modern locales (modern India) where animals have been regarded as more than animals. As I've ridden in scooter cabs on the streets of Delhi and Agra, I've watched the traffic bend its way around cows resting in the streets. No, we wouldn't let humans do that, but Hindu belief in reincarnation can generate this annoying curiosity.

Of course, the Bible believer simply has to go to Genesis 1:26–27 to see that man and not beast was made in the image of God. And Genesis 9:6 says that the death penalty is due for shedding man's blood, since man is made in the image of God. No such pronouncement covers the killing of animals.

Crusading vegans (as distinct from non-judgmental, elective vegans) would be inclined to reject this as narrowly sectarian reasoning, but world history would argue otherwise. One simply cannot point to a vegan culture, apart from relatively small sects or cults within a larger carnivorous society.

Discussion Questions:

1. Some have argued that the evil in abusing animals, e.g., in bear-baiting, lies not in violating an animal's rights but rather in terms of the ruin such callousness brings to the human soul. Does this make sense?

2. Visiting my wife's extended family in New Mexico, we found ourselves in a pickup taking shots with a .22 at prairie dogs on her grandfather's ranch. He'd told us that his cattle would step in their burrows and break their ankles, necessitating immediate slaughter. Still, prairie dogs are so cute and innocent. That day, it occurred to me that the death of a prairie dog was quite different from that of a human, for dreams and projects are cut short for the latter, but not for the former. You can't speak of the "tragic" death of animal in the way you speak of the tragic death of a human (except, say, in terms of the way in which the untimely death of a Conestoga-pulling mule stranded a pioneer family in a prairie snowstorm). Right?

3. Are zoos *per se* cruel to animals? Are circuses? Are Central Park horse-drawn carriages?

CASES

4. Some pet owners are indignant and/or grieved at the suggestion that their cats or dogs won't make it to heaven. Is there any reason to think they will have an afterlife?

5. When New York billionaire Leona Helmsley died, she left twelve million dollars to her dog. A judge later determined that this was far more than was needed to take care of the pet, so he reduced the amount to two million. He wouldn't have done this had Trouble (the name of the Maltese) been human. Did he get it right?

6. In the Bible, God points to the admirable features of animals in a number of passages, e.g., the diligence of the ant in Proverbs 6:6 and the seasonal instincts of the stork in Jeremiah 8:7. Consider ways that such creatures bring glory to the Lord and blessing to us.

7. Darwinians teach that species (and kingdoms, phyla, orders, families, and varieties) emerge and advance through survival of the fittest. Wouldn't this mean that some types of animals are expendable? Isn't it easier to base endangered species (or at least endangered orders) legislation on the scriptural teaching that God created the *kinds* of animals, rather than upon a purely materialistic account of their emergence?

Owen v. Crumbaugh

Supreme Court of Illinois
81 N.E. 1044 (1907)

THE nephews and nieces of affluent Illinois banker and landowner James T. Crumbaugh were indignant that the family had been slighted in his will. Crumbaugh's wife and only child had died, and the estate would normally have flowed to his siblings and their offspring, but he went in a different direction, endowing the construction and sustenance of a Spiritualist church and a public library. The relatives argued that the will was based on a falsehood, namely, Crumbaugh's declaration that he was in his "right mind and natural mind" when he wrote it. They claimed that anybody who believed in communicating with the dead through séances was mentally unfit to bequeath anything to anybody and that distribution of his wealth should be determined by the courts, which gave preference to close kin.

Deciding in Crumbaugh's favor, the Supreme Court of Illinois rehearsed his life and faith, drawing on the testimony of dozens of witnesses in the trial court, and they reviewed the law of competency, including one of their own precedent decisions. They concluded that allegiance to a curious religious sect was not enough to declare one delusional.

Actually, Crumbaugh himself once thought the Spiritualist faith ridiculous, but he came around at his wife's urging and in response to some dramatic experiences of his own. Most striking was what he took to be communion with his son, who died in infancy, but who now lived maturely as "Bright Eyes" in the "spirit land." He was convinced that Bright Eyes had intervened to rescue him on several occasions, wherein he narrowly escaped damage from a flying object, a fire, and a fall.

Though the Spiritualists trafficked in alleged "clairaudience," that is, "clear hearing, rapping, moving of tables or moving of furniture, trumpet séance, materialization, writing, spirit healing . . . and spirit photography," the court said it was in no position to draw a firm line between acceptable and unacceptable belief and practice, whether Baptist or Swedenborgian, whether treasure hunting with a small metal ball suspended on a thread or water seeking with a forked wooden stick. When such luminaries as Sir William Blackstone, Sir Francis Bacon, John Wesley, Martin Luther, and Cotton Mather believed in witches, how could the court disallow a will on grounds that the subject had strong convictions regarding the supernatural?

Instead, they appealed to standards hammered out in previous cases, decisions that spoke of insanity in terms of a conception arising "spontaneously in the mind, without evidence of any kind to support it," of "something extravagant" which "has no existence whatever but in his heated imagination," and of a person "incapable of being permanently reasoned out of that conception." Besides, Crumbaugh was a model citizen and excellent businessman, and critics would need to prove his madness was isolated, a notion the courts didn't buy.

Philosophers have a similar challenge—determining what counts as rational, not only in particular instances but as a general matter. In doing so, they don't rely strictly, as philosophers, on Scripture to make their case. Neither can they settle matters by pointing to test results in the manner of metallurgists, electrical engineers, or geneticists. Rather, they work at a level of abstraction whose reception depends upon the audience's hunger for coherence, consistency, palatability, splendor, wholesomeness, simplicity, fellow-feeling, and other such desirables, which may or may not be in play in the culture. Their stock in trade is the *reductio ad absurdum* ("reduction to absurdity"), which presses proffered principles and proposals to the breaking point, if such can be found. For instance, when one says there's no right and wrong, that morals are relative, then a critic might reply, "Well, then, I suppose it's okay to murder you, right?"

Most would balk at agreeing to this, and would reverse themselves to abandon or qualify their initial claim. But there's the rub. Some won't do this. They'll double down on what strikes most as stupid, and you can't break the impasse by quoting the Sixth Commandment or detailing the physiology of death. Rather, you leave it to whatever audience there might be to roll their eyes and discount his value as a thinker. Maybe you'll say something gracious like, "Well, we'll just have to agree to disagree," but you're thinking, "This fellow's a Crumbaugh before whom I shall not cast pearls." More likely, you'll back up and try another line of argument, seeking to undermine the fellow's conviction with an analogy, a piece of definitional surgery, or another implication.

Fact of the matter is, these impasses are everywhere in philosophy, and so philosophers break down into schools of thought, wherein they can find aid, fellowship, and comfort. It's the sort of thing you find among doctors, where allopathics are not much impressed with homeopathics, and chiropractors and acupuncturists live in different therapeutic worlds, each gainsaying the rationality of the other. But philosophy departments typically have a mix of each—analytical, continental, Eastern, existential, etc.—with more or less grudging courtesies extended as they patronize the others' "wacky" enthusiasm for Anselm, Leibniz, Hegel, Berkeley, Wittgenstein, Husserl, Kripke, Quine, or Žižek.

So why bother with philosophy at all, given the lack of common standards of rationality? Because the issues are too important to ignore, and because God gave us reason, of which we are to be stewards, even if others don't appreciate our stewardship. Still, it can be a sweet thing to find accord with those who share your sense of what is absurd or what is plausible in the realm of big ideas. And, along the way, you may discover that you've been entertaining an absurdity unaware, and your former detractors can prove to be your deliverers, at least at one point or another.

CASES

DISCUSSION QUESTIONS:

1. Are some Christians less "rational" than others? If so, does this mean they're farther off the mark in their faith, or is this a sign that they're closer to the heart of things, where the cold intellect is unwelcome?

2. What should we make of the commendation, "You'll love our new youth director. He's crazy!"?

3. Many atheists and secular humanists pride themselves on being more rational than Christians, and some heap scorn on believers as mental lightweights. What then shall we make of such distinguished scholars as Blaise Pascal (who invented a mechanical calculator in the 1600s) and the Oxford don C. S. Lewis? Were they smart and accomplished in spite of their faith or, in measure, because of it?

4. Saints Augustine and Anselm said that they believed that they might understand. For them, acknowledgement of God and Christ were the proper beginning points for learning. Does that make sense?

5. Some critics lump faiths (whether Christian, Hindu, Muslim, Buddhist, or Mormon) together as absurd and toxic (cf., Christopher Hitchens's *God Is Not Great: How Religion Poisons Everything*). But aren't there great differences in reasonableness among the various beliefs?

People v. Elmer

Supreme Court of Michigan
67 N.W. 550 (1896)

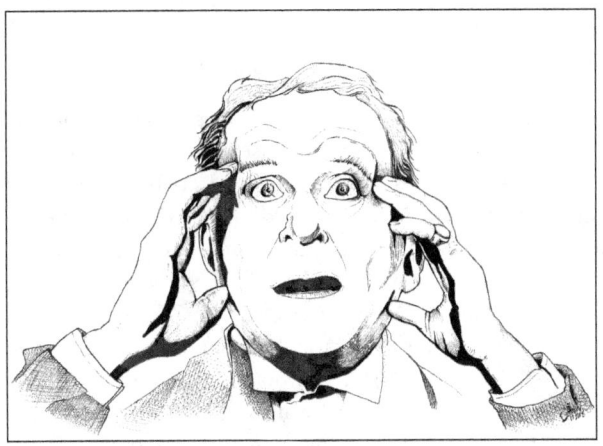

Arthur Elmer was convicted of being a "disorderly person" when he published a newspaper ad saying:

> Will Arrive at Ionia, Mich., July 23, 1895. A modern day seer is now in the city, and can be consulted on all conceivable affairs of life and human destiny. This strange gift, which he only uses to the advantage of the human race, excites the wonder and admiration of the most skeptical, and will drive doubt from your mind, and slay skepticism on the threshold of the interview. Being born with this marvelous power, and thoroughly conversant with the occult science, his revelations are truly wonderful, and acknowledged to be of the highest order. It has been said of him: "Never in the annals of clairvoyancy have future events been so truthfully foretold." He permits you a peep through the keyhole of the mysterious future, by which you may obtain the key of your future life and

success. Advises you with a strange certainty of the proper course to pursue in life. If business affairs concern you, he gives advice on business transactions, lawsuits, wills, mortgages, speculations, pension claims, and other financial difficulties. If affairs of the heart or emotions of love interest you, he gives you some astonishing revelations of courtship, marriage, divorce, and domestic troubles. Restores lost affection, peace, and confidence to lovers and discordant families on a positive guaranty. Tells the name of your future husband or wife, and date of marriage. Locates lost, stolen, and buried property and treasures, on positive guaranty. No money taken until goods are in your possession. Also locates friends and relatives. No charge until you find them. Psychometry, or soul reading. Doctor gives delineations of character, and tells what you are best adapted for.

The court then summarized his further claims:

The respondent also advertised himself as a "magnetic healer" and "clairvoyant physician." This advertisement was accompanied by several letters from those who claimed to have been treated by him and cured. Several witnesses testified that they went to the respondent; that he pretended to go into a trance, and that, either while in it, or after he came out of it, he told them what would happen to them in the future. One witness testified: "He said the reason he went into a trance was to tell the future and the past." The justice of the peace before whom the respondent was tried testified that the respondent was a witness for himself upon the trial in justice court; that he there testified that he had advised Mrs. Webber, a witness for the people, "to leave her husband; that he had been in a trance, and had seen her husband in the act of killing her; that he called his business "prognosticating"; "looking into the future"; not "telling fortunes."

The appellate court affirmed the conviction, both citing English law, which said that "every person pretending or professing to tell fortunes . . . shall be deemed a rogue and a vagabond" and favorably citing the observation, "No person who was not a lunatic could believe he [the defendant] possessed such power."

Elmer was making some fantastical claims, but did his presumed failure to have these powers mean that they were impossible? Is it conceivable that a person could "peep through the keyhole of the mysterious future"? Could even God? That question seems odd, even blasphemous, but it surfaces in what's called the philosophy of time.

Philosophers, Christians included, have been puzzling over the nature of time for ages. Augustine wrestled with it in *Confessions* in the late fourth century, and today members of the Society of Christian Philosophers and the Evangelical Philosophical Society still tackle it. Among the questions, we find:

- If the past is gone and the future isn't yet, then is the present all that really exists currently?
- If so, how long is now?
- If the future does not yet occur, then how could anyone, including God, see it when there's nothing there to see?
- Besides, wouldn't God lock in the future if he saw it, for he couldn't be wrong about what he saw? So what room would there be for human freedom and moral responsibility?
- We hear sometimes that God created space and time. What sort of thing is time that he might create it? Eden and Adam and aardvarks are tangible things, but what is time?

Regarding the last of these questions, Aristotle suggested centuries before Christ's birth that time was somehow tied to motion, such as the movement of heavenly bodies. For instance, a rotation of the Earth could mean a day's worth of time, and its revolution around the sun could mark a year. (Of course, Aristotle didn't grasp the structure and operation of our solar system, but the idea still carries over.)

In the sixth century A.D., in an effort to maintain God's omniscient foreknowledge, Boethius pictured God outside of time, as if on a hill viewing, all at once, the whole span of history, with 400 B.C. and 400 A.D. simultaneously available to his gaze. (And yes, we have to use time talk, such as "simultaneous" to explain time here.) So it's no problem for the Lord to be looking directly at our next year as he looks directly at our previous year. And this solves the problem of our being brutally predestined to make damnable choices, for there's no genuine "pre" to our predestination. We just do it, and he sees it and says, "So be it," with consequences to follow.

Others have no problem with the notion of a God who indeed shapes us and our destinies, who is able to "see" the future because he knows precisely what he will *do* and *do with us* in the future. Still others choose a mediating account associated with the sixteenth-century's Luis de Molina—Molinism. Knowing our natures, God works with "middle knowledge" or "counterfactuals" (if-then truths) whereby he can channel our choices in directions he desires without violating our wills. (It's not entirely unlike my knowing that *if* I tell you not to think of an elephant, *then* I know you will.)

Those who construe God as "atemporal" locate him before and outside of time, with the opening "a" (or "alpha privative") signaling that he is not "timeish." (Note the way the "a" in "atheist" signifies that the person is not God-accepting.) But there is an option, that of calling God "everlasting," not outside of time, but the eternal master of it. According to this way of thinking, time is essentially a matter of transition—of any sort—and the sequence of thoughts and acts of mutuality among the members of the Trinity before creation insured that time was flowing. Things were going on, one after another—hence, the passage of time, albeit without creation and its populace present.

Not surprisingly, Christians aren't the only ones at work on these matters. For instance, in 1908, British philosopher J. M. E. McTaggart wrote a piece with the self-explanatory title, "The Unreality of Time," in which he distinguished two sorts of temporal series: "A," consisting of future, present, and past events; and "B," which speaks of earlier and later events. In B, the Normandy Invasion is fixed in time, always later than Pearl Harbor and earlier than the Inchon Landing. In A, the Normandy Invasion was "on the move" in 1945, transitioning from future to past as the Allied troops moved off the beaches into the French countryside. He concludes that neither A nor B, nor both together, can get a fix on the nature of time. And then, of course, there are the scientists who preach the relativity of time and a time-space continuum.

Well, Arthur Elmer didn't lose any sleep over these distinctions and problems (though he likely lost some sleep over what repercussions he might face should people judge him a "lunatic" or a "rogue and a vagabond."). But, before proceeding, we should ask what the Bible has to say on this. After all, being a Christian philosopher entails taking the counsel of Scripture seriously.

Discussion Questions:

1. What would it be to experience every measure of a symphony at the same moment? Wouldn't it be a thunderous, incoherent mishmash of sounds? Then what sense can we make of God's experiencing every moment of human history at the same time, not strung out in

episodic sequences? Wouldn't this be chaotic? If so, how could we use it as a paradigm of his non-coercive sovereignty?

2. What are some Bible verses that speak of time? Do they settle the "everlasting"/"atemporal" dispute one way or the other?

3. If someone objects that God must not be bound by time, what sort of limitation would they suppose this entails? What exactly do they suppose he couldn't do under these circumstances?

4. Arthur Elmer spoke of the ability to look forward in time. What if he had claimed to travel forward (or backward) in time? What sense could that possibly make? Could God go forward or backward in time?

5. If everything stopped everywhere—the motion of objects; perceptions; thoughts; actions, both human and divine—would time stop?

6. We talk of "phenomenological" time—experienced time. A thirty-minute sermon can seem like twenty minutes or forty minutes, depending upon its content and delivery, plus our own physical or mental condition. The Bible says that a thousand years is like a day to God. Is there similarity between his and our experience of time? We can get bored, and time seems to drag. Can God ever get bored?

7. Could God go back and change the past? How would we know it if he could and did?

People v. Nathan F. Leopold Jr. and Richard Loeb

Cook County Criminal Court #33623 and 33624

In May of 1924, two college graduates, Nathan Leopold and Richard Loeb (who'd earned their degrees, respectively, and in their late teens, from the Universities of Chicago and Michigan), committed a horrific crime. They'd kidnapped and murdered, for the intellectual challenge and thrill of it, fourteen-year-old Bobby Franks, dumping his body in a marshland culvert in northwest Indiana. In doing so, the pair failed to notice that Leopold had dropped his glasses near the corpse, a clue enabling the police to track them down.

The ensuing trial garnered a great deal of notoriety as these two privileged, despicable characters faced what promised to be execution for their deed. Yet their families secured the services of star attorney Clarence Darrow, who would go on, the next year, to defend Tennessee school teacher John Scopes in the famous "Monkey Trial" in Dayton, Tennessee. Instead of seeking release for the two young murderers, Darrow had them enter guilty pleas, and then focused on winning them life imprisonment rather than the death penalty. In this, he succeeded.

Darrow used every angle he could muster to sway the judge, arguing, among other things that massive and unfair coverage had driven the public to reflexively demand the death penalty; that Loeb was an avid reader of crime stories, a practice known to warp the character of young people; that there "was not a particle of hate . . . not a grain of malice" in this "senseless, useless, purposeless, motiveless act"; that as a spider kills a fly, "they killed him because they were made that way"; that the wealth of their families had corrupted their minds, protecting them from the challenges that shape ordinary lives; that execution would deter no one, but rather it would stir a "weak-minded person" to replicate their act; that execution wouldn't bring back the victim, and besides, Bobby had suffered little before he died; that youth were beset with powerful emotions; that World War I had made the nation callous toward life; that execution would bring unfair disgrace upon their two families; that resentment of their wealth was driving the call for execution beyond what it would have been had the boys been poor; that the hard lesson had already been learned—parents and society must attend more closely to the nurture of their children; that reading Nietzsche corrupted Leopold's mind and spirit; that Illinois had not executed men their age, and it would be turning back the clock toward the time when children were executed in England; that life imprisonment was plenty grim; that we must follow the path of love, not the one of bloodlust.

Thus it went on and on, for two days, a *tour de farce* more than a *tour de force*. Darrow had rejected a jury trial by having the boys plead guilty, becasuse, as he explained in flattering terms to the judge, "his Honor" had the wisdom of years that would allow him to rule with equanimity rather than hysteria, especially when he heard such exalted rhetoric as this:

> If there is such a thing as justice it could only be administered by one who knew the inmost thoughts of the man to whom they were meting it out. Aye, who knew the father and mother and the grandparents and the infinite number of people back of him. Who knew the origin of every cell that went into the body, who could understand the structure, and how it acted. Who could tell how the emotions that sway the human being affected that particular frail piece of clay. It means more than that. It means that you must appraise every influence that moves them, the civilization where they live, and all society which enters into the making of the child or the man! If your Honor can do it—if you can do it you are wise and with wisdom goes mercy.
>
> No one with wisdom and with understanding, no one who is honest with himself and with his own life whoever he may be, no one who has seen himself the prey and the sport and the plaything of the infinite forces that move man, no one who has tried and who has failed—and we have all tried, and we have all failed—no one can tell what justice is for someone else or for himself—and the more he tries and the more responsibility he takes the more

> he clings to mercy as being the one thing which he is sure should control his judgement of men.
>
> Thus are we tutored in the demands of "justice."

Philosophers have been at this project since Socrates' day, when, in *The Republic*, Plato shows him both rejecting bad definitions of justice ("that which is in the interest of the powerful") and proposing his favorite (popularly rendered as "everyone's minding his own business"). And, in the centuries since, the topic has been broken down into a range of genres, whether retributive, distributive, compensatory, procedural, comparative, or restorative. And the schools of thought on these desiderata fall into two broad categories—teleological (with focus on consequences) and deontological (with focus on duty).

Darrow rang chimes in both venues. In the teleological halls, he made claims about the level of suffering the parents and miscreant sons would endure; about lessons learned for going forward; about the impossibility of bringing back the victim; about the slim prospects for deterrence; about the slippery slope back toward the execution of minors. Meanwhile, over in the deontological academy, he dismissed the demands of the *lex talionis* ("eye for eye") with mitigating/extenuating (lessening) and exonerating/exculpatory (dismissing) factors. He argued that the boys were simply not responsible for what they had done; rather, the blame rested upon all the physical, historical, and cultural forces that had shaped them. Furthermore, the people were in no position to secure justice, given their fevered state of mind and epistemological limitations. Retribution was simply a nonstarter on Darrow's model.

In pleading for mercy on account of their inability to do otherwise, he echoed a ruling that came down some eighty years earlier in England, the M'Naghten case, wherein Daniel M'Naghten, who shot the wrong man while trying to assassinate the prime minister, was spared execution on account of insanity. According to the court, a defendant could be excused from responsibility for his deed (though not from incarceration for the sake of public safety) if, "at the time of the committing of the act, the party accused was labouring under such defect of reason, from a disease of the mind, as not to know the nature and quality of the act he was doing; or, if he did know it, that he did not know he was doing what was wrong."

It's pretty clear that the "M'Naghten Rule" alone would not have sufficed to save Leopold and Loeb. Not only did they know that what they were doing was wrong; they gloried in it. After all, their mentor, Nietzsche, had written, in *Beyond Good and Evil*, "The great epochs of our life come when we gain the courage to rechristen our evil as what is best in us" (the same Nietzsche who celebrated the "Superman," who turned the clock back to the day when "good" meant "intimidating," a time before sniveling Jews and Christians had recast character defects such as kindness and gentleness as virtues).

Interestingly, C. S. Lewis argued (in "The Humanitarian Theory of Punishment") that those who dismissed the death penalty in order to serve love and kindness were misguided, for there was no limit to the horrors that could be visited upon defendants if "enlightened" criteria such as rehabilitation, incarceration, and deterrence were allowed to hold sway. In contrast, only retribution insisted on limits while recognizing the dignity of the malefactor.

Those familiar with current social discourse are aware that the term "justice" is invoked *ad nauseum*, with a good deal of hyperbole and nonsense mixed in with insightful talk on the subject. Furthermore, it's used with reference to everything from taxes to wages to wars to college admissions to police profiling to immigration to the admissibility of evidence. And various champions are knighted to carry the conceptual causes into battle (such as, for instance, the Harvard colleagues John Rawls and Robert Nozick, respectively the darlings of liberals and conservatives). But, again, it boils down to whether justice is essentially a matter of principles and rules (deontology) or impacts and outcomes (teleology).

Discussion Questions:

1. It strikes me that "social justice" boils down to "equality or similarity of outcomes." If so, is this teleological approach Bible friendly?

2. Robert Nozick constructs an example wherein a lot of fans pay a little more to see a basketball star perform. The player makes a ton of money; the spectators are out only a dollar or so for the special performance. But there's vast inequality in outcomes. The star is very wealthy, the fans not so much. But everybody walks out of the arena happy. So where's the injustice, if any?

3. Some argue that there are more minorities on death row, not so much because of their ethnicity, but because of their inability to afford powerful lawyers. Yes, they have public defenders, but these are

not typically top-flight attorneys, but rather beginning counselors, not long out of law school. If this is so, where is the injustice, if any? Does this mean that we have a problem with guilty rich people going free or with innocent poor people being convicted, or both?

4. Against the death penalty, Cardinal Joseph Bernadin of Chicago introduced the notion of a "consistent ethic of life," whereby those who oppose abortion at the beginning of life should stand against execution to end it. This was a departure from the traditional teaching of the church, going back to the writings of Augustine and Aquinas, who allowed for capital punishment. An obvious objection is that there is a morally relevant difference between killing a baby in the womb and killing an ax murderer who took out a family of four in their living room. And does the Bernadin principle outlaw another classic Catholic teaching, just war (again, formulated by Augustine and Aquinas, as well as Vitoria and Suarez, along with Protestants)? Be that as it may, Illinois Governor Ryan commuted the death sentences of over a hundred convicted murderers, and garnered praise from Pope John Paul II. Was this moral progress or regress?

5. Atheistical, utilitarian philosopher Jeremy Bentham argued against the death penalty because it was irremedial. If you make a mistake imprisoning or fining someone, you can release or repay them; but once you execute and bury someone, there's nothing you can do to help him if you discover he was innocent. Of course, there are any number of government actions that are subject to error and which result in loss of life, e.g., setting confused safety standards which lead to dam failure or horror on the highways, or sending soldiers into battle on ill-conceived missions. Was Bentham being unrealistic?

People of the State of California v. Orenthal James Simpson

Los Angeles County Superior Court (1995)

For almost a year, Americans were riveted by the O. J. Simpson case. They'd seen the bloody crime scene photos and the slow-motion "chase" down an LA freeway, with Al Cowlings driving the suspect home in a white Bronco, trailed by a host of cop cars. Taken into custody, the ex-NFL star was charged with the knifing deaths of his estranged wife, Nicole, and a restaurant employee who was returning her glasses, Ronald Goldman.

Over the months of the trial, and thanks to TV coverage, we became familiar with an intriguing cast of characters, including Kato Kaelin, who lived in an apartment out back; Judge Ito; the prosecutors, Marcia Clark and Chris Darden; the defense attorneys, Johnnie Cochran and Robert Shapiro; and detective Mark Fuhrman.

It seemed that most of the nation was glued to the screen when Simpson's acquittal was telecast at 10:00 a.m. (PST), October 3, 1995. Though released that day, Simpson was hit, in 1997, with a successful "wrongful death" civil suit by the Goldman family. He wasn't in a position to pay the millions in penalties assessed, though he raised some money through auctioning memorabilia. Then, in 2007, he joined in a robbery to reclaim some items he felt were his, and he served nine years in a Nevada jail for that offense, going free in late 2017.

I think it's fair to say that most observers think Simpson "got away with murder" in the criminal trial, though Cochran and Shapiro wrote books defending the decision. (Clark and others have written books to the contrary.) The evidence, some of which was discounted in the initial trial, was damning, including DNA analyses of crime-scene blood and matching shoe prints. (Some say the fact there were only two college graduates on the jury reduced the impact of technical DNA testimony.) Perhaps the jury composition was decisive, in that eight of the twelve members were black, that the defense attorney Johnnie Cochran "played the race card," discrediting the testimony of Detective Furhman (whom he once typified "a genocidal racist, a perjurer, America's worst nightmare and the personification of evil"), and that Los Angeles was stewing from the police beating of Rodney King. Indeed, there was a level of telecast celebration in the black community, some even saying that it was high time that a black man likely guilty of black-on-white crime was released after so many whites guilty of violence toward blacks had been exonerated—"pay back," if you will. In a subsequent interview, juror Carrie Bess assented to that description, saying it was decisive in her decision, estimating that it was so with 90 percent of the jury.

Be that as it may, "mistakes were made" in the prosecution itself, most dramatically in allowing Simpson to try on the glove once soaked in blood and repeatedly frozen by its caretakers in the evidence process. With Johnnie Cochran declaring "If it doesn't fit, you must acquit," Simpson more or less struggled to put on the glove, the difficulty likely enhanced by the glove's soaking and drying, and perhaps by his calculated failure to take his anti-inflammatory arthritis medicine.

In the end, the jury didn't take long to decide that the prosecution had failed to make their case for Simpson's guilt "beyond a reasonable doubt"—less than three hours of deliberation after more than eight months of trial, which raises the question of how much doubt is reasonable. (Incidentally, a poll showed that two decades after the trial, Simpson's guilt had become the majority opinion among black Americans.)

Seventeenth-century French philosopher Rene Descartes argued that maximum doubt was reasonable, at least as a beginning point. Having heard all sorts of competing knowledge claims, having seen man's susceptibility to illusion and delusion, and wanting to find a solid foundation on which to build all respectable belief, he doubted everything he could (strategically if not genuinely), including God's existence and the reality of the physical world (as opposed to a dream state). He discovered that the one thing he couldn't doubt was that there was some doubting going on, so there must be a doubter, namely, himself.

That's not a lot to know, of course. The person who goes around saying that the only thing he really knows is that he exists as a doubter is a useless bore. Fortunately, Descartes thought he'd found a way out of his state of minimal (indeed, scarcely discernible) confidence. He figured that an infinite being had to be the cause/source of his thoughts of infinity (you can't get a greater from a lesser) and that this infinite being (obviously, God) must be perfect and thus disinclined to let us be systematically fooled by what seems to be a genuine world. So, using his reason, he climbed his way back to the surface where he could work and converse with those who hadn't gone through his descent into the abyss where everything was up for grabs.

Turns out, the world of philosophy was more impressed with his downward climb into skepticism than with the ladder he used to get back out. And they admired his search for something indubitable. "Reasonable doubt" wasn't satisfying; they wanted "impossible doubt." And so foundationalism was born.

Some would find certainty in sense experience at its most basic level, e.g., "I'm being appeared to redly" (which, philosophers argue, is even more certain than "I see something red"). Others were keen on such principles as "Everything has a sufficient reason for its existence and behavior" or "You can't have both X and not-X." And they would get busy building on these certainties. But then they would be confronted with fresh onslaughts from the skeptics, wondering, for instance, whether some of these necessities were really just definitional items or policy resolutions rather than descriptions of the world.

The bigger question was whether iron-clad certainty was worth pursuing in the first place. Wasn't it enough that a claim be plausible? Could

CASES

you really have more than probability? After all, didn't we work that way all the time, giving guesses our best shot and checking things out in the aftermath to see if our convictions could stand the test of time? Weren't we really following what philosophers called "inference to the best explanation"? If so, maybe Descartes sent us on a multi-century wild goose chase.

This isn't to say that doubt is a bad thing in itself—just that you can overdo it, as with the Simpson jury. Indeed, while they said the government lawyers failed to demonstrate Simpson's guilt "beyond a reasonable doubt," I'm more inclined to say that their failure to deliver reasonable justice is manifest "beyond a reasonable doubt."

DISCUSSION QUESTIONS:

1. In America, the burden of proof is upon the prosecution; in France, it falls upon the defense. (It's been said, concerning the American standard, "It better that a thousand guilty murderers go free than that an innocent man hang.") Which protocol is likely to produce more truth and justice?

2. Is it wise for a teacher to raise doubts for the sake of raising doubts, so that students will be challenged to "think for themselves" and not be captive to the accounts and principles they've inherited or been marinated in? Or is this too easy, like shooting fish in a barrel, and pointlessly provocative?

3. In addition to burden of proof, courts have a range of rules, such as the requirement for pretrial discovery (so that there are no big courtroom surprises for either the prosecution or the defense), the exclusion of testimony designed to impugn the character of the accused, dismissal on grounds that the accused was not properly advised of his right to remain silent, or dismissal of evidence discovered without a proper search warrant. Are such guidelines a hindrance to getting at truth or are they well conceived?

4. In the Socratic dialogues, the sophists (who served as lawyers in their day, essentially arguers for hire) were the villains, the enemies of the dogged pursuit of knowledge. Centuries later, a rough character in Shakespeare's *Henry VI*, part 2, suggested that to improve the kingdom they must first "kill all the lawyers." Today, there are

innumerable lawyer jokes (e.g., "How can you tell if a lawyer is lying? . . . His lips are moving"). How fair or unfair is this?

5. Whatever the proper burden of proof in the courtroom, how does one determine the burden of proof in an ordinary argument or a theoretical dispute?

6. Christian apologists speak of *proofs* for God's existence (e.g., teleological, ontological, cosmological, and moral), but few maintain that these are airtight. Rather, most describe them as *arguments*. And many philosophers are more inclined to work on "defeater defeaters," arguments meant to counter the non-believer's "proofs" against the faith, such as the problem of evil. That being said, did an apologetical proof or argument play a role in your own conversion or in the conversion of someone you know?

Ranieri v. Ranieri

Appellate Division, Supreme Court
of New York, Second Dept
146 A.D.2nd 34 (1989)

Two divorcees, Rocco and Rae, were wed in Suffolk County, New York, and thus became the Ranieris. Alas, the wedded bliss lasted no more than eighty-four days, at which time Rae sued for divorce, claiming to have suffered from Rocco's acts of cruelty. Complicating the matter was the prenuptial agreement they'd signed, one clause of which held that Rocco would give Rae $90,000 after they'd been married for ninety days. Rocco defended himself on several grounds, one of which was that the marriage was a nullity since it was performed by a bogus minister, one certified by the Universal Life Church, essentially a mail-order operation. (Their website keeps track of the legal fortunes of their "ministers" through the decades.)

Turns out, the vows and minister's pronouncement are examples used in the English philosopher J. L. Austin's *How to Do Things with Words*, a classic in what's called "ordinary language philosophy." This approach says that many of our philosophical puzzles can be solved by taking a closer look at the language we use, and one of his moves is to distinguish between locutions (the descriptive content: "He *said* to me, 'Shoot it'"), illocutions (the purpose of communicating the content: "He *urged* . . . me to shoot it"), and perlocutions (the effect of communicating the content: "He *persuaded* me to shoot it"). And his subsets had subsets, e.g., with verdictives, exercitives, commissives, behabitives, and expositives, each as a type of illocutionary act.

Then he discussed a peculiar sort of declaration:

> [Performatories or performatives] have on the face of them the look—or at least the grammatical make-up—of "statements"; but nevertheless they are seen, when more closely inspected, to be, quite plainly, not utterances which could be "true" or "false." Yet to be "true" or "false" is traditionally the characteristic mark of a statement. One of our examples was, for instance, the utterance "I do" (take this woman to be my lawful wedded wife), as uttered in the course of a marriage ceremony. Here we should say that in saying these words we are doing something—namely, marrying, rather than reporting something, namely that we are marrying. And the act of marrying, like, say, the act of betting, is . . . to be described as saying certain words, rather than as performing a different, inward and spiritual, action of which these words are merely the outward and audible sign.

He goes on give a number of prerequisites for these wedding vows to be valid, e.g., "There must exist an accepted conventional procedure having a certain conventional effect, that procedure to include the uttering of certain words by certain persons in certain circumstances"; and "The particular persons and circumstances in a given case must be appropriate for the invocation of the particular procedure invoked" (hence, the controversy in the Ranieri "wedding").

Thus, when the licensed minister says, "I pronounce you man and wife," he's not saying, "The knot is tied even as I speak" or "You must be man and wife." His words are neither a description nor a command, but rather an actual accomplishment of something by the very utterance of certain words in a certain context. (Elsewhere he notes the Muslim context in which the husband's statement "I divorce you" is also performative.)

Austin ventures an application to the notion of truth itself:

> The truth or falsity of statement is affected by what they leave out or put in and by their being misleading, and so on. Thus, for example, descriptions, which are said to be true or false or, if you like, are "statements", are surely liable to these criticisms, since they are selective and uttered for a purpose. It is essential to realize that "true" and "false", like "free" and "unfree", do not stand for anything simple at all; but only for a general dimension of being a right or proper thing to say as opposed to a wrong thing, in these circumstances, to this audience, for these purposes and with these intentions . . . This doctrine is quite different from much that the pragmatists have said, to the effect that the true is what works, &c. The truth or falsity of a statement depends not merely on the meanings of words but on what act you were performing in what circumstances.

In *Speech Acts: An Essay in the Philosophy of Language*, American philosopher John Searle picked up Austin's program of "linguistic philosophy," namely, "the attempt to solve particular philosophical problems by attending to the ordinary use of particular words and other elements in a particular language." Searle wrote of an "internalized set of rules," analogous to our instinctively running to first base instead of third, even though we can't cite chapter and verse in the rulebook. The point is how language is actually played on the ground:

> The unit of linguistic communication is not, as has generally been supposed, the symbol, word or sentence, or even the token of the symbol, word or sentence, but rather the production or issuance of the symbol or word or sentence in the performance of the speech act.

Hence, "a theory of language is part of a theory of action, simply because speaking is a rule-governed form of behavior."

Playing off Austin's taxonomy, he says that "utterance acts" (e.g., saying words) and "propositional acts" (arranging them meaningfully) issue in "illocutionary acts" (for the sake of a project, such as stating, promising, or commanding), which accomplish "perlocutionary acts" (achievements, such as convincing or scaring).

Both men worked in intellectual proximity to Austrian/British philosopher Ludwig Wittgenstein, who spoke of the "language games" we play according to certain protocols, but none of them thought of language as "just a silly game." It's right serious business, and they used their linguistic analyses to venture into metaphysics. For instance, in *Sense and Sensibilia*,

Austin worked out on the word "real," showing no patience for attempts to posit a transcendent thing, "reality," that all real things have in common. In his analysis, he spoke of "real" as "substantive-hungry" (needing a real something or other to refer to) and as a "trousers word" (with the negative side wearing the trousers, i.e., the sense in which something is unreal.)

Searle was also impatient with giving grand status to universals, to abstract concepts. For instance,

> "Kindness" is parasitic on "is kind"; "is kind" is prior to "kindness." A language would not contain the notion of "kindness" unless it contained an expression having the function of "is kind", but it could contain "is kind" without "kindness."

Which is essentially the opposite of Plato's view that we only understand an act as kind if we have some grasp of the "Form" of kindness.

One interesting spinoff is the way that biblical scholars have become enamored with "speech act" theory, seeing it as a way to protect us from treating the Bible woodenly as a collection of propositions or facts (though biblicists in the grammatico-historical school have always recognized different literary genres such as history, poetry, and parable). Some see it as a way to discredit insistence on biblical inerrancy, with its true/false fixation. And, as one put it, in pushing back against the "big idea" notion of sermon preparation, we should see the text as a stained glassed window to be savored on its own merits rather than as just a window through which we look to determine the propositional goods. Nevertheless, it's the *truth* that makes us free, and truth is propositional. Besides, unless the windows are Arabesque or similarly abstract, they can be quite didactic and propositional in their portrayals. (I think of the magnificent Jesse Tree window at Chartres.) Yes, the rose windows in Notre Dame are glorious, but they beg commentary. We need an answer to "So what?" or "Why is it here?" And so we might explain, "The beauty of the rose reflects the beauty of God's creative and salvific work, the glass is a conveyer of light, a central metaphor for the gospel, and the craftsmanship gives testimony to the excellence in stewardship of gifts due our Lord." When we read of Nehemiah's surveying the ruins of Jerusalem in preparation for rebuilding the wall, we grant that it is narrative rather than command, but we may still draw a lesson, saying that "Nehemiah provides an excellent model for research and prudence in ministry." So yes, speech act analysis is interesting and illuminative, but it is not revolutionary in framing doctrine or ordering one's Christian life.

Cases

Look, language is a curious bird, and if you don't have an ear for its variegated usage, you're in for spills. I remember one of my grad school profs who used to horse around with it. A colleague might ask, "Do you know what time it is?," to which he'd respond, "Yes," and then return to his work. He knew what he was doing. Someone had requested the time, but he'd treated it as a question about his competency at temporal awareness. He flipped a matter of serious inquiry into a joke, as he did when someone asked him, as he exited the department one mid afternoon, "Are you gone for good?" His reply: "I never go for evil."

I think too of a Chinese professor we knew in college. He and a friend had come to America for study, and they spent some time in San Francisco trying to figure out what the waitress meant by "With or without?" when they ordered hamburgers. They scrutinized their dictionaries, and on successive days they tried different iterations until they were able to conclude that "with" meant "onion" or "cheese" or whatever it was.

So philosophers need to be reminded, "Go ahead, ascend the heights of ontological and epistemological abstraction as you please, but remember you have used words in particular situations using language that is not your own special possession. Ignore this, and it can bite you and waste others' time."

Discussion Questions:

1. Might a gesture serve as a performative utterance? What if the groom gave a "thumbs up" instead of an "I do"?

2. Flight attendants won't accept nods from those sitting in an exit row when they ask them if they're able and willing to remove the window in case of an emergency. They insist on a verbal response. What illocutionary, perlocutionary, and/or performative utterances are in play here?

3. The story is told of a plaintiff seeking compensation for injuries he suffered when his car collided with a truck pulling a horse trailer, a truck which had crossed the middle line on a narrow road. The defense attorney pressed him, "But didn't you say on the scene that you were just fine?" Well, yes, but the context was important. Both horses were badly maimed but still alive, and the state trooper who arrived on the scene proceeded to put them out of their misery with

shots from his pistol. Coming to the plaintiff, who was lying bloody and broken on the roadside, he asked, "Are you badly hurt?" The response, "No. Just fine." Discuss.

4. Could silence be a performative utterance of sorts? If a pastor never preaches on tithing or on hell, could he be saying loud and clear that these are not things we should worry about? Might we call it a speech non-act that shouts?

5. I once heard a prof say of a reference letter that it was "damning by faint praise." In other words, since such letters were typically glowing and devoid of negatives (subject to a kind of "grade inflation"), then the use of mild words (such as "good" and "fine") instead of grand ones (such as "great" and "extraordinary") was tantamount to undermining the applicant's candidacy. The letter may begin with "I commend him to you," but the choice of adjectives says otherwise. Does this support Austin's notion that truth and falsity are tied to "what act you were performing in what circumstances"?

Repouille v. U.S.

U.S. Court of Appeals,
Second Circuit
165 F.2d 152 (1947)

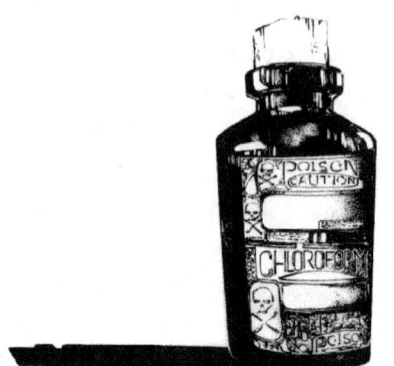

In October of 1939, Louis Loftus Repouille chloroformed his thirteen-year-old son to death. Four years and eleven months later, he applied for U.S. citizenship and ran afoul of the Nationality Act's rule that those seeking naturalization must exhibit "good moral character" for the five years preceding the application. If he had waited another month or so, he wouldn't have had the same problem. Nevertheless, the federal district judge said that Repouille was close enough to pass, but the U.S. attorney in New York objected, and the case moved up to the Circuit Court of Appeals, where the justices said they didn't have the data to make the proper call. They sent it back to the lower court with instructions that they do their homework and try again. The assumption was that Repouille would again be approved since another three years had passed, and the five-year rule was well-satisfied.

But what sort of homework did they have in mind? Well, they were appealing to a standard applied in an earlier Massachusetts case, one which tied judgment to the question of whether "the moral feelings, now prevalent generally in this country" would "be outraged" by the conduct in question; that is, whether it conformed to "the generally accepted moral conventions current at the time."

Judge Learned Hand, who wrote the opinion, left little doubt as to his own lack of "outrage" as he described the situation:

> [Repouille's] reason for this tragic deed was that the child had "suffered from birth from a brain injury which destined him to be an

idiot and a physical monstrosity malformed in all four limbs. The child was blind, mute, and deformed. He had to be fed; the movements of his bladder and bowels were involuntary, and his entire life was spent in a small crib." Repouille had four other children at the time towards whom he has always been a dutiful and responsible parent; it may be assumed that his act was to help him in their nurture, which was being compromised by the burden imposed upon him in the care of the fifth. The family was altogether dependent upon his industry for its support.

Furthermore, he noted the lack of enthusiasm for harsh judgment among the original jurors:

> Although it was inescapably murder in the first degree, not only did they bring in a verdict that was flatly in the face of the facts and utterly absurd, for manslaughter in the second degree presupposes that the killing has not been deliberate, but they coupled even that with a recommendation which showed that in substance they wished to exculpate the offender.

Instead of faulting the jurors, he compared them to other righteous, civilly disobedient figures, such as the abolitionists. And he underscored his own sympathy for Repouille by declaring,

> [W]e all know that there are great numbers of people of the most unimpeachable virtue, who think it morally justifiable to put an end to a life so inexorably destined to be a burden to others, and so far as any possible interest of its own is concerned condemned to a brutish existence, lower indeed than all but the lowest forms of sentient life.

He wondered out loud how one might take a proper reading on the national conscience, even mentioning the possibility of a Gallup poll.

One must ask whether Justice Hand had a firm grasp of the Bill of Rights, which were meant as a sea wall against the tides of public opinion, for there are a good many occasions when the public would not be "outraged" over discrimination toward those with strange religious beliefs (e.g., Santeria), repellant opinions (Holocaust denial), absurd associations (Flat Earth Society), or a different racial mix. In my own lifetime, it was illegal in some states for a black and a white to marry, and there was a day in America when the institution of slavery was perfectly acceptable to many. It's hard to see where things would stop if the standard were based on "the moral feelings, now prevalent generally in this country." Lynching enjoyed wide favor in some regions, and one has only to look around the world to see what damage the tyranny of the majority can do when the majority has lost (or never managed to secure) its moral bearings. The public conscience is fluid while the moral verities are fixed, and by tying the work of the court to the former rather than the latter, Hand did the law a disservice.

Be that as it may, this case puts focus on a concept philosophers have studied for millennia, the notion of "good moral character." It's returned to recent prominence through the discussion of virtue, thanks in large measure to the work of Alasdair MacIntyre (his landmark book, *After Virtue*, appearing in 1981). In the previous decades, ethical discussion was devoted to cases and issues, e.g., whether the Vietnam War was immoral, capital punishment unjust, abortion murder, or capitalism cruel. Focus was on the act, but then philosophers began to talk about the actor.

In doing so, they often returned to Aristotle's *Nicomachaean Ethics*, wherein this ancient Greek philosopher located the virtuous "Golden Mean" between two unsavory extremes. (See, below, the New London Channel discussion for more on this.)

A strong feature of Aristotle's theory is that virtue is a habit you can cultivate, and that the easier it comes to you, the more virtuous you are. Thus, though one may think that the person who fights against gluttony every step of the way is more heroic than the one who has no appetite for it (pun intended). But the one who's developed a spirit of moderation warrants the greater admiration. It's become ingrained, and so, in this respect, the diner is virtuous.

The virtuous person is not the one who sings "I gotta be me" or insists on being "authentic" when what he is authentically is inappropriate. Rather, he should be singing, "I gotta grow up."

On this model, a single sin in one's past does not render the actor a perennially bad person. The apostle Paul turned out well despite his earlier role in the stoning of Stephen. Just as "one swallow does not a summer make," "one goose flying south does not a winter make." So the five-year track record enshrined in law made sense, even if Justice Hand's take on the gravity of the murder in question was skewed.

It would be interesting to see how broadly the "good moral character" standard might be extended. Imagine that the immigration officials had said, "I'm sorry, Mr. Jones, but we can't accept slobs with a bad temper. And we understand you've been living with a woman out of wedlock. After all, we have the 'good character standard.'" The scenario's not a likely one.

Repouille v. U.S.

Plato, who was Aristotle's teacher, posed the case of Gyges' Ring in *The Republic*. This ring enabled the wearer to become invisible, and the question was how this might affect behavior. If you could slip behind the counter and put your hand in the till without detection; could slap without being caught someone you didn't like; become a peeping Tom without the need to peep—would you still remain morally upright? That would, indeed, be a test of character.

Discussion Questions:

1. In 1996, Lieutenant (and B-52 pilot) Kelly Flinn was charged with lying, insubordination, and "behavior unbecoming an officer" in connection with her sexual affair with the husband of an enlisted woman serving under her. She was finally discharged (but not dishonorably), with the chief of staff of the Air Force saying the problem was with her lying and not her adultery. The *New York Times* weighed in, blaming, in part, "antiquated adultery rules." So what makes them antiquated? And why was sex with another woman's husband not "unbecoming an officer"? Is respect for marriage a trivial virtue, if a virtue at all, and if it once was, what happened to vitiate it?

2. Gluttony is traditionally listed as one of the "seven deadly sins," along with pride, envy, lust, anger, greed, and sloth. But some quip that Baptists have turned what was once a sin into a virtue. In this connection, I think of the time I was speaking in a church and had supper in a church member's home before the service. I had a full serving of every dish, but that wasn't enough. The woman of the house pressed me to eat more, saying it would hurt her feelings if I didn't take another piece of chicken, more potatoes and gravy, etc. My moderation was being construed as a sin, and my caving in to her directions praiseworthy. Have we similarly, in effect, turned other vices into virtues, celebrating pride, envy, lust, anger, greed, and sloth? (See the Upside-Down Map for more on this.)

3. In *The Closing of the American Mind*, University of Chicago professor Allan Bloom argued that, in effect, we've become so open-minded that our brains have fallen out. He observed that the only universally recognized virtue on campus was tolerance; not chastity, honesty, industry, etc. Similarly, the only universally acclaimed vice

was perceived intolerance; not promiscuity, mendacity, slacking, etc. If you champion and exemplify tolerance (e.g., for the LGBQT agenda), and even if you are a drunk, a philanderer, and a plagiarist, you might be elected homecoming king or queen. Suggest that some of your classmates are doing wicked things (other than being tolerant of every perversity that might come down the line), and your continued matriculation in that school is in doubt. Is he right that this is the case, and, if so, that it is unfortunate?

4. A few years back, I was invited to contribute a chapter to a *Festschrift*, and my assignment turned me toward the public arena. I decided to write on the virtue of friendliness. (My interest, as a Southerner, was piqued by my seventeen-year sojourn in Chicago, where I found people much less inclined to smile, to greet you, and to say thanks for acts of consideration.) I wondered whether my thesis was merely a *cri de coeur* from a regional rustic, or rather tapped into a universal standard of goodness. The editor objected that "friendliness" wasn't on the standard lists (along with, e.g., prudence, courage, temperance, justice, love, hope, and faith), but I responded that enumerating virtues was an open-ended affair, with some writers listing as many as fifty. The editor admitted that maybe his Yankee upbringing had skewed his response, so he let me proceed. So how do we judge something to be a virtue, and, by extension, to say that Repouille was sufficiently virtuous to enter the country?

5. Several state legislatures have been weighing the legality of letting a baby be born and then, upon examination and reflection, ending its life if the mother deems it not worth the trouble or a heartache to raise. Does it make a difference that the child is five minutes old instead of thirteen years old (as in the Repouille case)? Why or why not?

ROBBIE v. CITY OF MIAMI

Supreme Court of Florida
469 So.2d 1384 (1985)

Because of a National Football League players strike in 1982, the Miami Dolphins (owned by Joe Robbie) did not play all its scheduled games at the Orange Bowl, which was owned by the city of Miami. Thus the city did not receive its contracted user fee for those games, and it sued. On the way to trial, the franchise and Miami reached an agreement—that an extra home game would be tacked on to both the 1985 and 1986 seasons, with $30,000 in rent due for each of the additional games. The team wanted a rider saying that they were not obliged to pay should these two games be cancelled due to an "act of God." Miami rejected this escape clause, and the courts had to sort things out.

Back in 1997, Mike Huckabee, then governor of Arkansas, objected to the wording of a bill designed to bar insurance companies from cancelling coverage on the basis of claims filed for storm damage. He didn't appreciate their construing "a destructive and deadly force" as "an act of God." Though the expression was common in the insurance industry, Huckabee countered, "I feel that I have indeed witnessed many 'acts of God,' but I see his actions in the miraculous sparing of life, the sacrifice and selfless spirit in which so many responded to the pain of others." He suggested, instead, that they substitute the expression "natural disasters." In the end, the legislators simply added his wording as option.

The expression "act of God" was meant to capture something not humanly foreseeable or controllable, for which men were not accountable. For instance, you wouldn't use the phrase to describe a fatal accident where the driver was drunk and speeding in a rainstorm. Still, it does seem a bit unfair to give the Creator credit for tsunamis but none for an unseasonably heavy snowstorm that saved the ski industry in Vermont. I suppose we reserve the term "miracle" for the *good* developments (thereby giving God credit), using "act of God" for the *bad* ones, where financial settlements are in play. Besides, we don't sell insurance to East Coast municipalities to cover their business losses if the snows are so good in Vermont that New Yorkers and Bostonians take their discretionary dollars to the slopes.

Be that as it may, we still have the question of God's sovereignty. Is he, in fact, responsible for all that happens and fails to happen on Earth? Might he cause the 100-mph winds that cancel an NFL game? Or does he at least have the power to stop them, yet doesn't? If either of these is the case, how might we still call him a *good* God, what with all the destruction? After all, don't we say he's all powerful and all good? Skeptics push this question rhetorically as a challenge to Christian orthodoxy, asking, "How can you presume to hold on to your notion of an omnipotent and omnibenevolent god when there is so much evidence to the contrary, so much pointless suffering?" The quandary is called the "problem of evil."

A variety of answers have been put forth. A popular one came from the pen of Rabbi Harold Kushner in his 1981 book, *Why Bad Things Happen to Good People*, written in the wake of his teenaged son's death. Kushner simply tossed aside God's omnipotence, saying the Lord was doing the best he could, and so we're fellow soldiers with our Creator in the struggle against the darkness. It made quite a splash, comforting some, but most believers in Yahweh, both Christian and Jewish, found it lacking, and not surprisingly so.

Among the more typical responses (some overlapping others) are the *free will defense*, which lays blame at the feet of man, whom God has endowed with the ability to choose wrongly and to harm others (though natural disasters are harder to accommodate on this model, even though a man can be faulted for building his house in a flood plain or "tornado alley"); the *soul-making theodicy*, which defends the moral rectitude/justice of God (*theos* + *dikaios*) by arguing that it takes trials and dangers to develop such virtues as faith, patience, prudence, and courage; the *downgrading evil* strategy, which either describes evil as the absence or diminution of God's good work (Augustine) or as an illusion (Christian Science's Mary Baker Eddy); the focus on *God's own suffering*, as in Christ's torture on the cross, thereby deflating our justification for holding him responsible for aloofness as we face dire straits; *universalism*, which argues that all will be saved unto eternal glory and blessedness, and that present sufferings are relatively trivial; the charge of *self-contradiction*, in that the critic obviously approves of his own life, which is the result of many tragedies (such as the death of his grandmother's sweetheart in WWI, putting his grandfather at the head of her courtship line); the *best of all possible worlds* approach, which "bites the bullet," arguing that if anything were different, the universe would be less wonderful than it is; the way of *voluntarism*, asserting that whatever God wills and does is morally right, by definition, since he simply is the standard for such judgments.

Of course, one might construct a God-excusing scenario for this or that catastrophe. For instance, what if the Lord knew that terrorists were prepared to detonate a nuclear device at the Orange Bowl, killing ten thousand outright and consigning another ten thousand to lingering, often fatal illness from severe burns and radiation poisoning? Might we then let God off the hook for sending a great storm their way, with the loss of fewer than a hundred lives and a few million dollars in damage? We may never know what he did for us in that case, but we either trust him or we don't to get it right. It's a faith thing. After all, it can be as hard to prove that there was *no* reason as that there was *some* reason.

The atheist's onslaught has been fierce, most notably in the person of David Hume, whose eighteenth-century *Dialogues Concerning Natural Religion* said the evidence against God's innocence was compelling. Two centuries later, John Wisdom mocked believers through a parable about an imaginary gardener, implying that Christians were immune to evidential difficulties and thus not intellectually respectable. His story can be employed to claim that Christians both lack positive evidence for their theistic assertions and ignore counterevidence when it arises. (Actually, I can think of several things that could falsify our goodness-of-God claim, including an eschatological shock where we found that faith in Christ had no effect upon a slide into hell. I'm persuaded this won't happen, but if it did, I would be prepared to say the goodness of God was a fraud.)

Another critic, William Rowe, constructed the case of a fawn trapped in a forest fire, who endured several days of horrible suffering to die. He then asked how that incident could make the universe a better place and, on the other hand, what would be lost if God intervened to free the fawn to outrun the fire. For you see, if there were even a single case of indifference or inaction on his part when he could have staved off needless torture, then he would not be morally perfect.

Of course, this raises the question of what sort of world the skeptic is prescribing. One in which natural laws are suspended and combustion stops in proximity to little animals? (Then perhaps California residents should tether fawns in their yards to neutralize wildfires.) One in which it's better to have the fawn escape, only to spend an agonizing month later on dying from the effects of a brain parasite? Farfetched? Well, we just don't know, and it's not at all clear we could run things better. (One thinks of the movie *Bruce Almighty*, where Morgan Freeman as God turns his powers over to Jim Carrey as Bruce, with chaotic results.)

This is just scratching the surface, but it's worthwhile to extend the challenge a bit. Hurricanes are one thing, but what about NFL labor strikes and management's pushback? Regardless of who was in the right, was the work stoppage an act of God? And how about its resolution? Were these ultimately acts of men, or even of Satan, with men as the devil's puppets?

Now we've gone deeper into theology, with questions about the sovereignty of God over the wills of men. Yes, they're free in that they do what they please, but are they really free to please what they please? (Compatibilists work with this distinction.) Are they victims of greed, or are they greed personified?

Proverbs 21:1 says, "The king's heart is a stream of water in the hand of the Lord; he turns it wherever he will" (ESV). What about the heart of Dolphins owner Joe Robbie; of Miami mayor Maurice Ferr; of NFL Players

Association executive director Ed Garvey? In whose hands were their hearts?

That's the way it goes with philosophy and theology. You start with football and contracts, and you soon find yourself in metaphysics (the study of ultimate reality).

Discussion Questions:

1. In *The Many Faces of Evil*, John Feinberg argues that there is not really a "problem of evil," but rather "problems of evil," difficulties on several levels. It's one thing to tackle the puzzles theoretically, but what about a personal tragedy that has drained the spirit and diminished the faith of a believer who cries out, "Why, why, God!?" And we hear of Christians who, facing the tragic loss of a loved one or a cancer diagnosis, are angry at fellow believers who blithely assure them, quoting Romans 8:28, "And we know that all things work together for good to those who love God, to those who are the called according to His purpose." Are the philosophers and theologians being insensitive, or are the victims being hypersensitive, letting their circumstances skew their understanding?

2. Speaking of weather-related "acts of God," the flood in Noah's day was surely the Lord's doing. It killed men, women, children, and animals (except for those in the ark) indiscriminately. A human would be condemned for this. How might God be excused?

3. Some argue that God permitted the Holocaust so that a sufficient number of nations could get behind the founding of the state of Israel, whose Zionist base resonated with God's purposes and promise. Is it appropriate to suggest such a thing for consideration?

4. Some argue that God, who foresaw all the evil and suffering that would eventuate in the world, had no business creating it in the first place. How about this?

5. Might the prophets of "anthropogenic global warming" start calling hurricanes "acts of men"? Would they be justified in doing so?

6. Is there a contrasting "problem of good" to be raised? Are there features of the world and human experience that are hard to explain apart from recognizing the existence of the God of the Bible?

State v. One "Jack and Jill" Pinball Machine

Missouri Court of Appeals
224 S.W. 2nd 854 (1949)

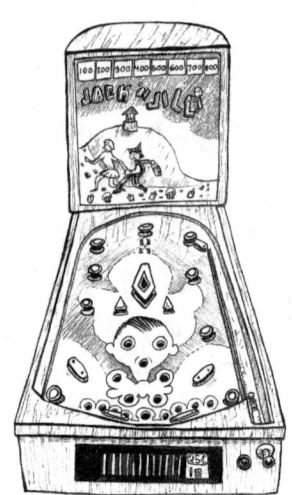

THE prosecuting attorney of Greene Country, Missouri, sought to destroy a pinball machine in play in his jurisdiction, arguing that it was a gambling device, prohibited by law. The defense responded that the machines only rewarded success with free games, and the Missouri statute merely proscribed payouts in "money or property," neither of which included extended play.

The eloquent Presiding Judge Vandeventer penned his opinion regarding this contraption "designated by [an] alliterative and euphonious cognomen." In doing so, he reviewed the corresponding laws in a variety of states, a number of which drew the line more generally against winning "things of value." Some of them counted extra games valueless within the purview of the statute, and he agreed. His discourse is worth reading:

> Does the player get property for his nickel? We think not. It is argued that he gets amusement. The vacuous mind that may momentarily be brightened by finding entertainment and amusement in watching a metal ball meander aimlessly over the surface of an inclined table and finally score by dropping from sight into an aperture therein, would be equally entertained by watching a certain species of scarabaeoid beetle aimlessly roll his putrid ball across the ground and into a hole where eventually it becomes sustenance for itself and young. Would not the entertainment and amusement in each instance be the same though five cents is paid to pull the plunger in the one and in the latter, the propulsion is

by the beetle and its accomplishments are not emblazoned upon an electrically lighted scoreboard. The privilege of watching either would certainly not be property . . . and we shall not dignify either by holding it to be "a 'thing' of value."

If a free game is property or a thing of value, what kind of value has it? Certainly it has no educational or intellectual value. How could watching a rolling ball bounce from peg to pin and then disappear, enrich the mind or broaden one's intellect? After its propulsion by the plunger, gravity moves the balls but that law of physics was discovered by Sir Isaac Newton and became common knowledge more than two centuries ago. Such information is not acquired by inserting a nickel in a pinball machine. From the beetle, one might learn some new fact relating to entomology but nothing from "Jack and Jill." If there is educational value in either, it preponderates in favor of the beetle. A free play certainly has not the educational value of a picture show, which in addition to entertainment and amusement, brings before the eyes and ears of millions, scenes and descriptions of faraway places, fine acting, historical facts and scientific maters that could be, by them, viewed or heard in no other way. Few modern developments have more education value than the cinema.

A free game has no physical value such as a game of golf, which by its pleasurable exercise, coupled with fresh air and sunshine develops the muscles, invigorates the body and creates a feeling of physical well being, thereby improving health and prolonging life. No such benefits appear here. To be allowed to do a useless thing free does not make that privilege property or "a 'thing' of value" because one has previously paid for doing another such useless thing. There is a vast difference between cost and value. Permission to use a useless device is not property or "a 'thing' of value," though the device cost money to construct.

Does the player receive anything of financial or economic value? Rather isn't this so-called recreation and amusement the antithesis of value? If one's time is worth anything, it is a loss instead of gain, a waste instead of reward. Hope of reward or gain, above the amount risked, is the lodestone of gambling. The fact that one has paid five cents for it does not conclusively fix that, or any other sum, as its value or any value at all.

In this connection, philosophers engage in what's called "value theory," a discipline that ranges across ethics and aesthetics. In the latter, the focus falls upon markers of quality and desirability in the arts and upon features of winsomeness in the natural world, whether people or landscapes. The

CASES

former concerns the highest goods and aims for humans. Aristotle was a "church father" in this regard, speaking of the *summum bonum*, the highest good, which, in his estimation, was happiness, which was not merely a pleasurable feeling, but instead the satisfaction of growing into all you were meant to be. It echoes in the opening words of the U.S. Declaration of Independence, which says government is designed to achieve and secure, for its citizens, "life, liberty, and the pursuit of happiness."

Of course, there is some danger of circularity in the definition since "to be happy" may mean essentially to get what one wants, so, of course, happiness is what we want. Be that as it may, this leaves open the huge question of what those secondary goods that lead toward happiness might be. And here philosophers have had a perennial workout.

In her 1998 presidential address to the Eastern Division of the American Philosophical Association, Mary Mothersill spoke on "old age," and asked, "Is longevity, other things being equal, a positive good? More generally, is sheer longlastingness ever a feature to be admired?" People seem averse to dying, but do they really want to live forever or even an inordinately long time? The Tom Hanks character in *The Green Mile* was not particularly happy with his long, slow aging process, whereby he outlived all his friends. And that doesn't even touch the special concern of Buddhists and Hindus to break the cycle of rebirth, gaining release into Nirvana.

Children have been known to play the Why Game, driving their parents crazy with deeper and deeper probes into the mysteries of everyday life:

> "How much farther is it to grandma's house?"
> "About an hour."
> "Why?"
> "Because we're about 60 miles away?"
> "Why?"
> "Because we left at 3:00."
> "Why?"
> "Because your soccer game wasn't over till 2:00."
> "Why?"
> Etc.

At a certain point, you just have to say something like, "Because that's the way it is." The same is true of value assessments. You enroll in college because you want a degree, because you need it to qualify for graduate school, because you want to be a teacher, because you want to live a life of study and discourse in philosophy, because you think it's your calling, because you . . ." After a while, you may simply come to something like the purported utterance of Eric Liddell in *Chariots of Fire*, when his sister urged him to go to the mission field directly instead of training for the Olympics: "God made me fast. And when I run, I feel his pleasure."

Protestant Reformers, speaking through the Westminster Shorter Catechism, said that "the chief end of man is to glorify God and enjoy him forever." Contemporary pastor/theologian John Piper has tweaked it to say that we "glorify God by enjoying him forever." And so we might ask if this is both compelling and operative in our own lives. And what this might say about the value of an extra pinball game or two along the way?

Discussions of value are far ranging, and the study is complicated by the fact that the word "good" is the most general term of approbation, applying to a good dog, a good man, a good milkshake, a good time, and a good statute as well as a good statue. Furthermore, there is a host of distinctions to be drawn in the discussion, e.g., the difference between intrinsic goods and instrumental goods (whereby Kant construed "rational nature" a good in itself, as opposed to a hammer's good as a means only), or between commensurable and incommensurable goods. But Judge Vandeventer's observations should give us a good (there's that word again) starting point.

Discussion Questions:

1. A colleague of mine puzzled on social media over why anyone would want to take a selfie. He saw no value (and perhaps some disvalue) in it. Was he right?

2. In his book *The Joy of Sports*, Michael Novak argued that watching a baseball game was something like getting a taste of heaven. Games operate on otherworldly time (innings instead of minutes or seconds, as in basketball or football), is played on an otherworldly field (with perfect grass, gratifying geometry, safe enclosure), by eternally youthful and fit participants (for the others retire or are cut as their powers diminish), displaying the splendor of eternal themes, such as the quest for perfection and the pleasure of community. Would Judge Vendeventer call attendance at a Cubs game at Wrigley Field or a Red Sox game at Fenway useless entertainment? Would he be right if he did?

CASES

3. Socrates said that "the unexamined life is not worth living." Was he right?

4. One of the most biting judgments one can say of a man is that he is "a waste of DNA." Is this true of any person? Or does every person have value?

5. In the 1970s, "values clarification" was all the rage. One exercise began with the sketch of a crest, with four empty quadrants. The student would then indicate his or her most treasured things by drawing in representative images of, say, the Yankees logo, a pet dog, or a rosary. One criticism of the activity was that it was strictly non-judgmental, designed to put people in touch with their preferences. So, theoretically, a swastika wouldn't be out of bounds. How valuable could such an exercise be?

U.S. v. Causby

U.S. Supreme Court
328 U.S. 256 (1946)

Justice William O. Douglas, who wrote this legal opinion, observed, "It is an ancient doctrine that at common law ownership of the land extended to the periphery of the universe . . . But the doctrine has no place in the modern world. The air is a public highway." Indeed, if everyone's property rights extended upwards infinitely, commercial aviation would be an impossibility, with lawsuits ensuing from every flight.

In this case, Mr. Causby was a chicken farmer whose property lay near the end of a Greensboro, North Carolina, runway, where bombers and other military planes landed day and night, missing his chicken house by only sixty-three feet. It drove the birds crazy, and over half of them bashed themselves to death against the barn walls in a panic. The Causby family was driven to distraction as well, not only from the collapse of their business, but also from the exhausting noise and, at night, annoying light. So he sued to protect his to-the-heavens airspace, and he lost.

Whatever the justice of it all, ancient doctrine citing "the periphery of the universe" raises the interesting metaphysical question of what shape this ownership might take. The full doctrine says property rights extend downward as well, so one can imagine something of an inverted cone or pyramid terminating at the center of the earth, where property lines from China would meet those from America, each coming to a fine point. But what about the other direction with its upward boundaries? Would it rise in the shape of a silo the width of the property at the Earth's surface? And how far would it go? The answers concern the metaphysics of space.

First, does the universe have a periphery? Say that we go out a gazillion miles and hit some sort of terminus to what we view as outer space, the darkness against which the nebulae and constellations shine forth in the night sky. Do we hit a wall of sorts? If so, how thick is the wall? Isn't it spatial as well? And, unless it's infinitely thick, there's something on the other side which continues the expanse. So shall we say that Causby's property is infinitely large?

And what do we make of claims that space is "curved"? We get that sort of statement from those who've imbibed Einstein's relativity theorizing, with its talk of a "space-time continuum." Textbook illustrations show a range of models, such as a steel ball resting on a flexible rubber sheet (the Earth's gravity bending light, whose speed is "the constant") or something like a saddle blanket draped over the back of an invisible horse. If space is really bent, then Causby's "silo" could be curved rather than straight-sided.

But those illustrations lie within the space of a book's page, which strikes me as a better representation of space itself, with the curved illustration speaking more to the behavior of bodies within certain regions of space, and with the understanding that the page extends infinitely in not only two but three dimensions. The relativity math can be helpful, even indispensable, in sending out deep-space probes and such, but, in the end, they don't give us the final word on capital-S Space. (And, incidentally, the speed of light—186,000 miles per second—is not an absolute constant but a contingent one. It could be 220,000 miles per second, or 27 miles per second, depending on God's good pleasure.) Science is good at helping us get around, but it's not equipped to address ultimate realities.

Metaphysics is devoted to sorting out the reality beyond and behind appearances, and there are plenty of wacky appearances to get behind and beyond, e.g., mirages, the Doppler effect, the sense that you continue to spin after you've stopped, *déjà vu*, the impression that your train is moving when it's actually the neighboring train that's in motion. Similarly, the apparent curvature of space can be a useful, albeit puzzling, fiction (or a useful reality if you define "space" a certain way), but it is ultimately nonsensical. We can't think it, and so, I'd suggest, we shouldn't say it, unless we're doing something specialized, where an as-if claim can help our math.

Immanuel Kant had an interesting take on this. He called space and time "pure forms of intuition," the theater, if you will, in which phenomena play, themselves subservient to such "categories" as causality and plurality.

On this model, space isn't a thing but rather a perspective from which we see (touch, taste, smell, and hear) all physical objects. It's that by which we experience things and not a thing in itself.

Fortunately, the Supreme Court excused Causby from these ruminations and contestations. Otherwise, the case could have run on through the ages as the parties brought in rival "philosophically expert witnesses" (an oxymoron, I fear) to settle the matter. Meanwhile, Causby might have shifted his complaint from the Greensboro bombers to the Cassini-Huygens Saturn probe, dragging NASA into court.

PS: The common-law expression that Douglas quoted in the decision was, *Cujus est solum ejus est usque ad coelom.* He left off *et ad infernos*, which would make the sentence read, "Whoever owns the soil, it is theirs up to heaven and down to hell." It was, indeed, a long-standing principle, applied, for example, in the 1587 British case *Bury v. Pope*, where a homeowner protested, unsuccessfully, his neighbor's decision to build a high structure which blocked out sunlight. The court ruled (citing *Cujus est solum* . . .) that he had the right to build as high as he wished on his own property.

Discussion Questions:

1. Is heaven "way out there" or is it a different dimension of space and time? Could it occupy the same space that we do but be imperceptible because of its radical disassociation with our earthly spatial reality? Does this question even make sense?

2. Does God see some things as close up and others as far off? Does he have spatial perspective, seeing things in relief? Or is everything equally near to him?

3. Could a soul fit into a grain of sand? Could it fill a domed football stadium?

4. For centuries, scientists thought that outer space must be filled with "aether" in order for light and gravity to make their way through it and do their work in it. Ocean waves needed water and sound waves needed air for motion and impact. So if there is no air in space, "no one can hear you scream," as the old movie line goes. But surely there

must be something as a means of conveyance for whatever forces are in play out there. Otherwise, space would seem to be nothing. So how could we talk about it? Right?

5. If the universe and everything in it suddenly doubled (or halved) in size, would it make any difference?

Whistler v. Ruskin

Court of Exchequer,
Division at Westminster (1878)

In 1875, the American painter James Abbott McNeill Whistler (who painted *"Whistler's Mother,"* i.e., *Arrangement in Grey and Black No. 1*) exhibited, in a London gallery, a painting he called *Nocturne in Black and Gold: The Falling Rocket*. It was a dark, impressionistic depiction of a fireworks show, with vague human figures in the foreground. John Ruskin, who held a chair in fine arts at Oxford and was the nation's most respected critic, lambasted the gallery owner, the painter, and the painting, speaking of "ill-educated conceit," "willful imposture," "Cockney impudence," and a "coxcomb" (pretentious fop). He expressed dismay at hearing they were asking "two hundred guineas for flinging a pot of paint in the public's face."

Whistler sued him for libel and won, but only a farthing (the smallest of coins). The loss drove Ruskin into depression, and the expensive victory, which didn't cover court costs, drove Whistler to flee English hostility for a more hospitable and pecuniarily viable Venice.

The painting incensed Ruskin since it violated what he and most people understood to be the proper standard of art: that its subject be both recognizable and edifying, and that its craftsmanship be unmistakable. Whistler had the temerity to "water down" his oils, deliver a "slapdash" image, and flirt with abstraction. It just didn't qualify as "serious art." It inclined the viewer toward a "retarding and vulgarizing" form of "self-satisfaction" (to use Matthew Arnold's earlier, popular language), the sort of thing that coarsened and even destroyed culture.

While the Brancusi case (discussed above) addressed the definitional boundaries of art itself, the Whistler-Ruskin case dealt with the question of what made art good or bad—aesthetics. And today, as in the era of that trial, the disputes can be vicious. Witness, for instance, the mix of cruel and ecstatic commentary on fashion choices for the Oscars red carpet. It's not enough to say you prefer x over y. Rather, you get TV time for declaring y to be "vomitous" and x "a stroke of genius."

Among the dismissive expressions is "kitsch," variously defined as "tasteless," "pathetically sentimental," or "tawdry." It's a good way to write off what you don't like and what you don't think others shouldn't like, e.g., the Precious Moments Chapel in Carthage, Missouri, or a Thomas Kinkade painting. But why should critics care if we drive miles out of our way to see the former and pay hundreds or thousands of dollars to acquire the latter? What's really at stake? Besides, isn't beauty simply in the eye of the beholder?

Indeed, the word "beauty" (as in "truth, goodness, and beauty") is central to the dispute. Are there universal standards of taste (as there are objective standards of morality and scientific postulation) to which we should hold ourselves accountable? Or is this simply a matter of harmless subjectivity, where you like Rocky Road, and I like Chunky Monkey, and it's no big deal either way?

Well, even if you think there are universal standards, you might not center your aesthetic on beauty. I prefer to speak of "enthrallment" or "fascination," for there are some magnificently ugly paintings (e.g., the Ivan Albright painting of Ida or of the shirtless old man in a bowler) that warrant and reward our attention and respect. And those who say that truth, goodness, and beauty are cut from the same cloth miss the point that something can be bogus and decadent while aesthetically engaging. Aesthetic goodness does not mean moral goodness. Indeed, the Bible warns against being deceived by appearances. (And, of course, it can work the other way, with a wonderful, true message presented in a clumsy or boring way.)

Of course, "beautiful" is a broad term, grander than "pretty." I suppose we could treat it as the most general term of aesthetic approbation, much as we treat "good" as the most general term of all approbation, whether we're talking about a good mother, a good hammer, or a good portrait. Terms of beauty can apply to an "elegant" mathematical theorem or a "lovely" act of sacrificial kindness. But again, a beauty-centered aesthetic can drive one to reflexively favor a Van Huysum still life with flowers and a Bierstadt Western landscape over Gericault's *The Raft of the Medusa* and Munch's *The Scream*. But not so fast.

The literature on aesthetic standards is rich and contentious, from Joshua Reynolds's insistence on a "pleasing effect on the mind" to Roger Fry's "significant form"; from David Hume's intersubjectivity to Leo Tolstoy's communitarian ideal. Some critics major on line, mass, rhythm, light and shade, space, color, etc. Others favor novelty or social impact. Some love narrative; others hate it. Some look for signs of seasoned and fastidious virtuosity; others couldn't care less, even celebrating the swirls and streaks of an ape's or pig's paintbrush. Is it process or product or impact or context? And so it goes.

No, aesthetic matters aren't everything, but they're not nothing either. They bear thought, investigation, and articulation, so that we might know how to talk helpfully when the zoning board is considering, for our neighborhood, a house that looks like a shoe; when the church building committee is proposing a paisley carpet for the auditorium aisles; when the new music minister favors polka for Sunday worship; and when the senior adult potluck includes a durian dish.

Discussion Questions:

1. Political scientist Wallace Sayre is credited with saying (and I paraphrase) that politics internal to the university is so bitter since the stakes are so low. Could this be true of aesthetic disputes? Is anything really important in the outcome?
2. Can aesthetic insensitivity rise to the level of sinful abuse? What about a pastor who delivers an utterly accurate but seriously boring sermon, oblivious to the stupor of the congregants; a husband

who lounges around the house like a slob, robbing his long-suffering wife of the satisfaction that she has married a thoughtful, presentable man? Are these men derelict?

3. Hitler is derided for fielding a "degenerate art" exhibition, one that featured non-representational art, such as works of surrealism, Fauvism, Dadaism, and cubism. But might he have had a point, that these movements ushered in a era where art did more to tear down the soul than uplift it? Peter Gay's 2007 book, *Modernism: The Lure of Heresy*, argues that that era's artists were typically determined to throw off old conventions, both artistic and moral. Hitler reacted to modernism with penalties and bans, but what if we react with criticism and shunning? Could that be sensible?

4. It's irritating to see how well done an ethically or spiritually toxic advertisement, television show, or novel can be. But must we, on aesthetic grounds, "give the devil his due"?

5. Might a harsh aesthetic judgment ever justifiably rise to the level slander or libel? Or should such matters stay out of the courts?

White-Smith Music Publishing Company v. Apollo Company

U.S. Supreme Court
209 U.S. 1 (1908)

In the opening decade of the twentieth century, White-Smith published sheet music from two compositions by Adam Beibel, "Little Cotton Dolly" and "Kentucky Babe." The company producing a player piano called the Apollo made piano rolls of the songs. White-Smith sued for copyright infringement and lost. The court said that, under current law, a copy was a tangible object that could be mistaken for the original, and that a white paper roll with holes in it could not be confused with a white paper sheet with ink marks on it. (The carefully spaced holes in the piano roll allowed jets of air to pass through, thus triggering the mechanism to sound particular notes.)

Attorneys for White-Smith had objected that the intention of copyright law was "to protect the intellectual conception which has resulted in the compilation of notes which, when properly played, produce the melody which is the real invention of the composer." The court insisted, though, that such a "musical creation which first exists in the mind of the composer" is "not susceptible of being copied until it has been put in a form which others can see and read." And in this case, what they could see and read was notes on a page. Indeed, it would be a very rare bird who could sight-read a piano roll.

Of course, copyright law has evolved and has had interesting tests in recent days over the property status of lines of computer code, but our concern here is with the metaphysics of the discussion. (Of course, matters of "intellectual property" bring questions of justice into play, but we'll focus here on philosophical questions of reality.)

For one thing, what's the status of an "intellectual conception"? Does it exist when no one has it in mind? If so, where? Take for instance, the opening notes of Beethoven's Fifth—duh, duh, duh, dum; duh, duh, duh, dum. What if no one is performing or humming it, all the sheet music is destroyed along with all the recordings, and no one is even thinking it? Does it cease to exist? Or is it just out there, wherever there is, waiting to be recalled?

Furthermore, we may ask whether Beethoven created the tone sequence or rather just discovered or came upon it. After all, if God knows all possibilities, physical and mental, and he knows the future, then this musical "ringtone" must have been in his mind long before Beethoven came on the scene. And, on this model, it would continue to exist if all earthly memory, reproductions, etc. were obliterated—exist, that is, as a concept without physical instantiation.

All sorts of theologians and philosophers have joined in the discussion (not of Beethoven's Fifth in particular, but of the "ontological" issues, those concerned with the "science of being"). Plato is a prominent case in point. He taught that there were non-material "Forms" (e.g., Justice; Friendship) which existed eternally and which we knew in our pre-Earth life. His teacher, Socrates, claimed to be a midwife who delivered his students' idea babies, the healthy ones originating in their earlier, clear-headed days. He worked by questioning—the Socratic method—with the conviction they already knew the important things and that they could remember them if they'd only follow his lead in chipping away the stupidity that had bedeviled them in their present, troublesome bodies.

A lot of Christians, including St. Augustine, have found much to like in Plato, though not his teachings about pre-existence. They're pleased to

White-Smith Music Publishing Company v. Apollo Company

locate the ideals of courage, knowledge, etc. in God's mind, secure there when cowardice and ignorance are rampant on Earth. But this raises the question of whether these concepts are coeternal with the Trinity, along with mathematical verities such as 2+2=4. That can sound impious, even heretical, as though there were other everlasting entities in the universe, even if they were only intellectual.

Some insist that those who wrangle over such abstractions are wasting their time. Some would ask, "What difference does it make if Ludwig hatched it or grasped it?" Some would say, "There's no way to settle this, so let's just quit talking about it; endless, irremediable disputation is toxic." Yet, that puts us onto another metaphysical question, or perhaps we should say a meta-metaphysical question, concerning whether this creature called man is constitutionally able to wrestle mentally with the ultimates.

Discussion Questions:

1. A 1980 court case concerned a General Electric genetic engineer named Ananda Chakrabarty, who had developed a bacterium which was effective in breaking down oil spills. GE filed for a patent, which was initially refused on grounds that life forms weren't patentable. Is there similarly something odd about patenting a notion, a concept? What about the quadratic equation?

2. Regarding numbers, some ("realists") say they are real, yet immaterial, independent of minds. Others (nominalists) say they are things in name only, merely human abstractions, useful fictions if you will. Still others ("conceptualists") say they are real, but that they exist only in the mind. What could possibly matter in this dispute?

3. Songwriters and musicians can be found in court claiming that others have plagiarized their work (e.g., when the rock group Spirit argued, unsuccessfully, that Led Zeppelin had stolen an opening guitar riff from "Taurus" to use in "Stairway to Heaven"). How should we judge when the similarity is sufficiently close to count as identity?

4. Copyright law says a copyright lasts for the lifetime of the author plus seventy years. Is this strictly arbitrary?

5. Philosopher George Berkeley faulted the mathematical calculus for speaking of infinitesimals. He reasoned that God alone was infinite. What do you make of this?

Worcester v. State of Georgia

U.S. Supreme Court
31 U.S. 515 (1832)

IN the early 1800s, Samuel Worcester, a native of Vermont, was serving as a missionary to the Cherokees on their tribal lands in today's northern Georgia. He was an agent of the American Board of Commissioners for Foreign Missions, which had grown out of a "Haystack Prayer Meeting" involving five Williams College students in 1806. Soon after graduation, they organized to send missionaries to India, most notably Adoniram and Ann Judson and Luther Rice, who subsequently became Baptists, as was William Carey, who had come to India from England. (Their denominational shift led to the establishment of the first American Baptist missionary society, which became the Triennial Convention, from which the Southern Baptist Convention emerged in 1845 on the eve of the Civil War.)

Worcester ran afoul of Georgia authorities operating under a new state law forbidding white men to live among the Cherokees without special license from the state. He and his missionary colleagues were convicted of illegal residence and sentenced to four years of hard labor. They appealed this ruling, and the U.S. Supreme Court took up the case, with Chief Justice John Marshall writing the majority opinion. He declared that the United States was the sole authority for legal dealings regarding the Cherokees, that the Cherokees were a nation under U.S. protectorate, and that the Indians had the right to determine who and who could not live in their midst. The opinion reviewed the history of colonial settlement, including the settlers' dealings with the Indians, and sketched protocols for interaction, including regard for their rights to property and political sovereignty, which, in the court's judgment, had been violated by the state of Georgia. So Worcester was set free.

This makes for a fascinating demonstration case in the philosophy of law. According to Marshall, Georgia had failed to make valid law, in that they'd worked at cross-purposes with the U.S. Constitution. But what made the U.S. Constitution valid? Was it because of its moral superiority? Well, certainly Marshall spoke to ethical matters, recounting the national practice of land purchase and treaty, not brute seizure and subjugation. But there are all sorts of wonderful policies we might imagine which do not constitute law. Just because it's a good idea, it doesn't follow that the citizens will fall in line with it dutifully. Lincoln's 1863 Emancipation Proclamation was a long time coming, and slavery was legal for ages. Indeed, law can be unsavory yet authoritative, as was shown to be the case in 1857 when the Dred Scott decision upheld the Fugitive Slave Law and disallowed the Underground Railroad, which was spiriting slaves to freedom in the North.

There are those in the natural law tradition who say that immoral law simply fails to be law, but most legal philosophers are inclined to say that immoral laws are nevertheless laws, though they should be changed and may well warrant civil disobedience. On this model—legal positivism—the content of law is determined by the authorities, whether kings, legislatures, or other magistrates. (A variant of this holds that it is not so much what's on the books but what the officials will actually enforce, e.g., when the speed limit is, in effect, more nearly 75 mph than the published 70 mph. It's called "legal realism," but it too depends upon the decisions and actions of officials, not the ethical winsomeness of their choices.)

This all raises the question of what, then, makes one a magistrate, able to make law. Is it moral grandeur, high IQ, or genealogy? No, for we can think of any number of ethically challenged, sub-genius, non-aristocratic men who became rulers. So what makes them the ones in charge?

CASES

As harsh at it may sound, the answer is power, and not just a measure of power. The power must be coercive, able to dominate. In the case at hand, it derived from the fact that the United States had military and police forces superior to those of Georgia (a fact borne out by subsequent battles in the Civil War, compliments of General William Tecumseh Sherman). That's what made the Worcester decision stand.

But that's not the end of the story. Though Marshall had declared the Cherokee territory a nation, he was powerless to override the executive power of President Andrew Jackson, a seasoned Indian fighter and a hero of the Battle of New Orleans in the War of 1812 against the British. "Old Hickory" pushed through a policy of Cherokee removal, forcing them to take a "Trail of Tears" to new land in Oklahoma. He had the "coercive sanctions" (which the Supreme Court lacked) necessary to back up this displacement of a "nation" from the east to the west side of the Mississippi.

As wrong as this may be, it shows that while "might does not make right," might does make property. Homeowners today in Dahlonega, Georgia, deep in the heart of the former Cherokee nation, do not need to surrender their lands to Oklahoma Indians seeking reinstatement of their property rights. These contemporary residents bought their houses and lots fair and square, as did the folks they bought them from. And so on back through the decades. So what was the base point for "fair and square"? Simply put, the U.S. policy which put Worcester's former mission field on the market for settlers to purchase.

Of course, it's not clear whether the Cherokees themselves acquired their north Georgia land in the purest of fashions. There may have been other native peoples residing there who themselves were pushed out or even killed by the Cherokees. It makes for interesting historical research, but it doesn't change the fact that those now in charge say the land no longer belongs to these pre-Cherokees either.

Of course, this cuts both ways. If the U.S. decided to reverse the Trail of Tears and re-establish the Cherokee nation, and they had the power to enforce it, that too would be the law. That's what law does, for good or ill—hence the need to be thoughtful and decent in the framing of law going forward, whatever the past may be.

As a side note, it's interesting to consider what sort of chaos we'd see in the Middle East if we tried to redistribute the land on the basis of original possession, ameliorating all wrongs committed in subsequent conquests. It certainly wouldn't go to the Palestinians, whose ancestors gained advantage

Worcester v. State of Georgia

and possession by Muslim Arab conquest. And the Jews would have to give way to the Jebusites or other Canaanite inhabitants, from whom they seized territory. The only reasonable approach is to say the land belongs to whom the land belongs to today by authority of the government. (Just ask the disgruntled, relocated homeowner who had to sell his land under the power of "eminent domain" to make way for an interstate loop.)

Discussion Questions:

1. Most think that it is morally permissible to fight for one's land when the one seeking to seize it is a murderous tyrant. But is real estate worth dying for if the one who wants it is not such a bad ruler (apart from the fact that he wants to take your land)?

2. Suppose a ski lodge developer needs to cut a road through what animistic Indians consider to be sacred land. What if the same tribe declared the entire state to be sacred and thus inviolate? How would one adjudicate such a claim?

3. Many Christians take trips to what they call the Holy Land. Is any land really holy? If so, what distinguishes it from unholy land?

4. John Locke argued that the original owner of a piece of real estate gained this possession (and the right to pass it along to whomever he pleased) by "mixing his labor" with the land, taking it out of a "state of nature." So we have the image of a pioneer in the wilderness coming across a promising few acres beside a stream. He clears the land, builds a cabin, cultivates a field, and brings in a crop. So it's his, even before government says so. Is this plausible?

5. Mound builders and other agrarian Indians developed extensive cities, some interlaced with canals. Their abode was more or less fixed. On the other hand, plains Indians roamed widely as they hunted buffalo. Suppose that a tribe from the latter group, in rotating their hunting expeditions from region to region so as not to decimate particular herds, visited a neighboring district, perhaps the size of Rhode Island, only every three or four years. Could they legitimately claim that land as theirs since they mixed their labor with it periodically?

6. In an earlier case, *Johnson v. M'Intosh* (1823), Justice Marshall addressed the issue of whether Indians could sell title to land. In his

decision, he rehearsed the history of land acquisition in the New World, and concluded that discovery and conquest gave the English (and later the United States) rights to the territory. Marshall wrote:

> We will not enter into the controversy, whether agriculturists, merchants, and manufacturers, have a right, on abstract principles, to expel hunters from the territory they possess, or to contract their limits. Conquest gives a title which the Courts of the conqueror cannot deny, whatever the private and speculative opinions of individuals may be, respecting the original justice of the claim which has been successfully asserted.

In other words, what's done is done, and the United States is now the arbiter of those lands (a principle he wielded against the state of Georgia in *Worcester*). In the course of his opinion, he used the example of the sea to argue that there is no basic right to possess it just because you fished in it (or in the case of the Indians, no basic right to possess the wilderness just because you hunted there). This was a landmark case. Should it have been?

Maps

PHILOSOPHICAL systems and concepts generate and, indeed, incorporate implications—if-then propositions—that tell us we will find this or that if we go this or that direction. They give us the lay of the land, but not just for contemplation. They also project journeys. And so we'll use maps to introduce a range of notions. Some are fair representations of actual working charts (e.g., the London Tube, the entrance to New London harbor); others are fantastical (e.g., the Land of Crest, the 1:1 version); and some represent interiors (e.g., the pineal gland, the auto assembly line).

In Christian literature, maps have been used to represent the conceptual landscape. For instance, artists have portrayed the journey through Vanity Fair and the Slough of Despond to the Land of Beulah, described in John Bunyan's *The Pilgrim's Progress* (1678). Then, taking his cue from Bunyan, C. S. Lewis gave us, in *The Pilgrim's Regress*, an allegorical map featuring the island of Wanhope, the town of Aphroditopois in the shire of Pagus, and the village of Ignoratia in the shire of Zeitgeistheim.

Though only one of the twenty-three maps featured below is explictly Christian (the "T and O"), I connect all of them to Christian puzzles and perspectives. I hope you'll enjoy the touring.

THE ASSAD/NUSRA/ISIS/KURD MAP

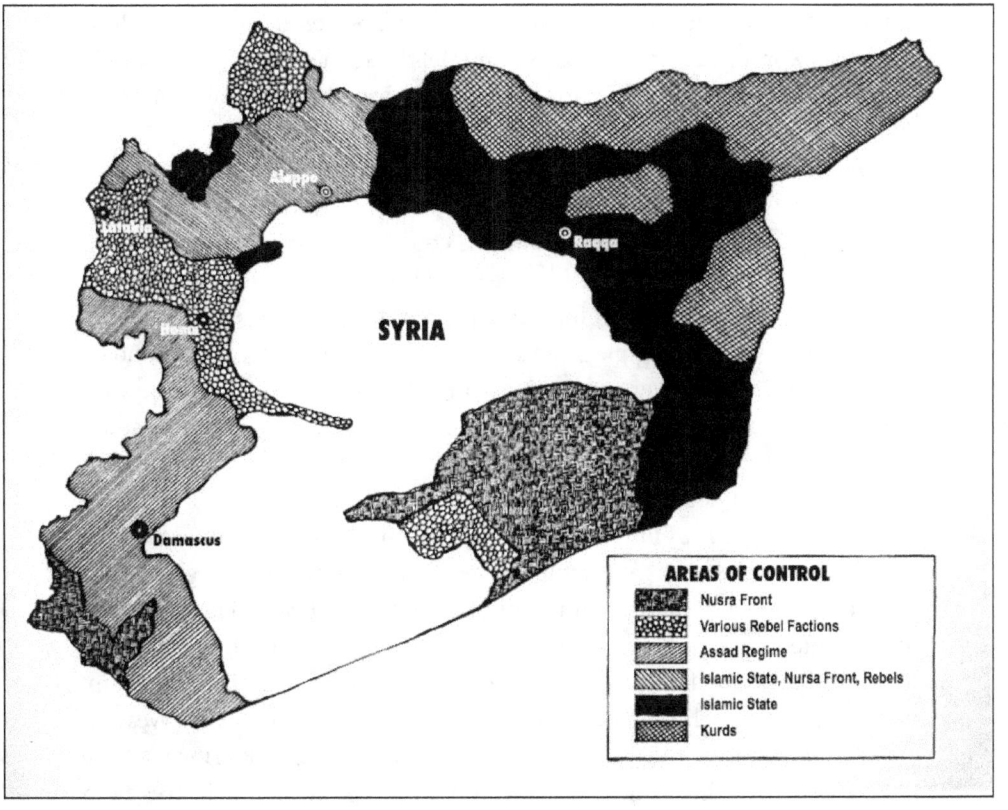

IT seems that every day in the second decade of this millennium, the sectors of control in Syria shift from one force to another, whether rebel, government, or ethnic in orientation. And it isn't the work of debaters, philosophers, or scientists trying determine the true contours of Syria's borders. Truth is not the issue; rather, it is power.

Such is the postmodern project, which rejects overarching accounts of reality in favor of relativism, with all sorts of tactics in play to gain advantage. (As Jean-François Lyotard put it, "I define postmodern as incredulity toward metanarratives.") While some applaud the way in which the shackles of "scientifish" modernism have been broken, leaving smug naturalists with less swagger than they once had, the newfound relief has come at a cost. For instance, while Christians used to reel under the lash of Hume, Kant, and their Enlightenment progeny, such as Bertrand Russell, they now they shudder in the creepy embrace of relativists who indulge their religious lifestyle with a patronizing, "Whatever works for you."

A number of thinkers have played into this dethroning of science. Thomas Kuhn, in his *The Structure of Scientific Revolutions*, showed how scientists worked under paradigms or models to do their "normal" research, but also how they also petulantly defended their perspectives against revolutionaries who dared point out difficulties in their conceits. This wasn't the pure system we'd been led to believe in, with courageous thinkers in lab coats going wherever the data led.

Wittgenstein also gets credit for his concept of "language games" and "family resemblances." While Plato believed he was looking for essences, Wittgenstein denied such things. Rather, we had to work with extended similarities, with overlappings and crisscrossings, whereby the boundaries of valid meaning were ever expanding. Nothing fixed about it. As for religious speech, it was just a language game you could play, as others could play commercial and political language games—not so much linkage with reality as maneuvers on a chessboard.

In *The Closing of the American Mind*, Allan Bloom explained mournfully that now the only true virtue on the American secular college campus was tolerance—not chastity, integrity, industry, or sobriety. He concluded that, in effect, we'd become so "open minded" that our brains had fallen out. Feelings had won. Truth was irrelevant. Enamored with multiculturalism, universities have eliminated requirements and even courses in Western civilization. Who's to say that Christian perspectives are superior to those of animism? All the while, the sensitivity police patrol the halls, ready to discipline those whose speech is deemed micro-aggressive, its utterances making classmates feel "unsafe." (Of course, the irony is that these indignant, tolerance champions have gone aggressively tribal, making life miserable for those who don't toe their ideological line.)

Into the mix have come varieties of the "hermeneutics of suspicion," of "critical theory," where you read power plays into every text (e.g., "We hold these truths to be self-evident, that we are endowed by our Creator . . ."

prompts the audience to bark, "*We*, is it! And who might that be, big shot?" and "How dare you try to co-opt us for a patriarchal religion!") We "deconstruct" texts by means of an ancient logical fallacy, *ad hominem*, whereby we defame the writer as we seek to impose our own social agenda.

The honorable craft of epistemology, with which we try to establish "justified, true belief," is consigned to the ash heap of history, for it's been exposed as a way to force "dead, white, European male" perspectives upon aggrieved people not adept at playing treacherous academic games. Logic itself, including the essential principle of non-contradiction ("It cannot be the case that both the cat is on the mat and the cat is not on the mat"), is cast aside as imperialistic, insensitive thuggery. So discourse degenerates into "Gotchas!" and "How dare yous!" and "Take thats!" This is sectarian warfare, not the collaborative pursuit of wisdom.

It's reminiscent of the Arab Spring, where the populace cast off the tyranny of the Mubaraks and Gaddafis, only to find themselves under the thumb of the Muslim Brotherhood and their ilk. But in this case, humanities scholars dethroned the scientists, only to find themselves ruled by reason-hating community organizers and literati pandering to parties averse to transcendent verities, which might cramp their liberated style.

In its Classical, Medieval, and Enlightenment forms, philosophy has typically subscribed to the notion of truth as correspondence, that propositions should follow the contours of independent reality, in both mundane (phonebook listings and dangerous-curve road signs) and exalted (the existence or non-existence of God) matters. But post-modernists have been called "antiphilosophers" (by themselves and others) for their assault on schools of thought presuming to seek and grasp overarching truth. Relishing the intellectual chaos that ensues and stepping into the gaps with transgressive/alarming assertions, such figures as Jacques Derrida and Michel Foucault come at Western civilization with a scythe, inspired in part by Friedrich Nietzsche, whose turn-things-upside-down approach is discussed below under a cockeyed world map. What you get are scrappy fighters, but belligerence is not a virtue in itself. Alas, this nicety is not their concern.

Discussion Questions:

1. John Cusack and Ione Skye starred in a 1989 romance film called *Say Anything*. Today, politicians seem to be following that dictum, and

it's not at all romantic. It's brutal. The point is not so much to make whatever helpful contribution you might have to reasoned discourse, but to brazen out absurdities, double down on exposed folly, circle the wagons around flapdoodle, go off half-cocked, and throw whatever mud you can find up against the wall in hopes that some of it might stick. The point is getting over on the opposition, whatever the cost in decency and plausibility. Do examples of this come to mind?

2. Some say that postmodernism resides essentially in the halls of academe, notably in the literature, philosophy, and social science departments. Others suggest that it's the operative perspective in the culture at large. Which is the case?

3. Is a hermeneutic of suspicion self-destructive, in that it cannot itself withstand the vicious scrutiny it imposes upon other writings?

4. What good might one say about postmodernism's crusade to get scientists and traditionalists off their "high horses"? Or are the postmodernists the ones on high horses, given their contempt for the labors of more conventional theorists?

5. In years past, students were encouraged to avoid such informal fallacies as *argumentum ad hominem* (attacking the person instead of the argument), *ad populum* (playing to the unreflective and easily manipulated enthusiasms of the mob), *ad misericordiam* (trotting out a sob story to divert attention from the real issue), and *ad baculum* (threatening the other party with harm). Have we turned these sins into virtues in the quest for political dominance?

Auto Assembly Line

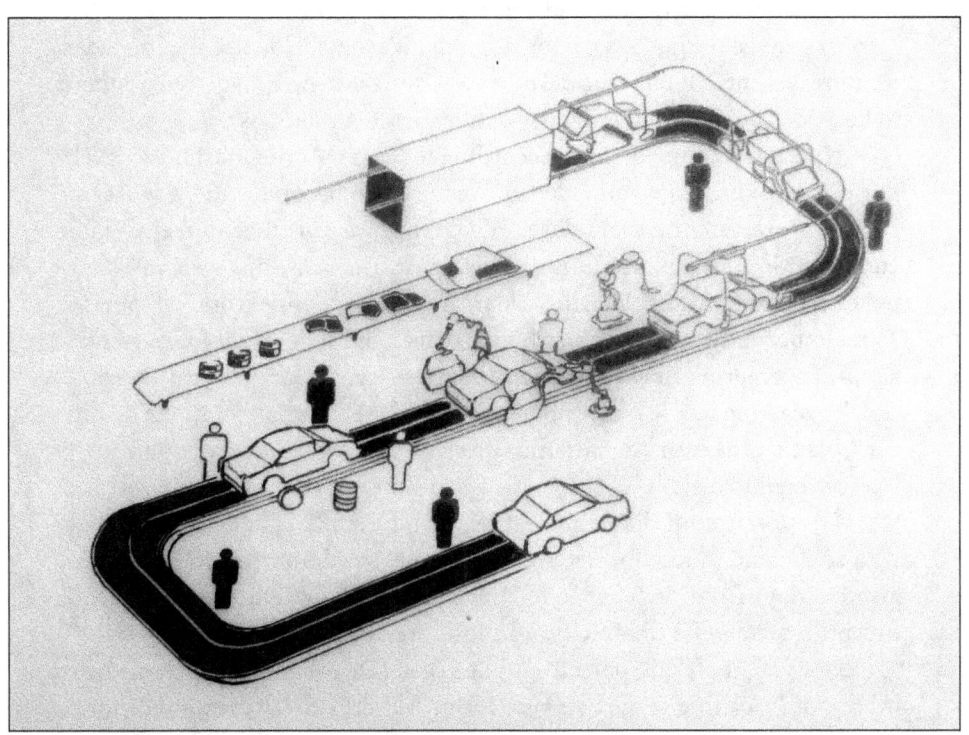

SINCE Henry Ford established the first automobile assembly line in Highland Park, Michigan (a town within metropolitan Detroit), this approach has become the industry standard. The "map" you see features cars, but, of course, we could have chosen a similar layout tracking the manufacture of air conditioners, furniture, or paper cutters, this last product used by French philosopher Jean-Paul Sartre as an example to answer the question raised in his essay "What Is Existentialism?"

So, what's with the paper cutters? Sartre explained that their "essence" preceded their "existence." By this, he meant that their nature and purpose were "set in stone" before the first one rolled off the assembly line. The manufacturer had to work with design engineers, prototypes, materiel suppliers, machinists, accountants, marketing representatives, personnel managers, and government regulators to make sure everything was in order before the product was good to go.

I'm thinking of the sort of paper cutter familiar in classrooms and offices throughout the world, the one with the square base marked with a measurement grid, plus a long blade along the right edge and a handle at the top to grasp for raising and slicing. Of course, one could use it for all sorts of strange things—as a door stop, a cudgel or shield, or a staging table for refreshments. But its true destiny is set by its design. It may have wanted to be a coat, a television, or a tasty entrée, but it is what it is.

Not so we human beings, according to Sartre. At the most basic level, our existence precedes our essence. We're free to become and do what we choose, at least on the moral level. (Of course, we can't turn ourselves into combination locks, aluminum cookware, or baseballs, but we can channel our energies into soldiering, eldercare, culinary endeavors, or sports.) More importantly, we can "make" a particular "lifestyle" right for ourselves simply by entering upon it without excuses (e.g., "I was raised that way" or "I'm reacting to my harsh upbringing" or "Well, I'm only human"). You can't blame others or the circumstances of your life. You are, in a sense, "condemned to be free."

Freedom sounds like a good thing, not the stuff of condemnation, but it's a scary kind of freedom. It means not only freedom from coercion, but also freedom from the chance for transcendentally salutary achievement, except in terms of authenticity. You lose the opportunity to "get it right," since, for you, there's no objective right to get. (Or you might say that whatever you do can be right on these terms.) There's no overarching moral system, no creation order, no natural law, no human nature. You're making it all up for yourself. So, you can be a thief (as was the lowlife Jean Genet, who gloried in his wickedness, and whom Sartre admired) or, if you wish, a sacrificial disaster relief worker. One's not better than the other. There's no yardstick, either externally or internally, by which you should be judged.

So, Sartre was perfectly free to fornicate with Simone de Beauvoir and then fornicate with other women to the dismay of Simone de Beauvoir. She had no reason to expect him to be faithful. There was no sovereign God on his throne casting a holy eye on the unholy mess. There were no universal patterns of human flourishing this behavior would violate to the ruin of the parties involved.

Of course, Sartre had a lot more to say about this "Wild West" perspective, and it was pretty gloomy stuff. In his play *No Exit*, he brings a variety of unlikable folks (a journalist, a postal worker, and a woman who murdered her own baby) together in "hell," and they torment each other with snarky conversation—the lesson being, as it is often expressed, that "hell is other people." Then there's the book *Nausea*, in which he teaches that this is the default mood when one takes a realistic view of things. And in *Being and Nothingness* he underscores the "absurdity" of it all.

Well, you might say that this is a bleak and untenable approach to life, but Sartre doubles down with the counsel, "Deal with it." If you try to perk it up with happy talk and hopeful schemes, then you're guilty of "bad faith."

Sartre had little or no interest in talking about things "out there," the typical topics of the philosophy of science, symbolic logic, theories of justice, metaphysical narratives, and such. Rather, he obsessed over the lived life of the will, moods, and directedness in our experience, deeming them the essential thing—a focus associated with what's called "phenomenology." And this puts him in the camp with others who've taken this philosophical turn, e.g., Edmund Husserl and Maurice Merleau-Ponty.

Let me hasten to say there are other existentialists, and some of them are more uplifting. Indeed, Sartre had a falling out with Albert Camus, who, in *The Myth of Sisyphus*, said that even acts of apparent futility (like rolling a stone up a hill only to have it roll back down from just short of the summit, repeatedly) are compatible with the happiness of "doing your thing." Also, Camus came out against revolutionary violence and communism, incensing Sartre, but Camus didn't mind.

Some existentialists—men and women who dealt with questions of meaning in life in terms of the states of mind and heart—identified as Christians, e.g., Gabriel Marcel and Miguel de Unamuno. And, in retrospect, many give credit to Søren Kierkegaard for pushing "subjectivity" as the key to wisdom. Contra Sartre, they say that when you dig deep, you can find gold and not just mud. (BTW, Sartre couldn't sustain his absurd moral nihilism, for he became a crusading anti-war activist in the Vietnam years, passing judgment on those who disagreed with him on the morality of the conflict.)

Existentialism is a slippery notion, so definitions proliferate. One way is to see it as the opposition of "essentialism," by which philosophers say there are eternal principles and verities, whether in the realm of concepts or the mind of God (Plato and Augustine) or woven into the fabric of the world (Aristotle and Aquinas). These are the essentialists, who say there is an essence to acorns, just governments, and, yes, humans.

I also heard it explained in terms of our appointment with death. For the objectivist, it's "All men are mortal." For the subjectivist, "I'm mortal." For the existentialist, "Oh, no! I'm going to die. It's haunting me. Will it hurt? Will I make a spectacle of myself when it comes? And what comes afterwards? I can hardly dare think about it, but I can't help it."

Of course, Christians can appreciate Sartre for mapping the soul of the lost man, for charting the emptiness and despair that comes from taking an honest look at the anxiety and loathing that arise in a godless universe. He gets points for candor. But he gets many demerits for acting like a hog eating acorns (or the repast he enjoyed at his favorite café, *Les Deux Magots*, "The Two Maggots," in Paris), oblivious to the oak tree under which he's dining. In the end, he's a fool, though a stylish and eloquent one.

Discussion Questions:

1. Sartre glorified the criminal Genet. Is that a common theme in film and television?

2. "Gender fluidity" is a hot notion, one that defies classic notions of maleness and femaleness. Also, homosexuality and heterosexuality are increasingly considered moral equals. All such talk is impatient with the concept of "human nature" and is devoted to magnifying "personal nature." Is this the right way to go?

3. Romans 2:14–15 says that the law is written on everyone's heart, with consciences accordingly accusing and excusing behavior. Is this a reality? If so, is it something to be ignored or scrubbed away?

4. Is hell "other people"? Is misanthropy a reasonable and fruitful perspective?

5. Oscar Wilde defended the literary work of a murderer by saying that the fact one was a poisoner was no reflection on his skill with a pen. Is this generally true? Is it beside the point to show that a philosopher lived an unsavory life, or, on the other hand, that he lived an exemplary life?

The 1:1 Scale Map

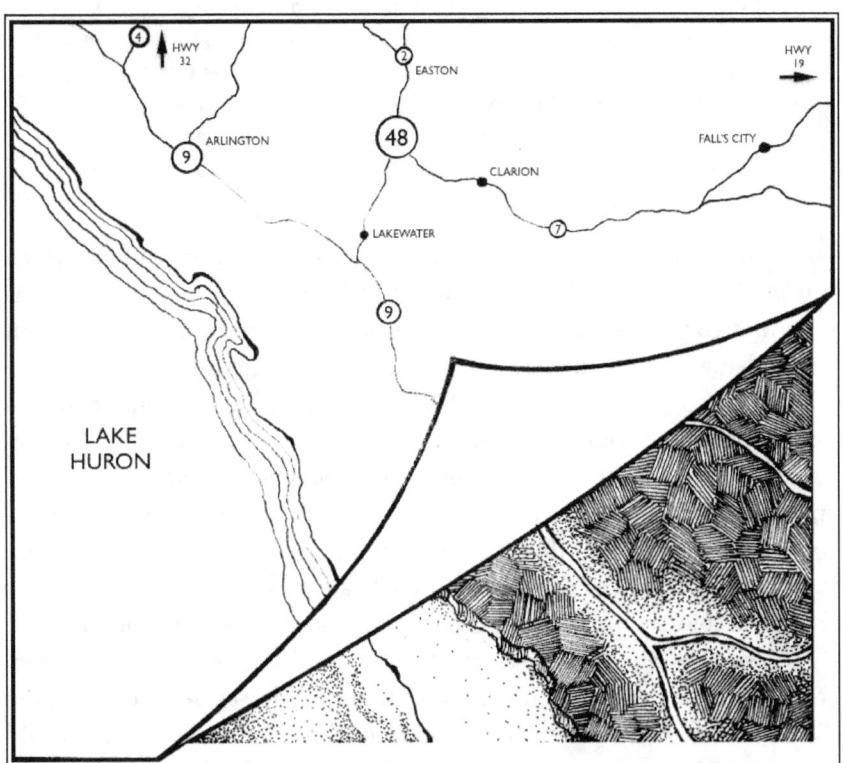

In 1893, Lewis Carroll, of *Alice in Wonderland* fame, imagined a 1:1-scale map in his book *Sylvie and Bruno*, and others have riffed on the idea, including Argentine author Jorge Luis Borges and American comedian Steven Wright. Here's the passage from Carroll:

> "And then came the grandest idea of all! We actually made a map of the country, on the scale of a mile to the mile!"
> "Have you used it much?" I enquired.

Maps

> "It has never been spread out, yet," said Mein Herr: "the farmers objected: they said it would cover the whole country, and shut out the sunlight! So we now use the country itself, as its own map, and I assure you it does nearly as well."

Well, actually, it doesn't do nearly as well, and Borges imagines more of the problem in his 1954 essay "On Exactitude in Science":

> In time, . . . the cartographers guilds struck a map of the empire whose size was that of the empire, and which coincided point for point with it. The following generations, who were not so fond of the study of cartography as their forebears had been, saw that that vast map was useless, and not without some pitilessness was it, that they delivered it up to the inclemencies of sun and winters. In the deserts of the west, there are tattered ruins of that map, inhabited by animals and beggars, in all the land there is no other relic of the disciplines of geography.

The point is that useful maps rely upon a level of abstraction, without which you would have to simply look to the ground in front of you to see what was next, though you would scarcely know where you were. A sense of location would demand context, generalization, and simplification.

The same goes for all theoretical thinking, including science and philosophy. You can't count each individual phenomenon and person as *sui generis* ("in a class by itself"), for then you couldn't speak meaningfully about anything. There would be no adjectives, no collective terms, such as "child," "blue," or "forest"—only this thing, that thing, and the other thing, for there is an infinite variety of each. You couldn't categorize them, respectively, as creatures, colors, or forms of vegetation, for those too are abstractions.

Instead of representing all rivers by a uniform blue line on your map, you would need to make the lines wider and narrower depending on the distance between banks in the various sections. But even when you did that, as on the 1:50,000 military topographical maps (such as those we used to study the Mekong Delta during the Vietnam War), you would still rely on blue to stand for rivers. The same goes for maps of Khartoum, Sudan, where the darker Blue Nile, rushing down from the Ethiopian highlands, meets the languid (and muddy) White Nile coming up from flatlands to the south. In a sense, the blue notation is a lie, for neither of the feeder Niles is really blue; but that's not the point. You don't need to know the pigmentation of this stretch or that, as much as whether or not there's a river before you, to travel or cross or tap for water.

And so we abstract. But what do we make of the status of those abstractions? And how do they relate to the specifics on the ground? Philosophers speak of these matters in terms of "universals" (general terms) and "particulars" (specific things). Nominalists ("name only" people, like Hume) say that universals are just useful fictions. Realists say they're real, as the name implies. Conceptualists say they're real, but only as concepts in the mind.

And the breakdown continues: Plato and Aristotle were both realists, but for Plato, the universals (such as friendship and horseness) were "transcendent," existing independently in an immaterial realm all their own. For Aristotle, they were immanent, written into the very creatures we see on Earth, e.g., horseness in Seabiscuit. And how exactly does this happen? What are the mechanisms for the "participation" of particulars in the universals? And what are the proper boundaries of application? When, for instance, does a river become a creek or an estuary?

For my money, conceptualism, with the universals residing in the mind of God, who creates and sustains all the particulars, makes the most sense. And thus one aims to not only "think God's thoughts [propositional] after him," but also to wield them in reflection and discourse concerning God's exalted universals (*Imago Dei*, anointing), along with his more mundane ones (lamb, sea), and even the dark ones (sin, delusion). Of course, if you don't believe in God, then things get trickier, more metaphysically daunting. If you take this atheistical tack, then, as my daughter says, "Knock yourself out."

Discussion Questions:

1. It's popular today to say that something is merely a "social construct," as opposed to a real thing, e.g., "race" and "gender." Well, certainly, all language is that to some extent, for it is a human enterprise. But does it follow that it is *only* a social construct?

2. Shows like *Modern Family* and *Big Love* have sought to normalize and celebrate what has traditionally been regarded as illicit (in these instances, respectively, homosexual and polygamous marriage). Is it tyrannical to insist that traditional "universals," such as "marriage" and "family," have limits in application?

3. Some leaders have deployed bogus universals to bolster their policies, e.g., Hitler spoke of the "Aryan race" to justify his brutality toward Jews and Slavs. Can you think of other universals which lack valid application?

4. It can be delicious to discover a concept, a universal, already at play in your language, or in a foreign language. It connects dots or shines light on phenomena you've noticed but haven't gathered together in your mind. In my own case, I think of discovering "ubiquitous" (appearing everywhere) and "obsequious" (flattering for the sake of favor); and, then, in German, *Schadenfreude* (delight at another's misfortune), and in Greek, *kairos* (momentous time). What are words that struck you as particularly insightful when you first came across them?

5. A thesaurus provides us word alternatives, such a "abode," "dwelling," and "residence" for "house." Have we just cluttered things up? The simplified language of Esperanto, whose vocabulary runs about 5,000 words, uses "domo" to stand for all house words. In contrast, Webster's unabridged dictionary contains around 170,000 words. Why not go with the leaner approach? If we stick with the richer vocabulary, are we saying that conceptual shades are important, that there is overlap without total duplication among concepts/universals?

Backstage

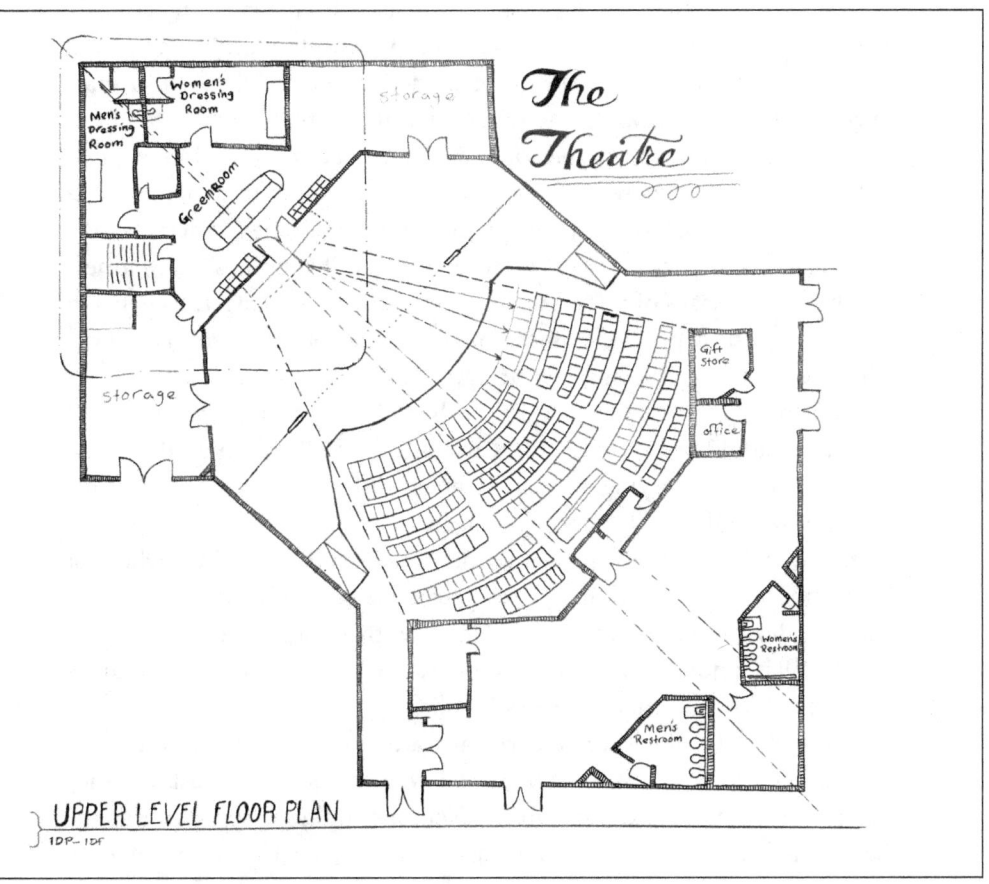

Here's the floorplan for a typical theater (this particular one drawn from Asheville, North Carolina). Of course, the stage and seating are the prime features, but the backstage is crucial. Without a place for the actors to get offstage, the play is ruined (unless you're in some sort of insufferable "art" production, pushing the boundaries of the medium just to show how clever or shocking you can be). Just imagine if there were no backdrop behind the stage, or that it was transparent. And what if the green room had only three walls, with one side open to the audience. And if the restroom and dressing rooms were mere kiosks so that the audience could watch it all—actors in their underwear, reviewing scripts, smoking and chatting. It would vitiate their performances.

Turns out, there is major application here to our own lives, to our own personhood. Indeed, the word "person" derives from the Latin expression *persona*, for the role one plays in a drama. And it's tied to masks; an actor adopts a persona when, for instance, he takes up the laughing comedy mask rather than the horrified tragedy mask. And though it may sound distasteful to say (given the way we've made "authenticity" and "transparency" to be fetishes), we do the same thing in the public presentation of ourselves. If we don't have a selection of persona at our disposal for dealing with the world, then we're toast, and we can do a lot of damage to others as well. Of course, Jesus was emphatic in his contempt for the hypocrisy of the Pharisees, repeatedly calling down woe on those "hypocrites" in Matthew 23. They wore masks of piety, but they were rotten and dangerous beneath them (the word "hypocrite" comes from the Greek for "judge from under"). But this was treacherous mask wearing.

Let me suggest that there is another kind that is characteristic of thoughtful adulthood. A baby cries when it feels like it; an adult can be pleasant when he's crying inside. A thoughtful pastor doesn't shake his head and say, "Oh, no, this doesn't look good," when he first visits a parishioner laid up in ICU after an auto accident. Neither did the EMTs who first came upon the fellow exclaim "Yikes!" And one of the serious life skills we learn in school is that of appearing/being attentive when we're exhausted or bored. Call it "phony" if you will, but these seem to be instances of maturity, fellow feeling, decorum, and professionalism.

But what if you had to be perky and attentive all the time? What if a camera were trained on you in your home with the feed broadcast in Times Square? Could you relax? And what if everyone could see you at every moment, whether with a bad-hair wakeup, a sneeze that left major residue on your upper lip, or . . . well, you can let your imagination run. The point is that we need to have time and place to retreat from public observation and judgment so that we might recoup our powers and recalibrate our behavior.

Think of David in 2 Samuel 12. God's judgment on the king's adultery and murder was the death of the child who issued from his treachery. As long as the boy's life hung in the balance, David prayed with tears, fasted, and slept in sackcloth on the ground. But when the child died, he cleaned himself up, began to eat again, and went to the temple to worship God. He reasoned that there was nothing else he could do, so he had to get on with being king before joining his departed son in the grave. Was he a counterfeit griever since he could set his pleas aside? No, for there is, as is said in Ecclesiastes 3, an appropriate time for contrasting behaviors on the stage of life.

This issue of the deleterious effect of stolen privacy has become more compelling in our day of increasingly dazzling technology. Writing for the U.S. District Court for the District of Columbia in the 2013 case *Klayman v. Obama*, Judge Richard Leon ruled that the government's "three-hop" gathering (the phone contacts of the contacts of the contacts of the "person of interest") of "telephony metadata" (who called, who was called, when, and for how long) was out of bounds, inconsistent with the Fourth Amendment, which outlawed "unreasonable search and seizure." Ah, but what's the problem if you have nothing to hide? Okay, then let's let the police go through your house whenever they please, looking for nothing in particular, but ever alert to what might turn up.

Just imagine the wreck you'd be if you were day by day open to "Where did you get this?" and "What's this for?" to the whims of those commissioned "to protect and to serve." Ah, but we should sleep like babies if we're innocent of any wrong doing. Right? But there's a big problem. For purposes of argument, let's say that we all do a thousand things a day, and that we're not particularly proud of at least one of them. Perhaps something muttered in traffic when the driver at the head of the left-turn line isn't paying attention when the light changes, or when, in that same turn lane, we pick our nose (a common activity captured in a photo book some years back). If someone is watching everything you do, they could capture that image and shoot it out through social media, to your mortification.

Furthermore, context is crucial. Our denominational press once asked me to consider writing an article on modern-day bestiality, and I had to wonder why they would pick me out of the millions in our fellowship. (Turns out, there was a resurgence of it in Illinois, where I lived, and the legislature was considering reinstating the prohibition, which they had tossed aside when repealing "sodomy" laws.) I did a little research and soon found that there was a subculture built around "zoophilia." Now, just imagine that one who wished me ill had perfect access to my search history, and he went grandly public with the report that I was looking into bestiality.

Maps

Well, yes, but not because I was aroused by it. "Riiiight. Suuuure." And then the burden of proof would be upon me to justify myself. Simply put, you cannot craft a life carrying around such burdens as might be gratuitously piled upon you by those who desire your ruin.

So our constitutional default is to honor privacy and to punish those who invade it—not only for the good of the state, but also for the dignity and viability of the individual citizen. After all, he or she is a "person," and it is crucial that they be allowed to choose the circumstances and manner of their appearances. Unless, of course, their activities seem quite likely to be nefarious. Yes, there's a place for police surveillance and wiretapping, but you'd better have a warrant (and not just one whipped up by your foes as a fancy tool of persecution).

As Harvard's Sissela Bok put it, "With no control over secrecy and openness, human beings could not remain either sane or free."

Discussion Questions:

1. A recent privacy controversy concerns police body cams. If an officer comes to your door and his body cam records part of the interior of your home, then, using the Freedom of Information Act (FOIA) regarding public records, the public is entitled to check out your décor. What other technologies might pose such problems, e.g., facial recognition software at sporting events? Can we become hyper-skittish or are there imminent dangers?

2. The Bible speaks of dramatic personality events, including King Nebuchadnezzar's episode of insanity (where he ate grass like an ox in Daniel 4), the Gadarene demoniac (who, possessed of demons, identified himself as "Legion" in Mark 5), and Pharaoh (whose heart God hardened according to Romans 9, so that he set the stage for divine intervention on behalf of the Israelites). How many "persons" can a human being be in the course of a lifetime, or simultaneously?

3. According to Calvinist doctrine represented by the acronym TULIP, man is in bondage to sin, and, indeed, something of a hellion, until God intervenes with irresistible grace, as when he "opened Lydia's heart" in Acts 16. Does God, in effect, choose our personas for us?

4. A dispositional view of emotions says it's not what's inside as much as what shows itself outside. On this model, possessing a repentant

heart is not just a matter of feeling sorry about sin, but about doing something about it, about turning from it in behavioral terms. What are other examples of the outward persona validating the claim of an inward state, such as love and fear?

5. In a cable television interview, a veteran actor said that his craft was not so much putting on a mask as letting the character already within him somewhere come out. So by this standard, Tom Hanks was "legion" in the sense that he had, inside, both some Forrest Gump and some Sully, along with a host of other characters. Is there something to this?

6. In infantry training, soldiers are tutored in "battle drill," reactions to coming under fire, e.g., through "fire and maneuver" or "fire and movement" toward the enemy. The exercises are run again and again so that they become automatic. They seem to evidence bravery when initiated in actual combat, but could it be that acting brave precedes being brave, so that the behavior precedes the persona?

The Cineplex

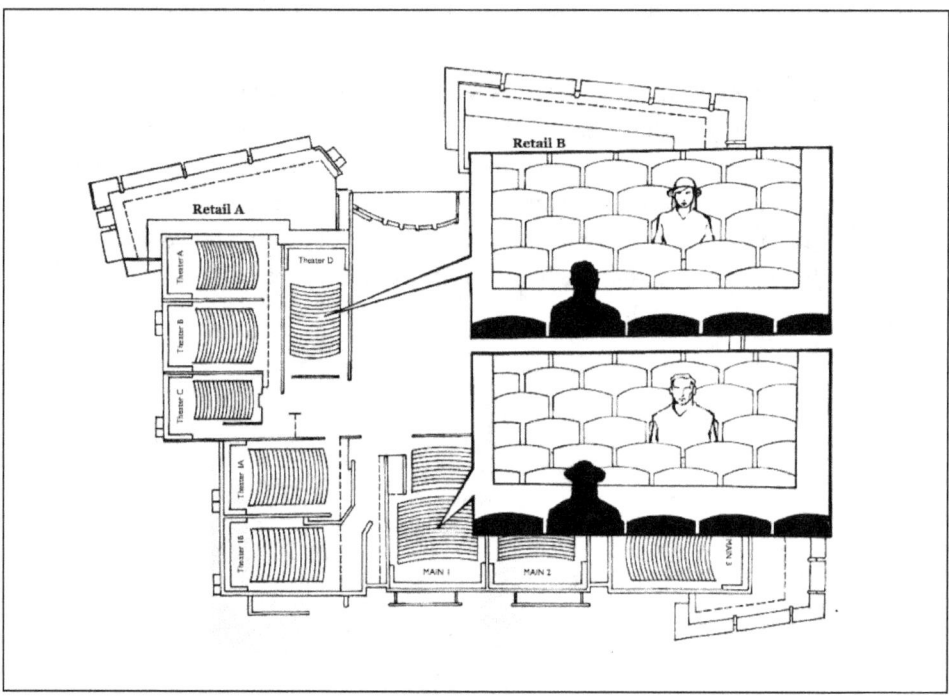

THE "cineplex" is a network of movie worlds unto themselves, so to speak. The occupants of each see their own film without access to what's being shown in the adjoining theaters. (Yes, I know that two or more theaters may be featuring the same film, but, for our purposes, we'll speak of a different one for each room.) This arrangement came to mind the first time I read *Monadology*, written in 1716 by the German philosopher Gottfried Leibniz. Therein, he said that "monads," which are centers of consciousness, "have no windows" and that one monad can affect another "only through the intervention of God."

The Cineplex

In this drawing, you see blowups of two of the theaters in the complex, with two characters appearing in each other's movies. They're not really present to each other directly, but only aware of the other by virtue of the projectionist's work. Now, imagine one's throwing a baseball at the figure on the screen, with the other seeing a movie of a baseball coming his way—and with 3-D glasses, if you will.

These monads, these little theaters or universes, are the building blocks or atoms of reality, created by God, with each having its own developmental "DNA," its engine of perfectability, which Leibniz calls its "entelechy." Their various internal unfoldings are engineered by God, even as he coordinates one monad with the others so that it appears that they are impacting each other. Nevertheless, the apparent human-to-human interaction is merely the result of "pre-established harmony." This model fits nicely with Leibniz's claim that this is the "best of all possible worlds," a notion mocked by Voltaire in *Candide* (1759), where Leibniz appears thinly disguised as Dr. Pangloss, who utters cheerful assurances in the face of disasters such as the Lisbon earthquake of 1755. Things may look out of control and evil, but you have to know the big picture to see the beauty of it all, a beauty insured by a God who is perfect in every way, including power and goodness.

Leibniz's philosophy is idealist as opposed to materialist. He says it all boils down to mental stuff, as opposed to physical stuff, the latter a view advanced by Thomas Hobbes in that same era, and which has been popular with some throughout the history of ideas, reaching back to Epicurus.

By Leibniz's account, animals are monads too, in that they have perceptions, desires, and memories. But human monads exceed these, for their souls are rational and reflective in a way that transcends mere animality. And at the top we have the being of God himself, whose "supreme substance, which is unique, universal and necessary, having nothing outside of itself which is independent of it . . . must be incapable of imitations and must contain as much of reality as is possible." It's unjust to compare the Lord to the cineplex projectionist, but perhaps there's something helpful in the analogy.

Of course, the real divine projectionist, who is both "architect" and "legislator" of all affairs, is properly "the whole aim of our will," the one "who, alone, can make our happiness," and the essence of "pure love, which takes pleasure in the happiness of the beloved."

The British philosopher Bertrand Russell said that "the Monadology was a kind of fantastic fairy tale, coherent perhaps, but wholly arbitrary."

MAPS

Well, perhaps so, or even probably so—at least with regard to the monads. Nevertheless, Russell, who wrote the famous/infamous essay, "Why I Am Not A Christian," committed the biggest possible metaphysical blunder in dismissing the reign of God in Christ. It was a mistake Leibniz did not make, to his everlasting blessing.

DISCUSSION QUESTIONS:

1. Might monads be compared to avatars, in that the appearance of you in my world and I in yours are stand-ins for the real you and me?

2. In his later years, Leibniz was embroiled in a controversy over whether he or Isaac Newton had invented the calculus. Most think they developed it independently. Be that as it may, here is an instance of a philosopher having another "job," in this case as a mathematician. There are other such cases, from pragmatist Charles S. Peirce (who worked as a scientist, including a stint at the U.S. Geodetic Survey) to Eric Hoffer (who labored as a longshoreman on the docks of San Francisco) to a range of priests and bishops (including Augustine and Anselm). It's interesting to see how "outside work" and philosophizing inform one another in a single life. (Leibniz's *Monadology* is a formal system, not unlike geometry and, yes, the calculus.) Can you think of other instances of philosophical cross-pollination?

3. Is this, indeed, the best of all possible worlds for this day because God is utterly sovereign in its operations?

4. My colleague at SBTS, Ted Cabal, has another analogy:

   > I thought of individual isolated musicians brought into the recording studio to play their part according to the score. They faithfully play what the composer has written. They also play their part right on time because they have a "click track" (or else someone starts a countdown to the beginning of the score and time is kept with a perfect metronome). But the players never hear the other musicians' parts, only their own. They do not know now the grand piece sounds nor are they able even to conceive what it would be like.

   Would this be a comforting notion?

5. Which would a sovereign God find more complicated or challenging—coordinating a world of matter and mind or coordinating a world of mind alone and its contents (e.g., ideas, perceptions, intentions)?

Eastern Kentucky Coal Mine

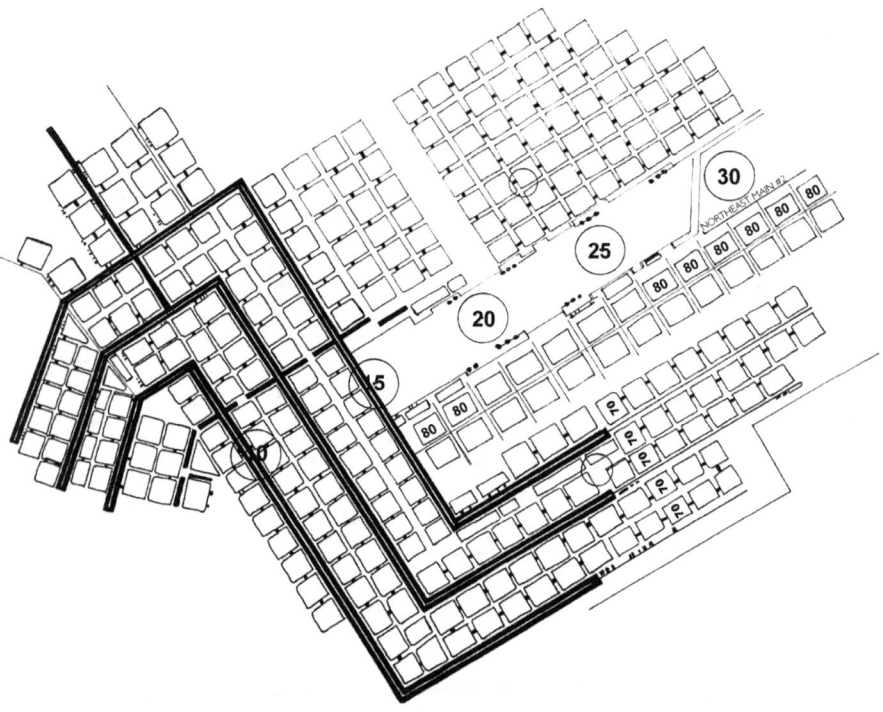

In preparation for a course on the ethics of work and leisure, I was able to videotape (by the light of our helmets) five miners in an eastern Kentucky coal mine. We were a half-mile back under a mountain, discussing both the satisfactions and the dangers of their labors. (They compared themselves to astronauts, who, every day, went "where no man had gone before.") And though we were surrounded by darkness at the end of a bewildering (for me) set of twists and turns, the whole thing was intricately and rationally structured. I knew this because I'd seen the map (replicated here) in the control trailer.

In this man-made cave, I thought back to Plato's cave allegory in the *Republic*. There, he pictured the epistemological plight of human kind, comparing us to prisoners chained and facing a wall upon which shadows played. These shadows were the product of items paraded over a bridge between the prisoners and a fire burning at the other end of the cave. Problem is, those in bondage didn't know these were shadows at all, for they were oblivious to what was going on behind—and above—them.

On Plato's model, the cave represents the world of human perception and opinion, ridden both by ignorance and ignorance of that ignorance. The answer is to break free of one's chains and climb out of the cave into the sunlight to see things as they really are. The ones who do this are the philosophers, who, through dogged dialogue, home in on the nature of the big things, such as justice, knowledge, love, and courage. These "Forms" are what they are despite what men may think. Indeed, there may be no justice whatsoever *on Earth*, but there's still capital-J Justice as an ideal existing in its own realm.

But back to the cave. While Plato pictured it as a natural cavern, I think we can extend the analogy to cover man-made subterranean rooms and tunnels. By this, I mean the web of popular conceits, the deliverances of conventional wisdom, and the structures of peer pressure and professional advance. It connects with the Christian notion of the big three sin inducers and seducers—the world, the flesh, and the devil—all at work to corrupt our understandings and behavior this side of the grave.

The Greek word for "world" is *kosmos*, from which the Russians got the word "cosmonaut" ("universe navigator") and from which, surprisingly, we get the word "cosmetics." In the latter case, it has to do with the facial arrangements involved in makeup, the presentation order of things before one makes a public appearance. Similarly, there is an array of things deployed against the truth of God (the "world" that we're told not to love in 1 John 2:15), and it's reasonable to say that much of what we find in the entertainment, educational, and political realms constitutes this "world." So, we see a range of film producers, tenured professors, veteran congressmen, bloggers, print journalists, pollsters, magazine publishers, tour directors, booking agents, gallery owners, ad men, novelists, spin doctors, religious gurus, vocal athletes, naturalistic scientists, talk show hosts, etc. cranking out an unholy mess. Of course, there are good folks in all these sectors, but the predominating perspectives are sub-Christian if not anti-Christian . . . and increasingly at odds with just plain common sense and decency (as, for instance, with the transgender normalization movement). So, right along, fools are digging shafts, bracing the current excavations with timbers, and chaining up the populace as best they can, so that they can extend and secure the ruinous error of their networks.

As in the coal fields, the culture is always opening new mines and closing old ones. In an appendix to his book *State of Fear*, Michael Crichton surveyed the American excitement over eugenics, which swept the nation (including the leading universities and courts) before World War II. Hitler gave the theory and practice a bad name, so that mine played out. Chattel slavery based on "the curse of Ham" was all the rage in the early eighteenth century, but the "worldly" notions that sustained it fell out of fashion. Still, other ruling stupidities (e.g., postmodernist relativism) rush in to keep the world in bondage, unable to "get it" in the most important ways. We're in a cave all right, but one of our own design.

Discussion Questions:

1. Are professional philosophers the ones best equipped and most inclined to lead the addled prisoners out of the caves and mines? If not them, then who? The clergy? Scientists? Homeschool moms?
2. Have you ever been chained up in a world of shadows constructed by fools, however well-meaning they may be?
3. Have you ever been party to putting others into a cavern of confusion or delusion?
4. Are there transcendent forms of negative and evil things, such as perfect ignorance or perfect greed? Or, might it be, as Augustine argued, that these are just vacuums or privations of a sort, with ignorance as the absence of knowledge and greed as the absence of generosity?
5. What disincentives are there to climbing out of the cave of popular foolishness?

Four Corners

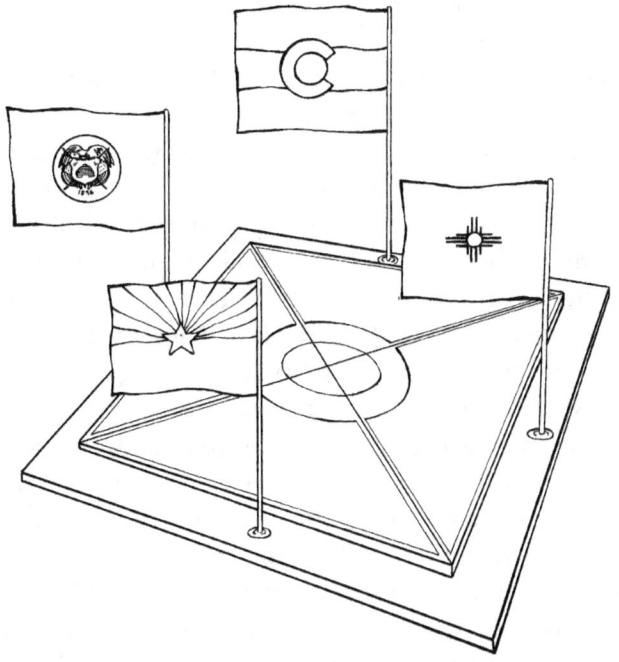

A good many tourists make their way to a remote spot in the American West, the point at which four states come together—Utah, Colorado, New Mexico, and Arizona (clockwise from the northwest). A monument marks the "quadripoint," with a bronze disk embedded in granite disk at the precise location. Visitors like to stand astride it, thereby being present in four states at once.

The site reminds one of Aristotle's view (spelled out in his *Physics* and *Metaphysics*) that four "causes" or factors are at play in all of nature. If we use, for example, the Statue of Liberty in New York Harbor, we can speak of the *material* cause (the iron, copper, asbestos, and shellac), the *formal* cause

(Bartholdi's models, sketches, and prototypes), the *efficient* cause (the casting, hammering, riveting, etc. by the metalworkers), and the *final* cause (to welcome newcomers to a land which shared France's love of freedom).

The first three are commonplace in our scientific age. Imagine, for instance, an evening newscast in which the anchor announces the discovery of a massive ice ball somewhere near Pluto. He might report that it was made of water (material), had a certain crystalline structure (formal), and resulted from the coalescence of moisture vented from a mysterious passing asteroid (efficient). This could be astonishing, but still within the range of expected explanation. But were he to add, ". . . and it exists to bring glory to God" (or "to provide aesthetic delight or a sense of wonder to earthlings," or "to prompt more deep space exploration," or "to provide for the development of life in the region"), we would find that very odd, indeed, unwarranted. You just don't talk that way when you do astronomy.

Of course, in ordinary discourse, these angles can make for some funny confusion. Picking up on an example supplied by philosopher Richard Swinburne, imagine a child coming down for breakfast and asking his scientist father, "Why's the water boiling?" The reply: "Well, the heat from the burner excited the molecules of water so that kinetic energy increased, eventually overcoming the surface barrier inducing phase change." The rejoinder: "No, Dad. I was wondering if we were having oatmeal?" The closure: "Oh, sorry. It's boiling because I asked your mother for a cup of tea."

Today, the courts are indignant when a school board wants to introduce a kind word for Intelligent Design in the classroom. (See the discussion of the Kitzmiller case above.) As the claims go, if you presume to extend ID talk beyond biology to chemistry and physics, then you've left the realm of serious thinking and entered the land of religious devotionals. But that wasn't Aristotle's perspective. He was no evangelical, but he saw purpose and direction everywhere.

Twentieth-century science historian Thomas Kuhn introduced the notion of "paradigms," models under which scientists operated, models which may be displaced by subsequent discovery and reflection. In this case, Aristotle's model for understanding nature was a vegetable, such as the acorn. The point of this little nut was to become an oak. It wasn't simply an inert item in the forest, but rather, it was pregnant with a *telos*, a developmental direction packed into a small kit. (This was before the science of genetics, but you didn't need the nineteenth-century work of Gregor Mendel to see that things were cooking in that little oak seed.)

Problem was, Aristotelian scientists applied the developmental *telos* to all matter, including metals. By their reasoning, a base metal like lead was yearning to become an exalted metal like gold. So they came up with the bogus science of alchemy to find a "hormone treatment" to help lower metals "be the best that they could be." But then, in revolutionary fashion, along came Isaac Newton, and the clock became the new paradigm. And no, hour glasses aren't yearning to become grandfather clocks, nor wrist watches aching to emerge as atomic clocks. That's Aristotelian vegetable talk, not Newtonian mechanical talk.

Still, Christians and theists in general are open to reflection on why God might have designed things as he did, what they're here for, and how the universe would be diminished if they didn't exist. And that includes humans. Witness the Westminster formulation that the "chief end of man" is "to glorify God and enjoy him forever." You don't exhaust the meaning of man by simply speaking terms of DNA, a nervous system, musculoskeletal engineering, and viscera.

In this connection, it's good to recall the work of Thomas Aquinas (thirteenth-century Dominican friar), who developed a system of thought, "Thomism," one which wedded the philosophy of Aristotle with biblical revelation. He picked up on Aristotle's four causes, applying them, for instance, to human law. In *Summa Theologica*, he said that all valid human law was based on reason (formal), applicable to a community of persons (material), the work of the magistrate (efficient), and directed toward the common good (final). So, if a crazy (non-rational) piece of legislation, which applied only to a single person (think Tom Hanks on a desert island with a soccer ball), was "enacted" by people lacking authority (non-magistrates), and meant only to serve special interests rather than the commonweal, the result wouldn't be bad law, but rather no law at all. No quadripoint, no law.

Discussion Questions:

1. Procrustes was a bad character in Greek mythology who made his visitors fit a guest bed by either stretching their limbs or lopping them off. So a "Procrustean bed" is a claim, theory, or policy meant to accommodate everything that might come along, but at the expense of mutilation. Are Aristotle's four causes a Procrustean bed, or are they matters of inescapable common sense? Can you think of something that lacks one of these causes or one that has more?

2. Roman Catholic ethicists can be quite insistent that they can read the *telos* of a thing, saying, for instance, that sexual organs are clearly designed for procreation and that any sexual activity outside the procreational context (for example, with employment of contraception) is illicit. Have they pushed the notion too far?

3. When God created the universe *ex nihilo*, out of nothing, was the only thing missing in his workshop the material cause, which he then supplied?

4. When we hatch a scheme to make money through offering a brand new sort of product, does our business plan follow Aristotle's four-part rubric? Or are own mental creations of a different sort?

5. Can Aristotle's four-cause system get off the ground without there being a God? Can it just run on nature? Some, like philosopher Jerry Fodor, suggest that there are naturalistic "telic" properties at work within organisms, endogenous forces which channel things onward and upward. But is this just *ad hoc* thinking in the absence of belief in a created design?

The Land of Crest

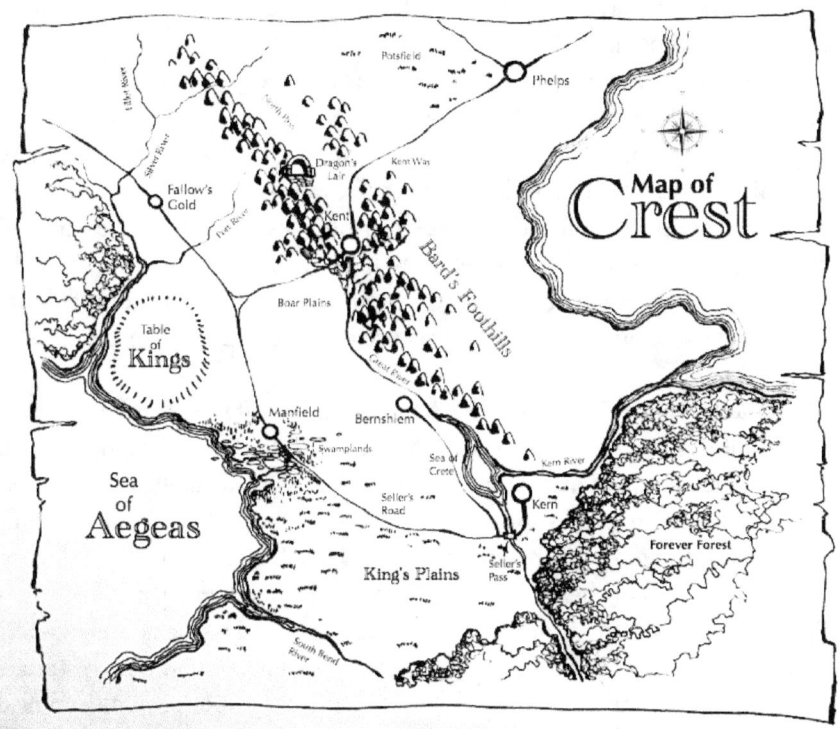

In the tumultuous 1960s and 1970s, some popular enthusiasm for "third way" philosophy surfaced in the counterculture. The names Georgi Gurdjieff and P. D. Ouspensky were tossed around with an aura of profundity. It was a time when old verities were questioned, and secular esoterica were in vogue. Gurdjieff and his devotees had come on the scene in the early 1900s, and their thought connected with some prominent cultural figures, including the architect Frank Lloyd Wright.

Gurdjieff's philosophy was a dog's breakfast of absurdities, with talk of "finer hydrogens," "astral bodies," and the cosmic "Law of Threes," which could be combined with the "Ray of Creation" to enable his students to locate themselves within the universe. He prescribed "sacred dances," which he would interrupt with the "stop exercise," requiring them to freeze until he released them for more motion.

He threw in study of the Kabbalah and numerology and drew disciples from those who had been studying eurythmics, a form of gymnastics designed to coordinate and empower the senses. He prescribed "duliotherapy" or the "slave cure," wherein he had them dig holes in the ground and then fill them back in.

It goes on and on, a testimony to man's ingenuity and capacity for self- and group delusion. But it hung together in its own way, with a place for every thing and a thing for every place. It was system, a worldview, a map to reality, if you will. The problem was that it was unfit to equip its followers to navigate within reality. They made terrible messes of their lives, missed real insight at every turn, and fell prey to ever more exotic forms of babbling. Of course, much of it was so vague that you could claim compatibility with whatever came along, but it was useless as a guide to the universe or well-being.

The literature is full of these bogus, though often charming, worlds, philosophical counterparts to A. A. Milne's Hundred Acre Wood, wherein Winnie the Pooh and his friends played. Some, like Gurdjieff's, are a laughing stock among professional philosophers; others, like Spinoza's pantheism, are treated with reverence in privileged corners of the academy, including offices of the secular environmentalists. One might think that a Spinozan who said that rocks, spiders, pine trees, and humans were equally divine would have trouble getting a hearing, but one would underestimate the intellectual impressiveness of a systematically rendered philosophical conceit, no matter how shaky the proofs or wacky the resulting scheme.

Discussion Questions:

1. All philosophical systems are abstractions, but some are tethered more securely and demonstrably to reality than others. Among the models noted in this book, which are most plausible and which are most unhinged?

2. Popular culture is awash in metaphysical curiosities, including Dianetics, theosophy, Gaia worship, and Wicca. What's the appeal?

3. It's sometimes said that if something is sweepingly new in theology or biblical interpretation, it's probably wrong. After all, Christian scholars have been at work on these matters for millennia, hammering out creeds, writing books, debating, and so on. The vocabulary of dispute and assent is seasoned and the propositions familiar. Yes, there are fresh means of expression, fresh arguments and declarations here and there, but a massive overhaul or an extensive new glossary signals error, and perhaps a measure of vanity. (Often, the fancy new talk can be translated fairly well into the old terminology; otherwise, it would be unexplainable.) Could the same be the case with philosophy—that a package of revolutionary concepts and reference points signals a foolish disregard for terms which have stood the test of time?

4. Does the public at large think that philosophy is essentially a matter of spinning out "Crests" for the vain amusement of academics? If so or if not, why is this the case?

5. Spinoza fostered the development of what's called "higher criticism," in contrast with "lower criticism," which was a matter of determining which manuscripts were most reliable and what the text meant. The *higher* version pressed on to question the truth of what was said, and, in this vein, Spinoza took issue with aspects of his Jewish "Bible," our Old Testament. For this, he was expelled from the synagogue in Amsterdam. Was his pantheistic take on reality an outworking of his skepticism toward the Bible or was it something deeper, rather an outworking of his impatience with or rebellion against the God of that Bible? In other words, is philosophy driven more by reason or by one's psychological or spiritual orientation?

The London Tube

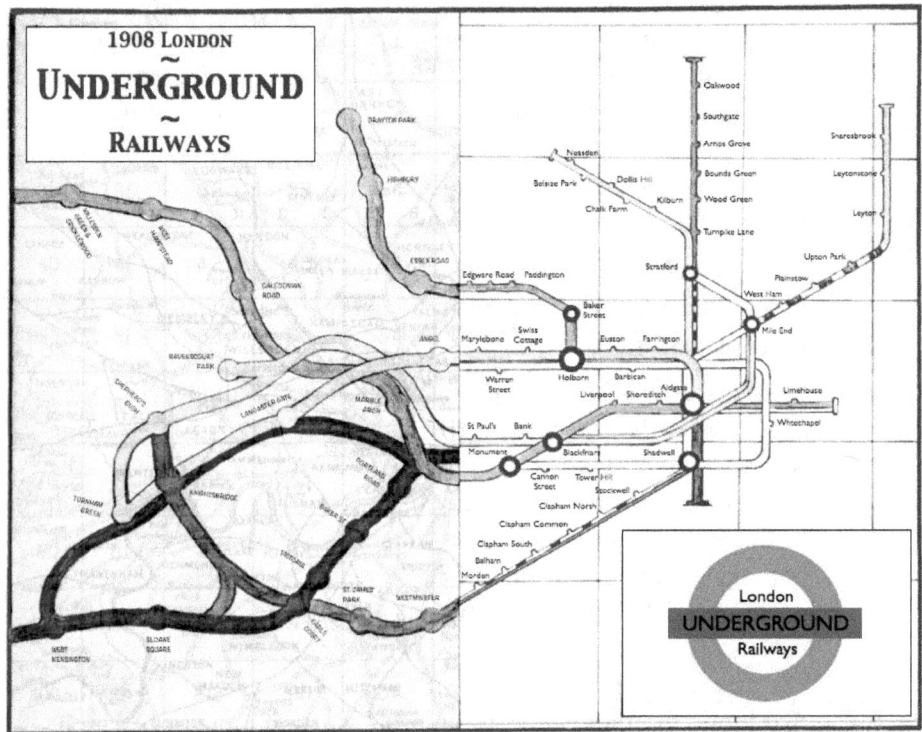

Until 1931, maps for the London subway (the Underground or Tube) were accurate tracings of the rail system, superimposed on surface maps, showing twists and turns, and station bunchings, as well as long spans between stations, whatever the case might be. It was problematic in several regards—to make room for crowded downtown details, they had to enlarge the central city portions, pushing suburban stations off the margins; they provided a lot of extraneous and distracting information; and they failed to supply critical, understandable data about transfer points.

The London Tube

Company engineer and draftsman Harry Beck came to the rescue in 1931, working without a commission and in his spare time. He designed a "topological" rather than a "geographical" map, and the 1933 pamphlet giving the public their first look at his work was an instant success. The Underground paid him a bonus of around $20 and had him supply updates and refinements through the years. Today, it is the standard look for subway maps, from Barcelona to New York to Tokyo.

Beck's design was a response to the pressing questions, "What difference does it make?" and "What do we need to get around?" That's the pragmatic impulse at work, and it shows up in many forms in philosophy.

Charles Sanders Peirce (pronounced "purse") birthed the term "pragmatism" in an 1878 essay, "How to Make Our Ideas Clear," advancing this maxim: "Consider what effects, which might conceivably have practical bearings, we conceive the object of our conception to have. Then the whole of our conception of those effects is the whole of our conception of the object." In this connection, he said that "hardness" was essentially a matter of what could scratch what, and not some abstract, idealized notion. For instance, a diamond was harder than a pane of glass since the former could mark the latter, but not vice versa.

This was the genius of Beck's design. People just wanted to know how to get around, which station was next and where they could jump from one line to another. It didn't matter that they were racing along under this or that park or building, but only how close they were to their desired stop. This new map let them easily check off the stations along the way. They couldn't care less if Manor House, Turnpike Lane, and Wood Green were actually equidistant on the Piccadilly line. They just wanted to know that the stations came in that order after Arsenal and before Arnos Grove on the way out to Cockfosters. And if someone said that the map was a lie because the Piccadilly tunnels were not dark blue, the public could counter that it didn't matter, for the coloration was only meant to distinguish one line from another, as from the light blue Victoria or the gray Jubilee. (Observers couldn't help but note that it resembled an electrical wiring diagram, a schematic drawing which fortunately doesn't follow the jumble and twists and turns of actual wires in a junction box.)

In the years following the publication of Peirce's essay, pragmatism found many expressions, associated with the likes of William James (who introduced a "pragmatic theory of truth"), John Dewey (who cast aside the "stuffy" schoolhouse memorization of historical figures and dates in favor of little workshops of childhood creativity and experimentation), C. I. (Clarence Irving, not Clive Staples) Lewis (with his "conceptual pragmatism," wherein words are seen primarily as tools), and Richard Rorty (who seeks to dismiss the traditional search for truth as bogus). As things developed, Peirce changed the name of his approach to "pragmaticism" to put some distance between himself and those who'd run away with his original expression. (He said his new word was so ugly that no one would steal it.)

Lewis's "pragmatic *a priori*" supplies the explanation for why we all can readily provide the name for the front of the hand—"palm"—but not for the back of the hand. Though we speak of a tennis "backhand" or of a mobster's "backhanding" an errant minion, we're still speaking by means of a compound made up of "back" and "hand." (I should note that a magician friend of mine says that in their specialized vocabulary, you find "back-palm," which is used typically as a verb in describing certain tricks.) Still, there is no single-word expression like "palm" (instead of "fronthand"). So what gives? Well, we use the front in so many ways that economy of expression is helpful. The highwayman growls, "Cross my palm with silver," the NBA point guard "palms the ball," and we extend our palm to get change at the cash register. (Imagine the clerk's dismay if we creepily extended our hand, palm down, to receive our change.)

James overdid it when, eschewing talk of fit or correspondence between a proposition and some feature of the world, he said we make things true by our action. For him, truth emerges as we proceed to carry out experiments and receive happy results. (The more normal way would be to say the results are happy because the initial proposition was true to begin with, a fact increasingly illuminated as we act on it.)

Pragmatically speaking, this approach to truth is workable when we focus on subway maps, cooking, and civil engineering. The "brute facts" keep us honest as we make our way around the world. But when you venture into the larger world of human values and public policy, it gets harder to say what "It works" means. Indeed, the Italian fascist leader Benito Mussolini, famous for "getting the trains to run on time," was a fan of James, taking comfort in outcomes when he squashed opponents as he consolidated his power and advanced his agenda. Besides, a lot of the people appreciated what Mussolini was doing. So what's not to like? Well, there's a lot not to like in Mussolini's program if we mean, by "It works," "It fosters human flourishing in accordance with the *Imago Dei* and a just social order." (Of course,

James did not back Mussolini, but it's a shame that his philosophy could so readily provide inspiration and comfort to a tyrant.)

Not surprisingly, "pragmatism" has become a dirty word in many circles, including churches, where the push for numbers and nickels can compromise preaching "the whole counsel of God." Of course, in the end, such shenanigans don't "work," so we might speak of a deeper pragmatism in terms of what brings lasting fruit, what pleases the ultimate judge, and what grows "oaks of righteousness" (Isaiah 61:3) instead of mushrooms.

Whatever the missteps and perversions there might be in this school of thought, it is still worthwhile to ask of a claim, "What in the world does it matter?"; to challenge grandiose abstractions with, "That's fine talk, but could you cash that in experientially?"; and to insist that disputants make sure they're not spinning their wheels over trivialities. Of course, much of professional philosophy could use a lesson in pragmatism. While papers read and published may "work" at padding one's resume in advance of promotion and tenure positions, it's fair to ask what good they do in the world and how they might actually help others live and achieve worthwhile things apart from maneuvering through the groves of academic esteem.

Along the way, philosophers might well turn back to James for a lesson in philosophical style. Most people could actually understand him, for he saw no virtue in pedantry. (May his tribe increase.)

Discussion Questions:

1. Proverbs 14:12 ("There is a way that seems right to a man, but its end is the way of death") and James 2:18 ("But someone will say, 'You have faith, and I have works.' Show me your faith without your works, and I will show you my faith by my works") have a "pragmatic" ring to them. Can you think of other verses or passages that sound a similar note, ones that speak of concrete, experiential, action-focused and result-oriented truth?

2. 1 Corinthians 13:1–3 pushes back against "pragmatic" success:

> Though I speak with the tongues of men and of angels, but have not love, I have become sounding brass or a clanging cymbal. And though I have the gift of prophecy, and understand all mysteries and all knowledge, and though I have all faith, so that I could remove mountains, but have not love, I am nothing. And though I bestow all my goods to feed the

> poor, and though I give my body to be burned, but have not love, it profits me nothing.

Do other verses come to mind in this connection?

3. Is the "health and wealth" gospel pragmatic, or is it counter-pragmatic?
4. Do biblical terms serve as better tools for getting a grasp on the world, e.g., "sin" instead of "mistake," "adultery" instead of "affair"?
5. Give a Christian evaluation of "What Pragmatism Means," Lecture II in William James's *Pragmatism: A New Name for Some Old Ways of Thinking* (you can find it at gutenberg.org).

Madrid's Art Museums

Within easy walking distance of each other lie Madrid's three great art museums of the Golden Triangle—the Prado, the Reina Sophia, and the Thyssen-Bornemisza. Though they occupy only a square mile in a city of over 230 square miles in size, this illustration shows them standing above the other buildings in the neighborhood. They're special, and so, for our purposes, they represent the place of the arts in the writings of German philosopher Arthur Schopenhauer.

Schopenhauer stands in the line of "German idealists," who, following Immanuel Kant, placed great emphasis on the human mind and spirit to shape the world. Their "school of thought" arose in reaction to the British empiricism of John Locke, who was himself reacting to philosophers who built great conceptual superstructures through reason alone (men like Descartes, Leibniz, and Spinoza). Locke said that thought that was not grounded in experience was literally nonsense, and that all meaningful talk about the world must start with perception, either external (like the appearance of trees or lightning) or internal (like the deliverances of memory or pain). And he pictured the mind as a blank slate (a *tabula rasa*) on which experience may write. From this, we mix and match what's been written and come up with useful concepts.

Kant argued that we're far from passive receptors of whatever may show up in our circumstances or observations. Rather, the mind is a very pushy entity, organizing the world before we're even aware of it. (We talk about this in the "Strip Map" piece.) And once his notion was on the table, a number of prominent German philosophers ran with it, with their own twists. Gottlieb Fichte preferred to speak of his own personal world-manufacturing, rather than of everyone's shaping the world in concert. He could even be construed as a solipsist, one who says he's the only one around. Furthermore, he extended the aggressive mind concept beyond the crunching of what was given to the actual projection of things with which the mind now must deal. For instance, it could generate illness in order to wrestle with it, growing yet stronger by the challenge. (I think of the days in the church nursery when we stacked up blocks for the purpose of knocking them down.)

Hegel (discussed in the "Oxbow" piece) construed the supervisor as the "World Spirit" (*Weltgeist*), wrestling history into shape through conflict between the old and the new, producing ever-more-exalted institutions. It involves a lot of crash-bang refinement, with many eggs broken to produce the omelet (nicely serving the communist and Darwinian notions of survival of the fittest and the march of history).

And then there was Frederich Nietzsche, who celebrated the "will to power," rubbing the nose of the weak in the tears of their own cravenness. Through his fictional character Zarathustra, he heralded the coming of the

Madrid's Art Museums

Superman (*Übermensch*), who would take us back to the time when "good" meant "intimidating."

Into this milieu came Arthur Schopenhauer, who was not as exhilarated as Nietzsche with unleashing the primordial will and parading the fruit of power. Rather, all this willfulness exhausted him, and he needed some relief. And this he found in the arts, which he called a "Sabbath," picking up on the biblical day of rest prescribed in the Decalogue. If you can just make it through the "six days" of the grind that mark our human existence and then stumble into the concert hall or gallery on the "seventh," you can restore your soul.

Not suprisingly, he had an affinity for Eastern thought. The Buddha had taught that suffering came from desire and caring, so if you jettison those concerns you will find serenity. Are you tortured by ill health? Stop desiring good health, and you'll be much happier. Do you want to be married and rich? Stop pining for matrimony and wealth, and you'll manage life much better.

In this spirit, Schopenhauer said, "Take a break. Get out of the rat race," at least for a season of sojourn in the arts. There you can give yourself over to things in themselves—the play of color, the surge of a symphonic movement—and stop worrying about whether the matter at hand will give you relief from your creditors or gain you entry to a profession or social circle.

Of course, Christians have their own Sabbath—the "Lord's Day," on Sunday, the first day of the week, when Jesus rose from the dead (instead of Saturday, the last the of the week, corresponding to the seventh day of creation). Its restorative power comes not only from rest from workaday labors, but also from worship and the communion of saints.

Yes, the arts can refresh the soul in their own way, but they don't stand so tall in the Christian worldview and pilgrimage as the museums in this illustration suggest.

Discussion Questions:

1. As it turns out, much contemporary art is preachy, ideological, confrontational, revolutionary, and insulting. Not much "Sabbath" there. Take (or recount) a trip to the museum or concert hall and size up the offerings in Schopenhauer's terms. How much provides escape from the wear and tear of the world? How much adds to it?

2. You might ask yourself if you find more "sabbath rest" in the deliverances of the arts than in a worship service, in the music and preaching of the church. If so, why? Is this a reflection of your worldliness? Or does it suggest that churches fall short of restoring the soul? Or is it to misunderstand the point to Sunday morning gatherings, which may, at the same time, "comfort the afflicted and afflict the comfortable"?

3. Does the relief/restoration view of the arts (including "escapist" movies) shortchange an important mission of the painters, composers, sculptors, etc.?

4. Aesthetic appreciation is sometimes cast as "disinterested," experienced as if one "doesn't have a dog in that fight." In this frame of mind, you don't care if the artist was a creep or his painting was meant to advance a controversial agenda. You simply attend to the beauty or grandeur of the piece. On this model, an atheist could appreciate Handel's *Messiah* and a devout Baptist could admire the Counter-Reformation work of Rubens or Bernini. Is this the right way to go about it?

5. If art is ideally a means of escape from the anxieties of the world, why not just turn to opioids? What's the difference?

Mount Peck

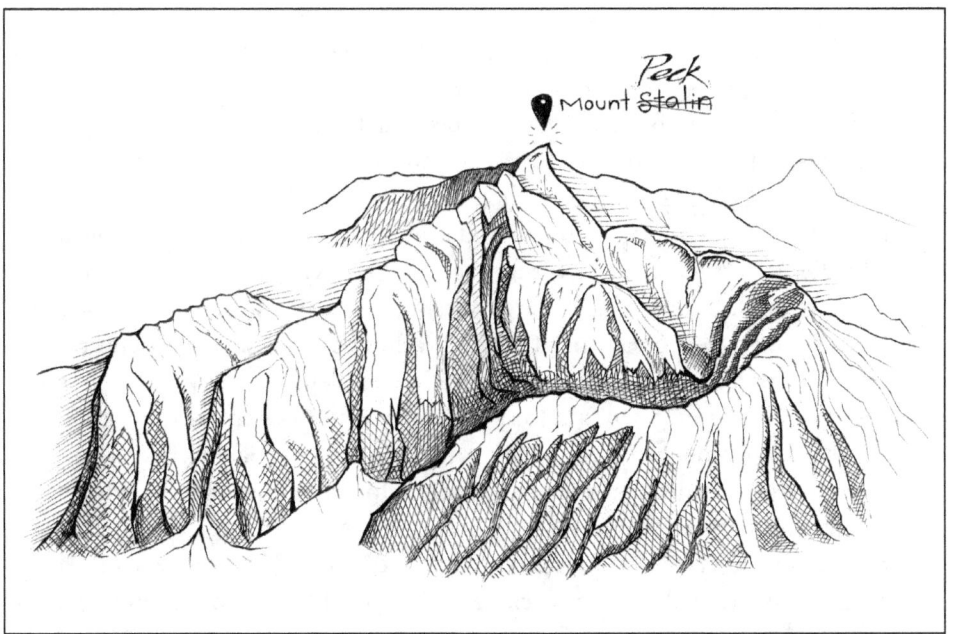

No doubt the Soviet Union, with Joseph Stalin at its head, played a major role in the fall of Hitler. *Der Führer* was a fool to invade Russia, and there he lost a million killed and another million either missing or taken prisoner. Russian deaths were upwards of eight million, so the nation was bled horrifically, even as it bled the Nazis. Thus we see the ally Stalin seated with Churchill and Roosevelt in photos of the 1945 Potsdam Conference, a meeting devoted to shaping the postwar world. Seeking, then, to honor an ally after the war, British Columbians were pleased to name a mountain for Stalin in the Canadian Rockies.

However, in 1987, representatives of the Ukrainian Canadian Civil Liberties Association objected so strenuously and effectively that Stalin had visited atrocities on their people (resulting in many more deaths than the total suffered in the Nazi-Soviet battles) that the BC government changed the name to Mount Peck, honoring trapper and guide Don Peck. (Incidentally, the majority of such geographical name changes are meant to erase vulgarities, whether sexual or racial, and I was thankful to find this "safe" one to open the piece.)

Suppose someone says, "I grew up within view of Mount Stalin." Do you respond, "Actually, you didn't. You grew up within view of Mount Peck." Who's right? Both? (And to complicate matters, might the First Nation people have had their own earlier name for the peak, as they did in the case of Denali, which became Mount McKinley, and then back again?)

Philosophers have puzzled over just how it is that language attaches itself (or is attached) to the world. Plato takes up the question in his dialogue *Cratylus*, with the parties trying to sort out whether the original linkages were natural (with fluid sounds tied to fluid things), divine (assigned by the gods), or purely conventional and arbitrary. Proper names have been a matter of particular interest. More recently, one view is that they are essentially descriptions, e.g., "George Washington" = "first president of the United States." So to say that George Washington had a set of dentures made out of lead, human teeth, cow teeth, and elephant ivory (or so says the *Smithsonian* magazine) is to say that the first president of the United States had such dentures. But along comes philosopher Saul Kripke in the 1970, saying, in effect, that George Washington could have died while he still had his baby teeth and yet have been George Washington, long before he could be described as "first president of the United States." So where is a proper name rooted, if not in a characterization of the person or object in question? Kripke said the linkup came at a sort of christening (or in Washington's case, perhaps, a literal one). From that point on, various depictions and narratives may accrue, but they don't define the subject in question, whose name is passed down through a "causal chain" (and since it is a "rigid designator," it would hold in every possible world). They merely summarize his life, however it may or may not have developed.

For an interesting analogue to the christening, philosopher/filmmaker Errol Morris proposes a photograph. Once taken, it portrays that particular subject, and whatever subsequent generations may make of it (perhaps mistaking Private Smith for Private Jones), it's still a photo of Private Smith.

Also interesting is the way that surnames "smuggle in" descriptions. In a medieval world, where there might be a dozen men in the village named John (with their "Christian name" honoring the "beloved apostle"), the people needed some way to designate one from the other. So they appended last names (surnames) according to where they lived (the one on the hill became "Hill"), their occupation (the one who stitches clothes became "Taylor"), their parentage (the son of James became "Jameson"), or a physical characteristic (the one with particularly strong arms became "Armstrong"). Of course, today's Bill Hill may live in a valley, but he's Bill Hill just the same, having been so labeled at birth.

Okay, but what if, as in the case of Mount Peck, there is a rechristening? And, again, what if indigenous people named it something else centuries before? Who wins?

What if we go "scientific" or "neutral"? What if we simply define Stalin/Peck as that peak located at coordinates 58° N, 124° W (in very round numbers)? Call it what you will, but it's still *that* peak, the one that the GPS will take you to if you key in the right latitude and longitude.

Ah, but what if there's a tectonic plate shift, and Peck drifts to longitude 125° W? And what if, in the process, it splits in two at the top, producing twin peaks? Does the "Mount" part of "Mount Peck" vitiate the name, meaning there's no longer such a place? Or do we designate one of the peaks "Mount Peck" and call the other one, its new sister, a brand new name?

Who cares? Well, there are interesting issues in play. On Kripke's account, salt was salt before people knew that each of its molecules was made up one sodium atom and one chlorine atom. So to define salt as NaCl is to say something factually true but not necessarily true in a logical sense. The sodium/chlorine structure is, in his words, an "*a posteriori* necessity," something discovered down the way. But for those who first identified salt (presumably Adam and Eve), the chemical composition was a total mystery. For all they knew, it had one atom each of potassium and neon (though, of course, they didn't have any notion of "atom" or those two elements).

If I may press this a bit, I think that Kripke overcommits to the "necessity" of physical laws, for they are utterly answerable to God's omnipotence. The Lord can perform the potassium/neon flip at will, with the tangible product remaining ordinary table salt.

One application is in questioning the claim that, contra Young Earth (or twenty-four-hour, "solar day") Creationists, the universe must be extremely old. Otherwise, light from some visible stars wouldn't have had time to make it to our eyes. Calculations depend upon a constant, a fixity, the speed of light, i.e., 186 thousand miles per second. But folks knew what light was before they had any notion of its speed (whether in wave or particle), and it wouldn't be a contradiction to say that at the time of creation,

MAPS

God made light go a trillion miles per second. The *universal constant* is really contingent, easily changeable according to the pleasure of God.

(I played with a similar notion in my dissertation, saying that "daylight" was essentially a *look* of things, such that if there were a dramatic shift in electromagnetic wave frequencies associated with that look, but the look stayed the same—e.g., with green bushes, white lilies, red roses—it would still be daylight.)

Though such matters may seem arcane, things got hot on a television show I saw recently. The topic was the imposition of pronoun gender neutrality (e.g., "xem") on the committee work of the California legislature. The consensus was that people have a right to be referred to as they please, and the discussion moved to the case of a former world heavyweight champion. The white host amiably said he was happy to refer to Cassius Clay as Muhammed Ali, and the black guest bristled. The problem was that the former had grounded the person's identity in Clay. This was a *faux pas*, for the boxer simply *was* Ali, not just *called* Ali, or so the guest insisted.

And there are theological questions in this arena. Do Christians and Muslims worship the same God? Do we humans get to name God, or does he uniquely get to "christen" himself "God"?

Of course, there are many John Smiths in the phone book, and they're not phonies. But just because they have the same name, it doesn't follow that they're the same people. But what of the many "gods" in the spiritual phonebook? It's fair to ask, "Which one is *the real* God?" Is it the one who self-identified as "I Am"?

DISCUSSION QUESTIONS:

1. Isidore of Seville (A.D. 560–636) was distinguished for his reliance on etymologies to get at the truth of things, and, indeed, word roots are interesting. For instance, "muscle" comes from "little mouse," the appearance suggested by shifting lumps under the skin when one flexed; and "hysterical" comes from the Greek word for "womb," supposedly suggesting that persons with wombs were more inclined to head in that direction. And it's funny how things can flip. When radio was in its infancy, those interested in its commercial use were looking for a word to describe how the waves emanated from a tower. Borrowing from agriculture, they likened it to the way a farmer "broadcast" his seeds. Now that's become the lead meaning, so much

so that someone might observe, "You say he broadcast the rye? That's so cool, like broadcasting a program!"

2. Kripke focused on proper nouns. What about common nouns? How do they pair with items and features of the world?

3. In 1973, psychologist Karl Menninger published a book with the provocative title *Whatever Became of Sin?* Of course, sin hadn't gone away, but its recognition had waned in popular culture. Increasingly, people were relativizing morality and rationalizing misbehavior so that talk of sin seemed archaic and plain wrong-headed. Here's a case of a word becoming, in a sense, detached from the world, cast upon the rubbish heap of absurdities. What are some other perfectly good nouns that have become the victims of indifference or contempt?

4. So what about it, do Muslims and Christians worship the same God? (By the way, in some Muslim regions, Christians are forbidden to use "Allah" ("God" in Arabic) in their public religious expressions, and some Christians happily accept this stricture, preferring a word such a "Lord" to signal their distinctives.) It's an issue that missionaries and Bible translators wrestle with.

5. Attending a Bat Mitzvah at a Reformed Jewish synagogue on Chicago's North Shore, I heard a young woman, under the rabbi's watchful eye, read portions of the Torah in Hebrew. In doing so, she said *Adonai* when she came to the tetragrammaton, *YHWH*. It was a matter of piety, of reverence for God's proper name. (By something of the same standard, I didn't call my father "Raymond," but rather "Daddy," in my childhood and youth.) It seems that the use of a proper name is governed by certain protocols. Can you think of other situations where you don't speak the "christening name" outright?

6. While some words, like "sin," can become extinct like dinosaurs, others can become culturally "radioactive" due to shifting sensitivities. When I was a child, "Negro" was a term of respect, in contrast with certain slurs I won't mention. But now its use is frowned upon, as we've come through a number of replacements, whether "black," "African-American," or "person of color." Are these the result of multiple rebaptisms, or altered descriptions, or what?

New London Channel

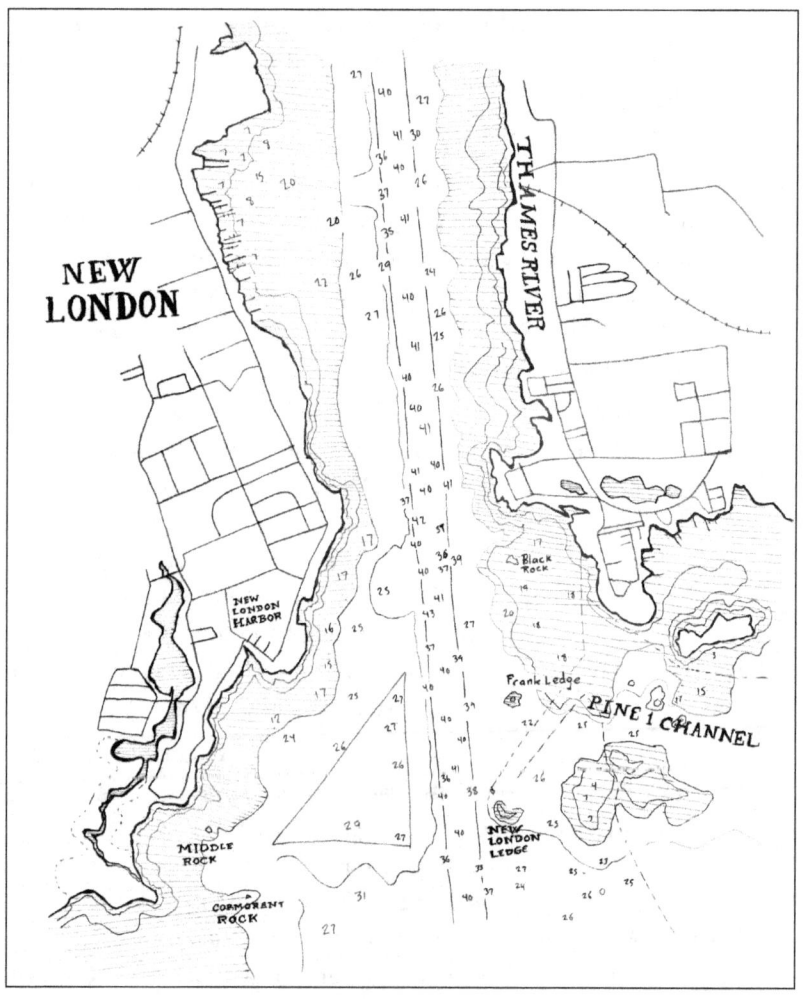

This nautical chart depicting the entrance to the harbor at New London, Connecticut, features depth readings which point mariners to the channel and warn them of the perils of the shallows, islands, and mainland. This counsel has been absolutely essential to the safe operation of the ships which have found port here, beginning with the whaling industry in the early nineteenth century, continuing with the vessels of the U.S. Coast Guard Academy in Groton, and accommodating the launch of the nation's submarines, designed and manufactured at General Dynamics Electric Boat facilities (in Groton, Quonset Point, and New London).

The map reminds us that there are "rocks on both sides" when we chart our courses in life. Aristotle made this point over two thousand years ago in his *Nicomachean Ethics* (so named because it was dedicated or directed toward Nicomachus, perhaps a relative). It's been said that "Aristotle takes what we all know and puts it into words we don't understand." Sure enough, some of his vast writings are hard to follow, but much of his philosophy, including this work, is quite accessible, clearly resonating with common sense and gratifyingly readable even as it expands our understanding.

In a nutshell, *Nicomachean Ethics* teaches that the path of virtue lies between two extremes. You can overdo it or underdo it. For instance, he observes that courage is an admirable mean, the middle path between a lack of courage (cowardice) and too much of it (foolhardiness). We praise the soldier who stands with the other troops in battle, but we condemn the one who runs away, as well as one who, abandoning his colleagues, makes a pointless mad dash toward the enemy. Both types are crazy, and crazy may be pitiable, but not admirable.

Following his template, Aristotle says it's good to have a sense of humor, but you can overdo it, making a joke out of everything. In that case you're a clown, a buffoon. But, on the far end of the spectrum, you don't want to be a stiff either. People welcome the middle way (sometimes translated "ready wit" in this instance) but shun both the humorless and the goofy person. The same goes for the virtue of generosity. Veer to the right, and you're wasteful, not unlike the Prodigal Son; veer to the left, and you're a miser. And so on down the line. (It's important to note that Aristotle wasn't applying his "golden mean" to obvious misdeeds. He didn't teach that a modest amount of adultery was desirable, as opposed to too little or too much adultery.)

But wait, isn't this the sort of cool Greek thinking that counted Christians foolish? What's all this business about a bloody trail to the cross, about pressing on in pioneer missions despite beatings and shipwrecks, about preaching so prophetically that they stone you to death? Wasn't the early church prone to overdoing things for the sake of the gospel? Point well taken, though, of course, Greeks knew what it was to lay their lives on the line for the motherland. But, yes, Christians could come off as quite nutty in their sacrificial zeal. Still, you can well imagine Silas saying to Paul, "Brother, you have to rest. You've been preaching and ministering for thirty-eight straight hours, and you have to take a break. I'm not urging you to be a slacker, but enough is enough."

Of course, we talk that way in our own churches, whether observing, on the one hand, that the preacher goes too long, "cramming" a twenty-minute sermon into forty-five minutes, or, on the other, that we're hungry for more than "sermonettes." Or, perhaps, we comment that one youth trip chaperon is a too-strict killjoy, while the other lets the kids run wild.

For purposes of comparison, let's take a look at the fruit of the Spirit in Galatians 5: "love, joy, peace, patience, kindness, goodness, faithfulness, gentleness, self-control" (ESV). All are wonderful, but what if the church treasurer embezzles funds and flees the country? And what if he returns to the states, does his time, rejoins the church, and then you make him treasurer again? And what if he again absconds with cash and makes a run for the border? Apprehended, convicted, imprisoned, and released some years later, he returns to the church as soon as he can and asks to be reinstated as treasurer. One dear soul, citing "patience" in the Spirit list, urges the congregation to say yes. Wouldn't it be not only permissible but also obligatory for the church to say no, that their patience wasn't infinite? Rather, to be responsible stewards of their offerings, they needed to decline his request, at least for the present.

I recall a chapel message at Wheaton, one where the president employed a nautical illustration to press us toward greater holiness. He had been a naval officer, one of several trainees on a ship off the New England coast. Their instructor told them to chart the best course they could manage around a rocky coastal promontory, and the students set to work with their charts and tools to sketch the optimum trip past the obstacle. Once done, they presented their work, only to have every single solution shot down. The problem was that they were trying to see how close they could sail to the rocks without crashing. He explained that they needed to allow for wide clearance and not flirt with disaster by seeing how tight they could cut it. The point was that we Christians had no business exposing ourselves to temptations as if we were moths gauging how close we could fly to the flame without being burned. Yes, but in many choices that we make, we don't have the broad ocean to one side and rocks to the other, but rather there are rocks on both sides. And Aristotle, working with common grace and rationality, which is available to all men since creation, even the unregenerate, could see that too.

Discussion Questions:

1. Where should we draw the line when it comes discretion in viewing movies? How close is too close? Or does it depend on the person, as it does with germs? Are some Christians more susceptible to infection than others?

2. At what point is a Christian's discipleship supposed to seem crazy in the world's eyes?

3. The military uses an acronym JJDIDTIEBUCKLE to teach leadership principles (justice, judgment, dependability, initiative, decisiveness, tact, integrity, enthusiasm, bearing, unselfishness, courage, knowledge, loyalty, and endurance). Are these all virtues which can be mapped onto the Nicomachean scheme?

4. Some soldiers have received the Congressional Medal of Honor for throwing themselves on grenades to save their buddies. Were these virtuous acts or were they irresponsible, with the right course being to do your best, along with the others, to flee the blast? Ethicists would call this an act of "supererogation," going above and beyond the call of duty. But might we count it a demand of duty, with the alternative being non-virtuous?

5. Immanuel Kant was not impressed with teaching ethics by means of lifting up heroes or exemplars. One could argue that inspirational stories divert one's attention from the method for sorting out the admirable from the deplorable; these tales could dazzle our imaginations and lead us to accept the faulty thinking and mixed motives of the hero or heroine. Be that as it may, who would you consider a model of virtue?

Outsized Texas

There's no denying that Texas is big and important (the biggest of the "lower forty-eight"), but the residents have been known to magnify its already considerable place on the national stage, to the point of parody. One reflection of this hubris is the comic American map with an outsized treatment of the state, to the detriment of its neighbors. And it's typically drawn by Texans, proud of what they're asserting, and not by critics who want to shame the Texans into humility.

Any number of philosophers can be charged with drawing outsized Texas maps of their own, exaggerating the importance of this or that feature of reality. Kant's ethic is a case in point.

A quick review: The sage of Königsberg was convinced you must build morality on reason alone, distilling his approach to a "categorical imperative"—a duty that exhausted the concerns of the whole category of ethical obligation. He actually had two versions: 1) that we should only use standards we could apply to everyone; 2) that we should treat people with special regard, as distinct from hammers or dogs.

Number 1 is incisive, in that I have no business saying it's okay for me to pilfer office supplies for home use while disapproving of others' doing the same. It's always germane to ask, "What if everyone did this?" Now, of course, you can game the thing to say, "What if everyone whose kid had a crucial assignment needing hanging file folders but whose wife had just lost her job, making this purchase difficult, took a batch of these folders from the supply cabinet?" But those serious about ethics know we can always make our case "special," granting us all sorts of immoral permission to do things we shouldn't.

Number 2 is also admirable, for Kant talks about the vital distinction between things we can treat as tools, useful but disposable when it suits our purposes. You don't have to keep a dry ballpoint pen around out of respect for its dignity, and it's no big deal to cage a chicken, pending its use for chicken soup. But you mustn't think of such behavior toward an inconvenient neighbor or elderly relative, though they seem to be "more trouble or expense than they're worth." You don't run those calculations on a person.

So far so good, but you can push back against trying to base all this on reason, and Kant's applications reveal the fault line. For number 1, he asks us to consider suicide. What if everyone did it? On his account, that would be crazy because it would mean the end to human reasoning, which is the basis of ethics itself. But I can imagine an environmentalist or two who would find this just ducky, for it would rid the world of "anthropocentric" abusers of the biosphere, leaving Mother Earth and her innocent and winsome fawns and seedlings to themselves.

He also mentions the squandering of one's powers through lassitude. What if everyone were a slacker? But what he takes as an obvious absurdity some would find idyllic, particularly in temperate or tropic climes with fruit and vegetables handy for the picking.

Something's missing in Kant. A yuck factor grounded in a created order, a sense of indignation, compassion, and the counsel of decency. For reason alone is something like a computer program—"garbage in, garbage out." If you have a dark heart, you can crank out all sorts of "rational" solutions, as Hitler and others have shown us. And if your heart is basically sound, you can stumble into an admirable life with the only the slimmest notion of what you're doing.

The slacker needs a sense of stewardship, of accountability for the gifts he's been given. It's not enough to figure, "Well, I have that ginormous trust fund, and I can jet around the world doing whatever I feel like doing with impunity." You need a broader context to banish this thought, one involving a Creator God who's blessed you with talents and opportunities, the appropriation of which contributes to human flourishing and greater fellowship with the source of your being.

Kant hints at this in talking about the value of the concepts of God, freedom, and immortality, but at the crucial point of anchoring ethics, he brushes God's hand aside and says, in effect, "Thanks, but I've got this." It's almost as though he's joining the atheist Voltaire in saying (reputedly) that he was glad he had believing servants because otherwise they might steal the silverware. Useful idiots, if you will.

Number 2 is also problematic, for in defining the inviolable beings, he turns to "rational nature," making reason an idol. Yes, but isn't that the heart of what it means to be a person? Doesn't this set us apart from rusting iron and migrating birds? Not if you think the Bible is authoritative and revelatory. For it says that our human specialness is based not on our skills at ratiocination, but rather on the fact that we're made "in the image of God." And though the elements or essence of this image are not spelled out, the Bible does not encourage us to think that it boils down to reflective cleverness.

This may seem a quibble, but Kant shows that it isn't. He called the "negroes of Africa" incapable of "feelings that rise above the trifling" and says that the difference between blacks and whites is "as great in regard to mental capacities as in color." (I wish he could have met Ben Carson and Denzel Washington, for starters.) Now it doesn't take a big step to see that this stupid and evil racism was groundwork for treating blacks as lesser beings. For if you think they, or any people for that matter, have less "rationality" than you do, then you might think they are less human. The same would go for the retarded or the as-yet-unborn. The Bible says they're worthy because they're made in the image of God. But Kant doesn't have room for this "foolishness." Kant's "outsized Texas" of rationality crowds out essentials, such as love and holiness and piety and creatureliness. Now who looks not so rational?

Of course, this isn't to glorify irrationality, for that can crash and burn too. And, yes, in the last analysis, the "Divine Comedy" along with its moral precepts is sweetly reasonable. The problem with Kant was not that he honored reason, a God-given capacity, but that he supposed he could sort things out by his own reason irrespective of revelation.

Discussion Questions:

1. On a scale of one to ten, how rational would you say man is? Or a particular set of men or women?
2. The French philosopher Blaise Pascal said, "The heart has its reasons, which reason does not know. We feel it in a thousand things. It is the heart which experiences God, and not the reason. This, then, is faith: God felt by the heart, not by the reason." So how can he have *reasons* that are not matters of *reason*? If Pascal's distinction is right, which are more important and reliable, heart reasons or intellect reasons?
3. If a skeptic didn't believe in the image of God in man, how might you persuade him that it was wrong to euthanize those who are radically deficient in reason, the profoundly retarded?
4. To join Mensa, you must score at least in the ninety-eighth percentile on a standard IQ test (e.g., 132 on Stanford-Binet). Does this mean that its members are remarkably rational?
5. William F. Buckley said, "I would rather be governed by the first two thousand people in the Boston telephone directory than by the two thousand people on the faculty of Harvard University." Is that rational?

The Oxbow River

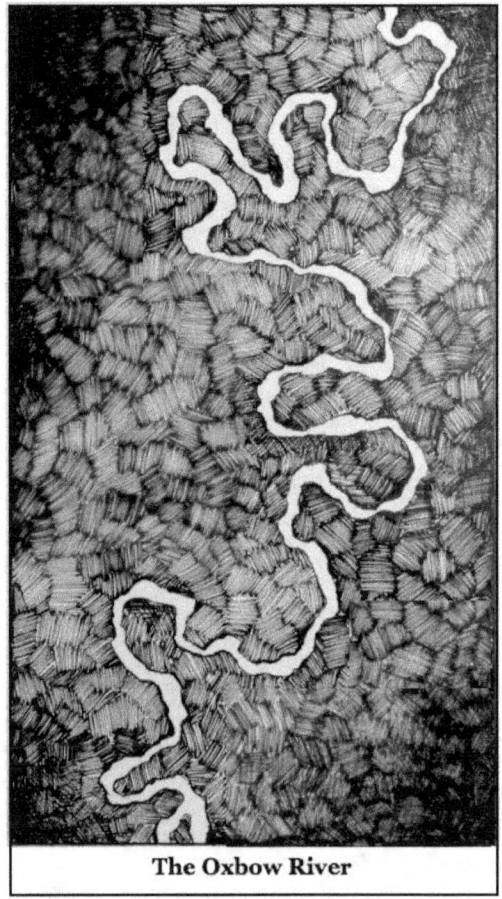

The Oxbow River

WHILE the northern, western, and southern borders of Arkansas are drawn with straight-line geometrical precision, the eastern border is a mess, for it traces the meanderings of the Mississippi River. Such twists

The Oxbow River

and turns are commonplace throughout the valleys of the world as gravity and topography work their power on descending bodies of water. Back and forth, back and forth, as they make their way to the sea.

Hegel's philosophy of history bears similarities, for it centers on "dialectic," a sort of conversation between realities and emerging, contrary possibilities, resulting in new realities, which will in turn be confronted by new, conflicting possibilities—thesis, antithesis, synthesis/thesis, antithesis, synthesis/thesis . . . and so on. Marching onward, ever forward; progress through struggle. It's grounded in a sort of conceptual ping-pong game between the being of what's happening now and the non-being of mere-potential, but it also plays out on the world stage in the affairs of men, or so the account goes.

Over a hundred years after Hegel laid out his theory of history, Karl Marx and Friedrich Engels, drawing heavily on Hegel, hammered out the doctrine of "dialectical materialism," wherein matter, beginning with some sort of primordial stuff, has a long-running "conversation" with itself, evolving, if you will, into better and better circumstances for the working man. But Hegel's dialectic was *idealistic* rather than materialistic, the manifestation of a world spirit, or *Weltgeist*. (Kant got things started in this direction earlier in the eighteenth century, declaring the power of mind to shape the world.)

So, much like a section of the river, a particular form of government, religion, art, family, industry, etc. runs its course until it hits an obstacle and is turned in another direction. But unlike ping-pong, play continues off the table onto other tables. And the river ever alters as it negotiates these reversals, for it may widen, pick up fresh pigmentation from a new sort of soil, or gain speed as it follows a new azimuth.

Unlike the Mississippi, the dialectical flow of history goes uphill rather than down. (Though, I've read that the silt buildup in the Mississippi as it reaches New Orleans is so considerable that, in places, the river is forced to flow uphill as it punches its way into the Gulf; but by this time, it has so much heft and momentum that it can do this without diversion.) In Hegel's case, the Gulf of Mexico is called "Absolute Spirit."

This notion has charmed a lot of philosophers and, "downstream," a lot of laymen whose fancies are tickled by the thought that history is on the side of trashing what they don't like and delivering what they favor. So they take to the barricades to confront "the man," confident that he'll be ground to dust in the march of events. Lenin preached it. So did Mao.

The twentieth-century British philosopher Karl Popper was a fierce critic of this mindset, first in *The Open Society and Its Enemies* (1945) and then with *The Poverty of Historicism* (1957). Popper was known for his insistence that serious scientific theories needed to be "falsifiable"—that something could possibility count against them, for otherwise, they were gaseously compatible with whatever came down the pike—and that the predictive power of Hegel's fantasy was zero. But more than this, it tended to trample men, since social planners, who thought they saw the future and marched in that direction, stomped on and over folks who wouldn't get with the program. This included at least fifteen million recalcitrant kulak farmers in Stalin's Ukraine and seventy million or so victims in communist China. After all, "You have to break some eggs to make an omelet."

Of course, Christians believe that history is marching toward its proper culmination, but not at the beck of an impersonal spirit. Rather, the centuries are in the hands of the personal God, one whose Scripture reveals that utopian zeal is both stupid and cruel. The Bible teaches that a fallen world will not perfect itself, and those who presume to usher in its perfection are servants and masters of tyranny and brutality.

Back in the 1970s, *New York Times Magazine* featured an article about the conceptual roots of political conservatism. The writer argued that it all came down to belief in original sin. If you didn't believe in it, then you thought government could produce a truly "great society," a "workers' paradise," or some other wonderful state of affairs by bashing the status quo and by both proliferating and growing social programs. Hegelians resonated with such talk.

Not so the original sin folks, who took a more skeptical approach to public policy. Yes, pursue justice, but don't think you can achieve heaven on earth in the process, and don't think you're entitled to visit injustices on those who get in the way.

Discussion Questions:

1. Is there evidence that the world can regress as well as progress?
2. In the political realm, "progressives" talk about "being on the right side of history," as though human affairs were headed in a direction they favor. Thus they deem as dinosaurs those who refuse to get on board. Is "right side of history" a tricky expression?

3. Whatever the truth of Hegel's grand projection, there are, indeed, good developments that have come through the clash of the old way and the shock of a new notion or movement. Does anything come to mind in this connection?

4. Do old ideas and ways really go away, or is there really "nothing new under the sun"? In the Old Testament, covering events well over two millennia ago, children were sacrificed to Moloch to insure a better life for the people; today, we countenance infanticide to remove a hindrance to a better life. Bestiality was condemned in the Torah; today, some states have had to reinstate bestiality prohibitions in their criminal codes since there has been a resurgence of this practice. (They had been eliminated some years earlier in the rush to repeal "sodomy" codes. Through repeals, legislators had meant to address homosexuality, thinking that bestiality was not really an issue.) Yes, there are new technological developments, such as pacemakers and smartphones, but people, with fresh health from their electrically regulated hearts, use those fancy phones to send and receive drivel, lies, and worse. Same old same old, right?

5. What leads young people to wear a Che Guevara T-shirt? Why did Sean Penn, Michael Moore, Danny Glover, Noam Chomsky, Danny Glover, Oliver Stone, and Naomi Campbell visit and lionize Hugo Chavez in Venezuela? Do they really think that the Marxist-Leninist approach holds great promise if applied purely?

6. Martin Luther King Jr. said, "The arc of the moral universe is long, but it bends toward justice." President Obama had the quote woven into a rug in the Oval Office. Is it true?

Palestine

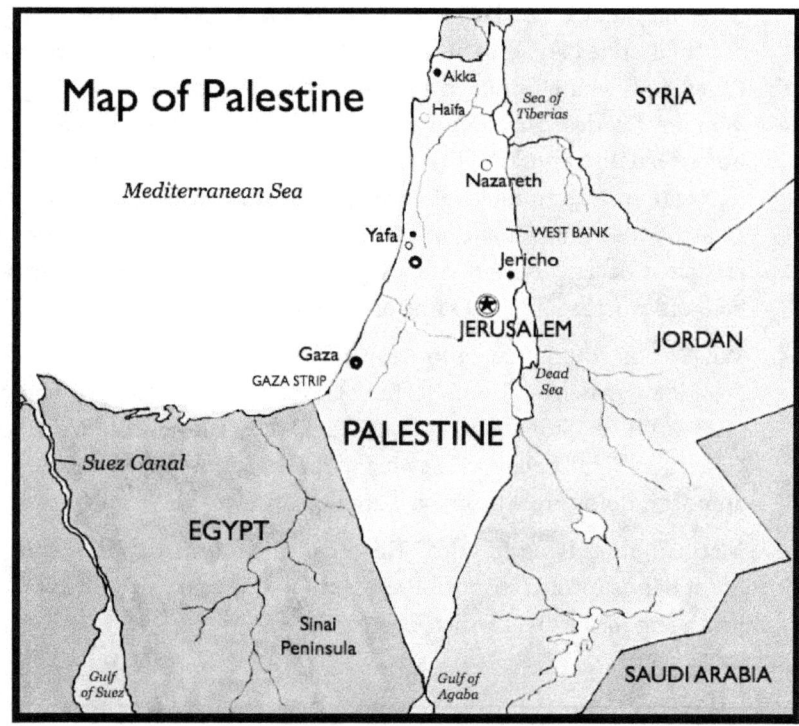

VARIOUS mapmakers have scrubbed the modern state of Israel from regional maps, turning its territory over to the predominantly Muslim Arabs who call themselves Palestinians. This is not the first attempt to cleanse the land of Jewish influence, for the very word "Palestine" is a Roman slight. As Rome solidified its rule over Jerusalem and the nations that surrounded it, they renamed the district *Palestina* in honor of the Jews'

ancient enemy, the Philistines. In this same vein, the city of Shechem became the Greek/Hellenistic *Neapolis* ("new city"), which today is Nablus.

Philosophers do that sort of thing as well, most notably, I think, in the case of the logical positivists, with the British philosopher A. J. (Alfred Jules) Ayer as a prime exemplar. He worked in the empiricist tradition, begun by Christians John Locke and George Berkeley, who insisted that all meaningful talk derived from actual or potential experience. They were concerned that we not talk "non-sense."

On this model, Berkeley, a Protestant bishop, faulted the Roman Catholic doctrine of transubstantiation, the one that said Communion wine literally turned into the blood of Christ, despite the fact that it continued to look, smell, feel, taste, and sound like wine. He counted as nonsense the Catholic insistence that, though the appearances stayed the same, the underlying "substance" changed. Berkeley said he had no experience of such substance because it was, indeed, a fiction.

Fast forward to the twentieth century, where many European and American philosophers were in the thrall of science, based on empirical testing, with confirmation and disconfirmation of various hypotheses. By their light, we couldn't run a check on the claim that God existed, that adultery was evil, or that a sunset was more beautiful than a rotting possum. All the hopeful religionists, moralists, and aesthetes had to go on were moods, faith projections, and feelings of disgust and delight—but those were subjective, not objective. So the positivists were happy to relegate books on metaphysics, ethics, and aesthetics to the fiction shelf. Accordingly, Christians were mocked as foggy-headed dreamers, and those making moral and value judgments were counted as "emoters." Hence, "Adultery is evil" amounted to nothing more than "Adultery? Boo!" (A convenient conclusion for the adulterous Ayer.)

The positivists, in their haste to dismiss religion and ethics, didn't do justice to their own principle—that a meaningful statement must be at least possibly testable, if not actually testable in the foreseeable future. By their guideline, though we may never be able to run tests on the exact makeup of the interior of a planet detected in another galaxy, we can at least imagine going there in an advanced space ship, boring to the core, and taking readings. That's good enough for a logical positivist to treat as meaningful (even if implausible) the statement, "The center of Planet X is mainly molten zinc."

But, by that standard, the Christian has grounds to say, "Jesus will one day return and the saints will ultimately be gathered to the Father in heaven." That's a possible experience, one with "cash value." So it's meaningful to talk that way. (Several philosophers speak of "eschatological verification" in this connection.)

So when they try to use the reign of current science and its parochial testability as an overlay to obscure territory properly belonging to the "things of God," they transgress. At this point, doctrinal statements may well involve faith, but it is *propositionally meaningful* faith, faith that we believe will one day "become sight."

Another problem with logical positivism: It's self-referentially inconsistent, for their own dictum (that only experientially verifiable statements are meaningful) is not experientially verifiable. It's merely a stipulation, a policy commitment. So it's meaningless?

Discussion Questions:

1. Apart from eschatological verification, are Christian claims testable on Earth? For instance, does the Bible's claim that all believers are indwelt by the Holy Spirit face refutation if the majority of Christians on Earth commit suicide in the face of grave difficulties, including persecution, poverty, and family tragedy? And what about Philippians 4:6–7?: "Be anxious for nothing, but in everything by prayer and supplication, with thanksgiving, let your requests be made known to God; and the peace of God, which surpasses all understanding, will guard your hearts and minds through Christ Jesus." Does the "peace of God" testimony of a host of Christians facing grave difficulties count for anything in defending the meaningfulness of "Jesus loves me"?

2. The comedian George Carlin said that the expression "jumbo shrimp" was an oxymoron, but there are more serious examples in play in the culture. For instance, "African-American racist" is declared a nullity since, on one definition, a person can only be a racist if he or she is able to oppress those of another racial group. Can you think of other attempts to gain advantage in an argument by claiming, through a charge of contradiction, that a certain set of entities doesn't exist?

3. There's something of a curious Christian counterpart to logical positivism, one that claims the absurdity/impossibility of genuine knowledge outside the revelation of Scripture, that secular morality is a wasteland (or an unwitting theft of Christian insight), and that attempting apologetics with an unbeliever is like trying to teach algebra to a pig. Can we go too far in denying respectability to irreligious thinkers?

4. Is there any form of literature—philosophical, religious, poetic, etc.—which is essentially meaningless, incapable of rising to the level or truth or falsity?

5. We hear that ideas have consequences, but I sometimes flip the maxim, saying, awkwardly, that consequences have ideas. The formulation came to me when I was reading E. Michael Jones's book *Degenerate Moderns: Modernity as Rationalized Sexual Misbehavior*. His thesis was that a range of anti-Christian opinion shapers (e.g., Alfred Kinsey, Pablo Picasso, Margaret Mead, and Sigmund Freud) ventured into decadence, and then fashioned ideologies that reflected, excused, and normalized their wicked behavior. Is it fair to suggest that A. J. Ayer would craft and advance a philosophy that let him off the moral hook for his infidelities?

Pineal Gland

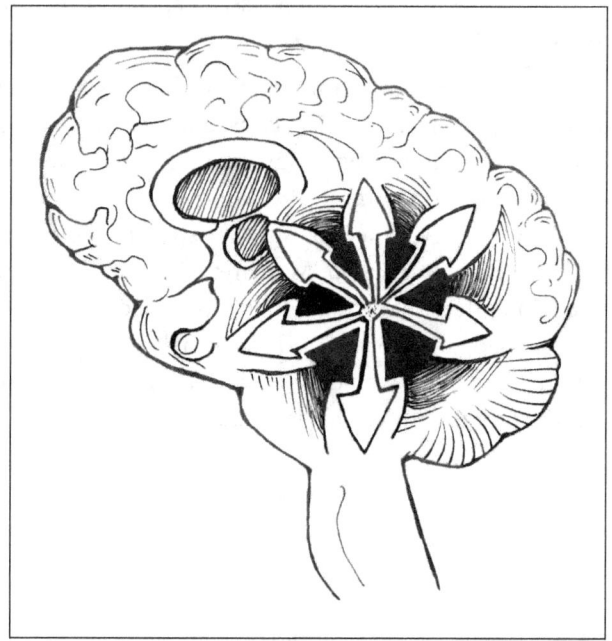

Today, we know that the pineal gland, located deep within the brain, secretes the hormone melatonin, which helps us sleep. But three centuries ago, René Descartes believed it was where mind and body interacted. By "body," he meant things that had weight and three dimensional "extension" (took up space), and this included the brain, which occupies about eighty cubic inches and weighs around three pounds. On the other hand, the "furniture" of the mind lacks volume and heft. Thus, it makes no sense to ask, "How many inches wide is that fear?" or "Did that inspiration weigh more than a pound?" So the physical world is one thing, the mental world another, but they're not insulated from one another, and, for Descartes, the pineal gland is the transfer station, the key to "interactionist dualism."

The notion of two separable components is captured in such songs as "I'll Fly Away":

> Some bright morning when this life is over,
> I'll fly away.
> To that home on God's celestial shore,
> I'll fly away.

It echoes the message of Psalm 90:10: "The days of our lives *are* seventy years; And if by reason of strength *they are* eighty years, Yet their boast *is* only labor and sorrow; For it is soon cut off, and we fly away." In other words, like John Brown (in Pete Seeger's words), our bodies may be "mouldering in the grave." Nevertheless, "we" (minds) will fly away (from our bodies) to something much better.

As with virtually every claim in philosophy, options, rivals, and critics abound. Among those in play have been:

- *Materialism*, which claims that there's only body, just the physical, and when the body rots, that's all she wrote. Mental states are nothing more than brain states. (Sometimes it's called the "Mind-Brain Identity Theory".) Incidentally, one might think that a naturalistic atheist would default to this position, but Thomas Nagel is a recent prominent exception. He saw consciousness as an irreducible reality.

- *Idealism*, which claims that talk of physical bodies is translatable without loss of meaning into talk of experiences. For instance, once you describe the look, smell, taste, feel, and sound of an apple, you've exhausted the meaning of "apple." On this model, you have actors/experiencers and experiences, none of it physical in the materialists' sense. Death is simply transition from one sort of experience to another.

- *Epiphenomenalism*, a form of dualism, which recognizes the distinctiveness of mind and body, but with mind/consciousness "supervenient," simply along for the ride, as it were. The brain does its thing, and the mind experiences it as an act of will, an episode of worry, etc.

- *Neutral monism*, which says there is only one thing of which we speak, but in two different ways—using "P-predicates" for physical properties (such as the average length of the adult brain at 6.3 inches) and "M-predicates" (such as the feeling of satisfaction over vindication).

Of course, mind-brain dualists don't have to sign off on Descartes' pineal gland hypothesis. The aforementioned epiphenomenalists don't, but neither do the *occasionalists*, who say that God manages all the interactions. For instance, when I decide to lift a pencil, he (on that occasion) prompts the body to lift it. And when someone jabs me with a pencil, he (on that occasion) gives rise my pain experience. That's a lot of work for God, but he's up to it, being omnipotent and omniscient.

Furthermore, idealists can have their own sort of mind-body dualism. For them, the experience of excruciating pain is utterly different from the experience of seeing a thumb banged by a closing car door. The former is mental, the latter physical.

And so it goes, with tweaks and reformulations and "breakthroughs" of one sort or another.

One surprising development is the emergence of "Christian physicalists." Papers on this approach have surfaced at meetings both of the American Philosophical Association and the Evangelical Theological Society. Pardon my skepticism, but I don't see that they succeed in "saving the appearances," as they used to say, i.e., for making sure that no phenomena were left hanging out there, whether in the form of consciousness or biblical texts. And it seems to me they've gotten reckless in wielding Ockham's razor (so as to not "multiply things beyond necessity"). In trying to trim fat, they've cut out muscle . . . or rather spirit.

Discussion Questions:

1. Which of the mind-brain options we've noted could most readily accommodate mental telepathy? Psychokinesis?

2. In 1848, Phineas Gage was seriously injured in a railroad construction accident. A spark ignited a demolition charge that drove an iron rod through his head, destroying much of brain's left frontal lobe. Though accounts conflict, the general take was that Gage suffered a dramatic change in personality for the worse, such that friends said he was no longer himself. Psychologists used this case to argue that there was a strong link between personality and parts of the brain. Would this be a problem for Descartes, particularly in his capacity as a Christian?

3. In drug tests and the practice of medicine, benign placebos are often employed to provide contrasting data for the medication in question, or to stimulate the psyche to so as to bring about improvement in the absence of ailment-specific pharmaceutical therapy (for instance, a patient gets a "sugar pill" instead of an antibiotic). What do you make of the "placebo effect"?

4. Quite apart from such drugs as Prozac and Zoloft, back rubs and massages have been shown to alleviate depression. How does this work?

5. Descartes believed that animals were like machines, without consciousness of pain, so beating a draft horse was similar to banging on a malfunctioning soft drink dispenser. Is there any reason to believe this, or to doubt it? And if animals have minds/souls, where do they go when the animal dies?

6. Doctors used to declare a person dead when the heart stopped. Today, they employ the "Harvard criteria" for "brain death" (including pupils being dilated and fixed and flat EEG readings taken a day apart). Is the brain, indeed, the key indicator of life and death?

7. In 1901, Massachusetts doctor Duncan MacDougall weighed six bodies just before and after death and found a discrepancy, pegging it at twenty-one grams. This he postulated as the weight of the soul. Since then, the notion has been repeated in a range of media, including film and popular music. (And, of course, it has not fared well in scientific circles.) Could there be anything to MacDougall's approach and conclusion?

Prester John

THE legendary Prester (*Presbyter*/Elder) John shows up in the writings of Shakespeare, Robert Lewis Stevenson, and Umberto Eco, and in the pages of Marvel and DC Comics. In the Middle Ages, he appeared on maps which were meant to be serious, maps which variously located him in Central Asia, India, and Ethiopia. Many believed that the spiritual progeny of the Apostle Thomas had somehow carved out a marvelous somewhat-Christian kingdom (the citizens being Nestorians, who had trouble with the divine/human unity of Jesus' nature) in the midst of Muslim lands, and that this John now presided over it.

Which brings us to a curious proposition upon which British philosopher Bertrand Russell worked out, namely, "The present king of France is bald." No, Prester John was not the king of France, but both figures were non-entities, the king of France in Russell's day and Prester John in any day. And, for our purposes, we may apply the same analysis.

Philosophers of the logical persuasion have been interested in the "truth value" of each proposition. (By the way, a proposition is not the same as a sentence since the same proposition may be expressed in very different sentences—"It's raining"; "Es regnet"; "Il pleure.") That way, they can be rolled into chains of thought and argument. Take, for instance, what's called *modus ponens* (from *modus ponendo ponens*, meaning, "By affirming, I affirm"). It simply says that the combination of "If A, then B" and "A" will give you "B." Fill in whatever you want, and it works. Start with "If my dog has fleas" for "If A"; for "then B," add "then I'll give him away." So it's spring-loaded. Affirm that your dog has fleas, and it follows that you're giving him away. The same goes for other setups, e.g., "If you heat water to 100 degrees centigrade, then it boils." And there are other such logical rules, expressible in different schemes, with names like "disjunctive syllogism" and "De Morgan's laws." But to make them work, you need to have propositions which are either true or false (according to the law of excluded middle) and not both true and false (according to the law of non-contradiction). It's like a binary, digital computer program.

So what shall we make of "Prester John is bald"? (And I don't mean "Prester John" as a strictly literary figure; we're not asking whether Hester Prynne and Superman were wearing red letters on their chests.) It hard to say whether it's either true or false, for there's no such person as Prester John. It's a non-starter when it comes to truth. But Russell pressed ahead. He said that we should treat "The present king of France is bald" as the conjunction of three propositions:

a. There exists something that is the present king of France.
b. There is only one thing that is the present king of France.
c. Anything that is the present king of France is bald.

This, then, would render the proposition false. Done and done. Crisis of indeterminacy averted.

Alas, there are other troublesome propositions to bedevil the logicians and those who dream of a comprehensive systemization of knowledge, with everything in its proper place. The most prominent one goes back to the ancient philosopher from Crete, Epimenides, who said, "All Cretans are liars." The problem was that he himself was a Cretan, and if what he says is true, then it's false; it's a lie. But if it's false, it's true, since it makes the point of Cretan mendacity. (By the way, some say that the Apostle Paul was confused about this in Titus 1:12, when he was criticizing Cretans. They say he mistook Epimenides' philosophical puzzle for a moral pronouncement. But I think it's the other way around. Epimenides was simply playing off the well-deserved reputation of his people, a reputation with which Paul was well acquainted.)

The puzzle has been refined to the statement, "This sentence is false." (If false, true; if true, false; so both—a contradiction.) And it's been mapped onto a number of enterprises, including mathematics (by Kurt Gödel) and set theory. In this later connection, Bertrand Russell (according to Martin Gardiner) asked us to consider the barber who shaved every man in town who didn't shave himself. So does the barber shave himself? Well, if he does, he doesn't, but if he doesn't, he does. Doh! Or, to put it otherwise, is this barber to be found within the *set* of those whom he shaves?

To address the paradox, set theorists have simply disallowed the membership of a set within itself. It's a little bit like the scene where Groucho Marx is playing a doctor: The patient lifts his arm and complains it hurts when he raises it. "Dr. Hackenbush" responds, "Well, don't do that" and then asks for his fee. (The same goes for "This sentence is false." Declare it bogus and move on.)

The big problem is that if you allow a contradiction into the system, you can prove anything. To demonstrate, let's stipulate that "B" means something crazy, like "Chickens are whales." So here goes, a look at the logical fallout of contradicting oneself:

Premise: A and not-A. (a contradiction)

> Step 1: A. (If, following the premise, both A and not-A are true, then A alone is true all by itself.)
>
> Step 2: A or B. (If A is true, then it doesn't matter what you put for B; all it takes is for one side of the "or" to make the whole sentence true.)
>
> Step 3: Not-A. (If both A and not-A are true, then not-A alone is true all by itself.)
>
> Step 4: B. (If, as it says in step 3, that it's either A or B or both, then by eliminating the A side, with the "trump card" of step 3, you're left with B, which, again, is crazy. But it's been "proven.")

So a contradiction is like a virus. Let it into your computer, and it'll eat everything.

Of course, this leaves open the question of whether language and knowledge are so orderly as all that, or if this is even an ideal. Metaphors, for one thing, are right unruly, yet sentences containing them can be quite meaningful. So too paradoxes. How about the opening to Dickens's *A Tale of Two Cities*, "It was the best of times, it was the worst of times . . ."?

Discussion Questions:

1. What about a logical rule that reads, "If A then B; then if not-A, not-B follows"? Does that work? Insert some actual propositions for A and B to check it out.

2. What do we make of the truth status of verses such as Proverbs 22:6, "Train up a child in the way he should go, and when he is old he will not depart from it"? If the man turns out bad, the parents must have blown it. Right? And Proverbs 6:10–11: "A little sleep, a little slumber, a little folding of the hands to rest—and poverty will come on you like a thief and scarcity like an armed man" (NIV). If a sluggard gets rich, is the proposition false?

3. The precision of logic and the complexity of language can make for a bad fit. For instance, the symbol "v" ("or") allows for "either/or" or "both." It can be used to represent the true proposition "Dogs are not cats, or clarinets procreate" (since the A is true and the B is false). But that sounds weird, since we hear the sentence to say there is some sort of connection between the A and B, which there isn't here. But, for purposes of symbolic logic, it's perfectly well formed as an either/or statement. It just takes either a true A or a true B to make the whole thing true, and, *voilà!*, "A or B" is true. So are we trying to put a square peg in a round hole when we seek to force our talk into symbols?

4. In our seminary doctoral program, you may take symbolic logic toward satisfying your foreign language requirement, as a substitute for German, French, or Latin. Does this make sense?

5. Some missiologists are unenthusiastic about defining the church by a clearly circumscribed set, an us-versus-them approach that puts the heathens outside and the faithful inside. In the late 1980s, Paul

Hiebert spoke of these as "bounded sets," as opposed to "centered sets." The former thinks of corrals, the later of open prairie with an attractive water well at the center. The former asks who's in and who's out (with, of course, the aim of inviting others in); the latter speaks of who's closer and who's farther away from the source of life. Does it make sense to speak of a "centered set"?

6. There are other logics and other notations. Aristotle introduced syllogistic logic (whose propositions began with the words, 'All,' 'No,' and 'Some,' as in "All men are mortal"), and two millennia later, the Englishman John Venn showed how such sentences, in groups of threes, could be represented by interlocking circles. Some logics (called modal) deal with the meanings of possibility and necessity (with square, diamond, and fishhook symbols), with the connections between knowledge and belief (epistemic and doxastic), and with the play between that which is obligatory and that which is permissible (deontic). In the propositional logic discussed above, sometimes "and" is represented by a dot and other times by an ampersand . . . and even by a "K" in the "Polish notation" of Jan Lukasiewicz, where "Kab" means "A and B." Have you every dabbled in one of these systems of formal logic? Was it rewarding beyond the pleasure in monkeying with a new game or puzzle?

The Progressive Treasure Map

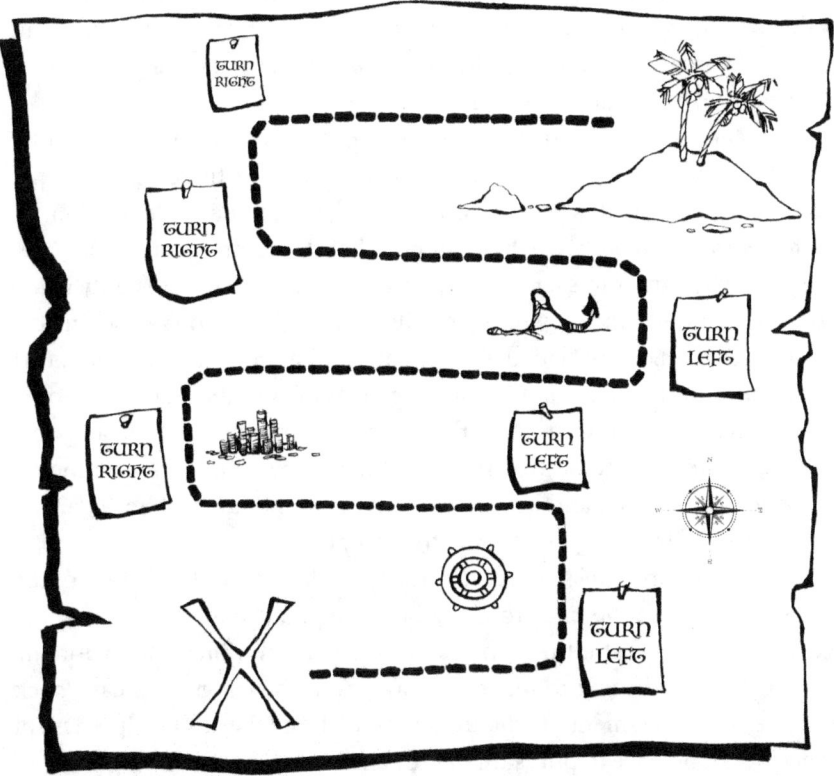

The Danish philosopher Søren Kierkegaard spoke of truth in terms of "inwardness," "passion," and "subjectivity," and is best known for urging a "leap of faith" into belief in God and Christ. Opponents of Kierkegaard and the Christian faith say this means that trust in Jesus is irrational and that one must simply make a mindless jump into the Kingdom.

Of course, SK meant no such thing. Rather, he held that no "proofs" could establish the soundness of an overarching worldview, with its supreme metaphysical commitments. Arguments come up short, whatever your "religion," including the religion of materialism. (Blaise Pascal had a similar stance, from which he proposed a "wager" wherein one sizes up the life outcomes of rival religious "bets.") But more than this, Kierkegaard showed no patience for those who suggested that we could be detached, disinterested observers, sizing up big truth claims from the sidelines, acting as if they were diving or gymnastics judges in business suits, holding up our score cards while the athletes tumbled and sweated in the arena. Rather, evaluators must have thrown themselves into the sport (with "blood, sweat, and tears") before they are qualified to comment on what's going on, before truth can become Truth for them, if you will.

His take on the state Lutheran church of his day was merciless, for he saw it as an institution of spiritual deadness, even where there was doctrinal correctness. Against this type of domesticated, safe, respectable religion, he wrote *Fear and Trembling*, which argued that Abraham's "crazy" and "deplorable" willingness to sacrifice Isaac was normative. For it was only when Abraham showed himself willing to follow through on God's shocking directive that the Lord provided an alternative. The order to kill Isaac didn't make sense up to that point, for the aged Abraham and Sarah had only one son to fulfill the promise that they would parent a vast nation, and now God was telling him to destroy that son. But God was building a nation on faith and not on flesh, and he insisted that the grandfather of both genetic and Christian "Israel" would be a faith exemplar.

Hence the "progressive treasure map." With our "Godlike" view of the sketch, we can see the end from the beginning, but the pilgrim can only see one instruction at a time, and he must enter upon the route before he gets what he needs next to make his way toward blessings. You can't stick with the cool assessment of a natural law ethicist or the aloof snippiness of an aesthete. You have to put "skin in the game" (the often terrifying game of radical discipleship) to really grasp reality.

Kierkegaard also had no patience for the wildly abstract philosophizing of Hegel and others who presumed to utter sweeping and detached descriptions and prescriptions for mankind. He insisted that wisdom comes at the gut level, and for this he has been labeled the "father of existentialism." (In this connection, Francis Schaeffer blamed SK, at least indirectly, for the dreadful atheistical work of Jean-Paul Sartre. But this is less than fair, something like blaming Paul for antinomianism, since he said we're "saved by grace, not works."

Kierkegaard's language was over the top, a linguistic overcorrection. He could have said that truth was, at base, correspondence with reality, but that one was in no position to appropriate and preach it until he had lived it, with some risk. Or something like that. Indeed, speaking of truth "as subjectivity" invites theoretical malpractice. But hammers aren't scalpels, and we're fortunate that he took up the hammer he did.

DISCUSSION QUESTIONS:

1. What aspects of the contemporary church would provoke Kierkegaard's rebuke?

2. One of my seminary professors observed, after years in the pastorate, that Christians typically stalled out in spiritual growth if they couldn't bring themselves to do two things—tithe and evangelize. What do you make of this?

3. Kierkegaard was a harsh critic of the church and the culture—for its superficiality, its pretentions, its aloofness, and its love of comfort. And, as one philosopher has observed, you probably wouldn't want to have him as a neighbor, for he wasn't particularly sociable. Could he still be described as "Christlike"?

4. Dietrich Bonhoeffer, another Christian thinker who wrote on radical faith (hence, the title of his book *The Cost of Discipleship*), went to the gallows for connections with the plot take down Hitler. Unlike Abraham, who was stopped from killing, Bonhoeffer understood his spiritual duty as one to work with assassination conspirators. Could passionate Christianity lead one legitimately to violence?

5. Does your own faith evidence the inwardness that Kierkegaard commended?

6. Kierkegaard's passionate discipleship suggests daring ventures such as missionary work among cannibals, refusal to recant the faith at the point of an ISIS sword, or selling all one has and giving the proceeds to the poor. Could one equally display radical servanthood to Christ by remaining silent when itching to speak a well-deserved prophetic word or sticking with an unpromising ministry when an exciting option beckoned?

The Strip Map

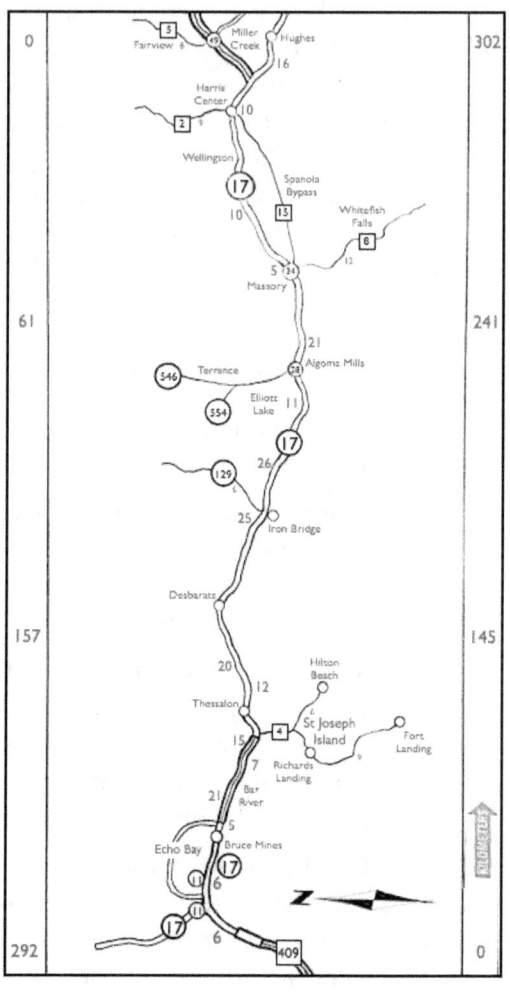

Years ago, when our family negotiated the two-lane highways of America to visit relatives from Michigan to Florida, we'd get help from one of our kin in the form of a AAA strip map booklet. The American Automobile Association would custom-make these for their members (and, by extension, their relatives, though probably not intentionally). Page after page, they centered on the desired route, with highlight markings to show detours, speed traps, and such. Unlike standard fold-out road maps, they didn't show the big picture. They didn't contextualize the roads, but only showed what came up next on the highway.

These strip maps have a Kantian feel to them, in that they help picture the distinction between the noumenal and phenomenal worlds in his scheme of things. Immanuel Kant was "awakened from his dogmatic slumbers" by Scottish empiricist David Hume, who said that experience gives us no grounds for confident belief in God, miracles, the substantial soul, or the laws of nature. He said we could only make sense of the soul or person as a bundle of disjointed perceptions, thoughts, and feelings, and that natural causes boiled down to the regular conjunction of events (e.g., water boiling whenever it reached 100 degrees centigrade at sea level); a conjunction on which we project causality, even though things could turn out quite differently the next time (e.g., water not boiling until it reached 200 degrees) with no "violation" of a law, which was, itself, nothing more than a useful fiction.

Kant, a devotee of science in proper "Enlightenment" mode, was shocked that Hume could make such crazy claims, but he struggled to say where the Scot went wrong. In due season, he came up with a radically different account of things, one that saved the sanctity of science from the skeptics. To do so, he had to effect what's called a "Copernican revolution." Instead of arguing that we can build our rock-solid devotion to scientific law from the testimony of experience, we should go at it the other way around: we can assume the inviolability of the causal system, and then figure out why it's inviolable. And so he cast a "transcendental" argument, claiming to find the ground of the possibility of what we know to be true.

His answer was ingenious. He said that the English philosopher John Locke was terribly mistaken when he said that the mind was a blank slate (*tabula rasa*) upon which experience would write. Rather, the mind was a reality-shaper itself, with inescapable categories of thought built right in. One of these was the category of causality. Thus, whatever we experience is already rigged to be causally related to other things in the world. And the world itself was cast within space and time, both of which are "pure forms of intuition," to use Kant's terminology.

He called this rigged world the realm of "phenomena." In contrast, the realm of things as they really, really were was called the "noumena." Though the noumenal world was beyond our experience, it was useful, even important, to believe in some notions "out there"—God, freedom, and immortality. These "regulative" ideas helped keep morals afloat, but they were nowhere as certain as the products of physics and chemistry, e.g., such "phenomenal" items as Bernoulli's principle or Avogadro's number.

This bifurcation sent shock waves through the philosophical world, with a host of subsequent philosophers extending or riffing on the scheme, including fellow Germans—Fichte, Hegel, Schopenhauer, and Nietzsche. Of course, others pushed back hard, including, in the late-twentieth-century, Christian theologian Francis Schaeffer, who said that Kant had drawn an arbitrary "line of despair," pushing really important matters, such as belief in God, out into a relative la-la land. And much earlier, back in England, Thomas Reid made a case for "common sense" philosophy, an alternative to both Hume and Kant. He argued that God had not put up

MAPS

comprehension of the world and its standards as a target we could not hit with our understanding.

So back to the strip map: Though your automobile journey might take you past suffocating green kudzu plants springing from red Georgia clay, over snow-capped peaks in the Rockies, down past the Grand Canyon, through the Mojave Desert, ever approaching the blue Pacific, your page of strip map gives you only black on white, a line winding up the middle of the narrow, rectangular page—some numbers and letters, but no topography or global context. It's "phenomenal," if you will, but not "noumenal."

DISCUSSION QUESTIONS:

1. Did Kant really prompt despair by saying belief in God was substantively different from belief in the law of gravity? What's the problem with saying that matters of faith are less certain than matters of science?

2. It's said that the victors get to write history, and so it was that humanists of the "Renaissance" and "Enlightenment" (*Aufklärung* for Kant) got to label their predecessors denizens of the "Dark Ages." Was calling those centuries "dark" and the current ones "reborn" and "light-blessed" fair? If so, in what sense and to what extent? If not, why not?

3. In one form or another, philosophers such as Leibniz and Parmenides (his version, *ex nihilo nihil fit*, i.e., "Nothing comes from nothing") have put forth the principle of sufficient reason, which I might paraphrase, "Things don't just happen." By this standard, a fire marshal will not answer the reporter's question "What started the blaze?" with "Nothing, really. It just started." Is this conviction, as Kant argues, "wired" into our makeup, or is it either the result of observations made throughout the years or a reflection of our doggedness in getting at the cause, if in fact there was one, leaving no stone unturned on the chance that there might be something to find under it?

4. Is Kant right when he argues that immortality is a morally compelling idea, helping to keep people from doing really bad things? A lot of folks talk as though it is nothing to fear, saying of ethically questionable and Christ-indifferent people, "Well, he's in a better place now," or (chuckling) "Heaven'll never be the same now that he's up

there." On the other hand, film villains about to die will shout cavalierly, "See you in hell!") What place does concern with the afterlife and eternal judgment play in the minds and hearts of most people?

5. What if someone argued that Kant had things upside down, that the world of real experience centered on God and that the natural world was just a dream, a noumenal realm of imagined challenges to perfect our souls? If they sing, "He walks with me, and he talks with me, and he tells me I am his own," are they right? What if the mystical testimonies of Teresa of Avila and John of the Cross were more epistemologically compelling than reports from a weather station on Mount Washington or experimental reports from Fermilab? May a Christian think such things? Must a Christian think such things?

Strongpoint Defense

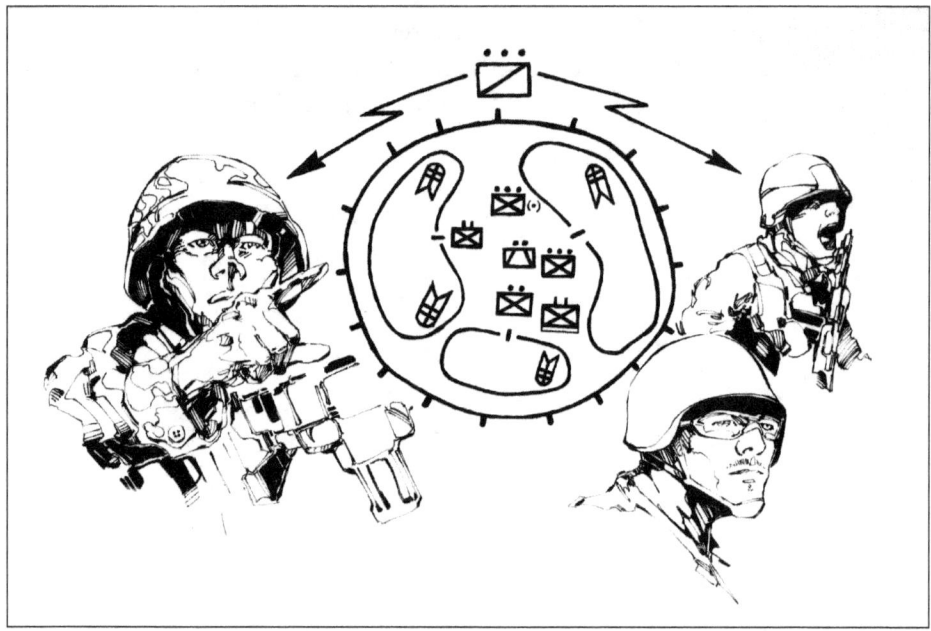

THIS map features standard military symbols for a strongpoint defense. It represents infantry and antitank units dug in within a circle, with perimeter screening from a cavalry unit, prepared to hold their position at all costs. (It's sometimes called the "die in place" defense.)

Elsewhere in this book, we look at a case of irrationality (*Owen v. Crumbaugh*) where a father changed his last will and testament to endow spiritualist enterprises, including their practice of séances. But a measure of irrationality has been at play, through the years, in so august a sector as the sciences, and Thomas Kuhn put the matter on the table with his 1960s book *The Structure of Scientific Revolutions*. In it, he argued that science didn't progress uniformly by building a great wall of wisdom, with current insights resting on those of early scientists, rows of bricks resting on rows of bricks, all the way down. Instead, it proceeded by a series of revolutions as one model ("paradigm") was overthrown by another.

Mars provides a case in point. In Aristotle's day, astronomers were convinced that everything in the heavens was round, whether as spherical bodies or circular orbits. But careful observation, night after night, revealed a problem, an anomaly or failure at lawfulness. The "Red Planet" wasn't behaving. When sky gazers connected the dots (say, concerning the position of Mars at midnight on successive evenings), they found an elliptical loop-the-loop instead of an orderly run along a wide arc. But instead of saying that they were wrong about necessary roundness (since Mars did non-round things), they doubled down on roundness, postulating a variety of circles within circles with off-centered axes to generate astronomical whirligigs for theory protection. It sort of worked on paper, but things got so unwieldy that by the time Kepler suggested that some heavenly movement was elliptical (as when planets slingshot around the sun and take long trips into space before gravity asserts itself and they return for another slingshot), astronomers were ready for a change. Furthermore, Kepler's model helped put to rest the notion that the Earth rather than the sun lay at the center of things. (The earlier confusion kept them from realizing that the retrograde motion of Mars was really a matter of perspective, of parallax, as Earth overtook Mars in its obit.)

One might think that the old scientists would simply say, "Oops. Never mind. Sorry. Now I get it." Rather, they dig in and defend their original system to the end. As Kuhn quotes Nobel physicist Max Planck to say, the scientific ruling class pretty much has to die off before the transition can come. After all, they've invested their whole lives in one way of thinking, and they'll fight tooth and nail on behalf of their convictions, their grants, their honor, their professional prerogatives, and their legacy, never admitting that they've been leading their students and the public on a snipe hunt all along.

Some of this is good. You don't toss off your deep commitments lightly. Indeed, you spend your whole life defending them against all sorts of gainsayers and critics. (Christians should be as familiar as anyone with the need for perennial apologetics, and no single observation, e.g., the death of a child despite the parents' prayers, should cause you to say, "Well, I guess God isn't good or all-powerful after all.") But, in some instances, there may come a time when you need to throw in the towel and consider that what you thought to be "inference to the best explanation" (IBE) didn't get you to

Maps

the best explanation after all. Of course, some do this, but a lot fight to the finish. Not strictly rational, but such are the creatures we are, notwithstanding all our degrees and awards and notoriety.

Discussion Questions:

1. Who has most to lose in the dispute over the age of the world, old earthers or young earthers? Who has a more workable fallback position? Are the answers different when it's a disagreement internal to the church, as opposed to disagreement between believers and non-believers?

2. How might Kuhn's observations be applied to the controversy over anthropogenic climate change?

3. Largely because of Kuhn, the word "paradigm" has come to enjoy (or suffer) wide usage outside the natural sciences, even with regard to church growth models. Have you heard the word in play in other contexts?

4. Max Planck spoke of old "experts" hanging onto their tattered paradigms until death, so as to preserve what they could of their dignity (which is not to say they aren't true believers till the end). Martyrs, such as those who went to their deaths in Roman spectacles, stick with their paradigms to the end, but their demise is hastened by their intransigence. Can you think of others who have been destroyed (literally or figuratively) by righteous stubbornness?

5. At a philosophical meeting, I read a paper arguing the failure of a classic pro-abortion essay by Judith Jarvis Thomson (one in which she asked us to imagine a dying violinist hooked up to life support in the form of another person, who didn't volunteer for the job). For the sake of analogy, I drew on "alimentary laws" requiring children to care for destitute parents. Whatever the merits of my argument, only one of the seven or eight comments in the Q&A session was even moderately friendly. When it was all over, an officer of the group took me aside and asked, in effect and rhetorically, "What did you expect? You rejected a chapter in the philosophical canon."

   In my theological work, I'd spoken freely of the biblical canon (from the Greek word for "measuring stick"), the collection of books that made up the Old and New Testaments, but I'd not heard that term used in philosophy. I'd always thought of philosophers as an irreverent, unruly bunch, not at all reluctant to puncture pretensions and subject anything that came down the pike to fierce scrutiny. But now I was being told that the profession had its "scripture," and that I had better gird up my loins if I presumed to question it. I'd run up against a paradigm of favored thinking on this grave moral matter, and I should expect as much blowback as a skeptic would face should he question the veracity of miracle accounts in the Gospel of Mark. So did Kuhn provide a handle for understanding schools of thought in the humanities as well as the sciences?

The T and O Map

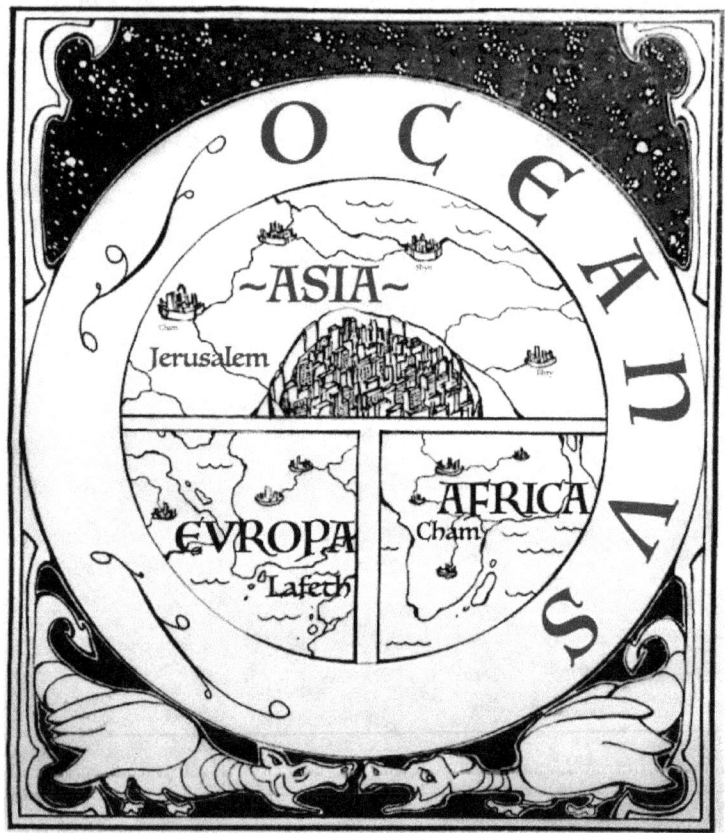

THE medieval T and O map of the "world" (the O) put Jerusalem at the top, with the Mediterranean (literally, "middle of the earth") forming the main post of a cross (T), the crossbars being the Don (Tanais) River on the left and the Red Sea or Nile on the right. This orientation gave primacy to Christ, the Jewish Son of God, the Messiah. It honored the Jesus of Colossians 1:15–20:

> Who is the image of the invisible God, the firstborn of every creature: For by him were all things created, that are in heaven, and that are in earth, visible and invisible, whether they be thrones, or dominions, or principalities, or powers: all things were created by him, and for him: And he is before all things, and by him all things consist. And he is the head of the body, the church: who is the beginning, the firstborn from the dead; that in all things he might have the preeminence. For it pleased the Father that in him should all fulness dwell; And, having made peace through the blood of his cross, by him to reconcile all things unto himself; by him, I say, whether they be things in earth, or things in heaven. (KJV)

I think the map is an admirable picture of the philosophy of Thomas Aquinas, whose take on the universe and truth and goodness was theocentric. In his "Treatise on Law" (Questions 90–108 in the *Summa Theologica*), he spoke of the way in which God, whose purposes are the eternal law, reveals himself through natural law (the created order and the moral code imprinted on the conscience—general revelation) and divine law (Scripture—special revelation). These apply, in turn, to human law (whose content we can mutually support with non-Christians because of a statute's deep-down reasonableness, as, for example, regarding the prohibition of incest) and canon law or church law (which deals with such things as ordination, worship, and mission).

By the way, followers of Thomas Aquinas call themselves Thomists instead of Aquinists. Movements are usually tied to last names, e.g., Lutherans (Martin Luther), Wesleyans (John Wesley), Kantians (Immanuel Kant). But Thomists, like Mennonites (Menno Simons), went the other direction.

This is not an otherworldly approach, focused on the content and activities of heaven (though this activity is immanent, eminent, and imminent), but rather it deals with the world as God's creation and as our current field of endeavor. It doesn't picture one continent (Europe to the left and Africa to the right) aflame in ruins and the other in verdant plenitude, but rather, it features both as habitable and instructive.

Aquinas gave us a philosophical "map," and not just a theological one, because it incorporates the deliverances of the "light of reason." It's a philosophical map which encourages Christian colleges to acknowledge, with Augustine, that "all truth is God's truth," and to press the faculty to "integrate faith and learning," bringing their disciplines to bear upon their understanding of Scripture and vice versa.

As testimony to his regard for both faith and reason, Aquinas wrote in dialogical fashion, acknowledging objections to his position, and then drawing on Scripture, theologians, and even world-class "secular" thinkers (his far-and-away favorite being Aristotle, whom he calls simply "The Philosopher") to parry them and forge his own declaration on the issue. The Protestant Reformers were not as keen as Aquinas on man's ability to sort things out for himself, so they insisted that the Bible alone is the decisive authority (*sola scriptura*) and not just a member of the steering committee. In his influential film series *How Should We Then Live?*, Francis Schaeffer was hard on Aquinas. In one scene, Schaeffer, in his alpine walking outfit, enters a room where the medieval philosopher is at work at his desk, and proceeds to fault him for the way in which he elevated reason to the level of the Bible. Well, yes, that's been a problem in Catholic theology/philosophy. But we need to be careful to not throw the baby out with the bath. Romans 1 and 2 give us good cause to respect the counsel of natural law, and Evangelicals, including the theologian Carl F. H. Henry, have noted this.

Discussion Questions:

1. Traditionally, Protestants have been more open to contraception than Catholics. How strong is the scriptural argument for rejecting birth control? How strong is the Catholic argument that sex outside the "procreative and unitive" context is "disordered" and "unnatural"?

2. Atheist Nat Hentoff joined religious leaders in denouncing partial-birth abortion. He argued from a position of secular humanism. Does general revelation provide other such grounds for co-belligerency with non-believers in the public square?

3. Tertullian asked, rhetorically, "What has Athens to do with Jerusalem?" His point was to reject philosophy and the products of unregenerate human wisdom. In his book *How the Irish Saved Civilization*, Thomas Cahill argues that since the Irish had not been brutalized by the Greeks and Romans, they were not as inclined to toss classical learning overboard. Did these Irish monks have more insight than Tertullian?

4. Some construe the doctrine of "the sufficiency of Scripture" as meaning that no other writing or teaching may presume to extend the canon. Others take it to mean we must not "go slumming" into

secular thought, searching for guidance in, say, psychological counseling. What do you make of this?

5. Try your hand at constructing alternative maps representing different worldviews, with, say Vienna, Rome, Mecca, New York, or Taos at the top-center of the T (or whatever letter or symbol you prefer).

The Upside-Down World Map

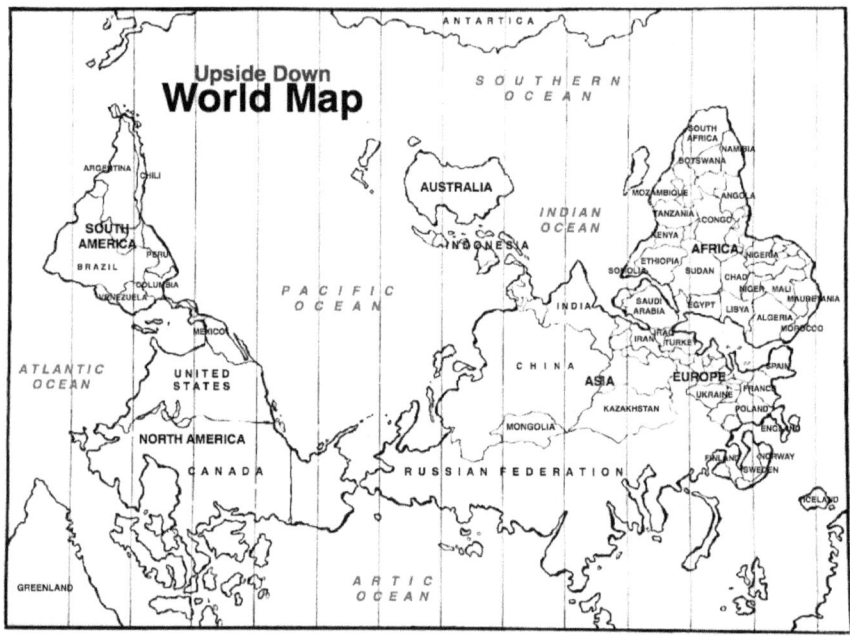

Sometimes called the "south-up map," the upside-down world map is meant mainly to critique or correct a bias toward northern, Western culture. Technically, it's a tossup which pole you put at the top, for there's no up or down in space (so far as we know, and whatever that means). An alien could just as easily happen upon planet Earth with a view of Antarctica at the top of his spacecraft "windshield" and Cape Horn at the bottom, and then orient his subsequent maps so as to place Hudson Bay well below Tierra del Fuego on the page. Nothing crazy about that. Of course, magnetism now draws compass needles north, giving that region something of a navigational cache, but I'm told that the poles could reverse one of these days, erasing that "advantage."

The Upside-Down World Map

Be that as it may, a south-up map provides us an introduction to the ethical thinking of Friedrich Nietzsche, whose book *Zur Genealogie der Moral* (*On The Genealogy of Morals*), argues that conventional moral thinking has things upside down. By his lights, "good" originally meant something like "intimidating." The "good" man was the one to whom deference was owed, the "alpha male" who could command the respect of the room, whether for his strength or guile—"the man of strife, of dissention ... the man of war," the one who delivers "knightly-aristocratic value judgments," which presuppose "a powerful physicality" and which show themselves strong not only in war, but in "adventure, hunting, [&] dancing."

Nietzsche goes on to say that a sniveling bunch of losers—Jews and Christians, to be specific—couldn't compete on those grounds, so they foisted a new concept of goodness on the world, and it stuck. Since they were weak and contemptible, they condemned physical domination and pride. In place, they enthroned such "virtues" as "love, joy, peace, patience, kindness, goodness, faithfulness, gentleness, self-control" (to quote from Galatians 5:22–23). After all, those "lame" postures were ones the Judeo-Christians could manage. They resented being counted disgusting under the old system, so they engineered an inversion to assuage their shame and demean their betters.

Nietzsche took it upon himself to put the willful, imposing renegade back on top, designating him an *Übermensch* ("Overman" or "Superman"), and celebrating him in *Also sprach Zarathustra* (*Thus Spake Zarathustra*). The Overman, following Nietzsche, would say, "The great epochs of our life come when we gain the courage to rechristen our evil as that which is best in us" (from *Jenseits von Gut und Böse/Beyond Good and Evil*). By this, he meant that we become magnificent when we say, in effect, "Put it on my resume," when critics tell us we're not nice.

Though Nietzsche enthusiasts are quick to protest that he would have found Hitler distasteful, Hitler was an unabashed fan, as were other fascists of the day. (In a famous photo, the Führer stands admiringly before a bust of the philosopher, and he was known to send flowers to Nietzsche's sister.) It's not hard to see why, for Nietzsche's disparagement of the Jews served nicely the program of a despot who commissioned Teutonic members of his "Aryan Master Race" to run the death camps at Auschwitz and Treblinka.

Though Jews and Christians were the villains in his story, many a nonbeliever has faulted the ethics represented in Nietzsche. For instance, in Plato's *Republic* (written in Greece centuries before Jesus's birth, a Greece which had no use for the religion of the Jews), Socrates made philosophical mincemeat of Thrasymachus' claim that "might makes right," a view akin to Nietzsche's. And, indeed, many men of war, adventure, and physical prowess have also been champions of Judeo-Christian values. Oliver Cromwell and George Washington are two cases in point. Furthermore, those who think the Jews are weak should examine the results of Israel's Six-Day and Yom Kippur Wars.

In short, Nietzsche got it wrong both morally and historically, and those who aspire to upend the ethical order in favor of the elites of their choosing embarrass themselves conceptually and place themselves in harm's way at the hands of "weak" peoples who refuse to suffer their stupid and, yes, "bad" tyranny.

Discussion Questions:

1. Has the term "Christlike" become so tenderized that we might be tempted to call the Jesus of the gospels "unchristlike" in upending the money changers' tables at the temple and calling the Pharisees "whitewashed sepulchers" (not to mention the triumphant, returning Christ of Revelation)?

2. It's reported that when British Prime Minister Margaret Thatcher heard that Germany was expressing pride at having beaten England at their national game, soccer, she replied, "They may have beaten us at our national game, but we beat them twice at their national game in the twentieth century." (She was referring to war.) If there is anything to this dig, could Nietzsche have played a part in setting his country's tone?

3. If we rank the world's moral orientation on a 1–10 scale, with Nietzsche at 1 and Jesus at 10, where are we? (Or pick a continent, nation, state, or city as your area of concern.)

4. What would you think of a pastor who, in Nietzsche's words, delivered "knightly aristocratic value judgments," which presupposed "a powerful physicality" and reflected an aptitude for "adventure, hunting, [&] dancing"? What about a parishioner with these qualities?

5. Does composer Richard Strauss's "*Also sprach Zarathustra*," the opening theme for the film *2001: A Space Odyssey* (1968), capture

the Nietzschean spirit? Could it just as well serve as the prelude for a Sunday morning church service?

6. British theologian Theo Hobson listed three marks of a moral revolution: 1) that which was condemned must be celebrated; 2) that which was celebrated must be condemned; 3) those who once condemned that which is now celebrated must now be condemned as well. What examples spring to mind? Are they fortunate or unfortunate?

Weather Map Copies

SEVENTEENTH-CENTURY philosopher René Descartes turned the philosophical world upside down (or right side up) when he said that we needed some ground of certainty for our knowledge claims. As it stood, thinkers could proffer all sorts of rival and extravagant assertions, citing this or that authority, running down this trail or that as far as their premises, concepts, and intellectual finagling could take them. For instance, Descartes' contemporary Baruch Spinoza cranked pantheism (all is God) out of the notion of "substance." How then might we adjudicate among theories and evaluate the thought castles of competing kingdoms?

Descartes' answer was to institute a sort of zero-based budgeting, whereby everything would be on the table for review. His approach was to doubt everything he could—the existence of God, the reliability of his senses and intuitions—until he hit rock bottom, which he famously said was the reality of some thinking going on. It didn't have to be correct thinking; just any old sort of thinking would do, for at least it showed that a thinker was at work. (*Cogito ergo sum.*)

Once he'd nailed that down as a certainty, he proceeded to work his way up—to a necessarily infinite cause (God) for his thoughts of the infinite, and then on to the reliability of his "clear and distinct ideas," since a good God wouldn't create and sustain a systematically deceptive world. Philosophers have not been as impressed with his climb out as with his climb down; the quest for bedrock certainty was just the thing. And historians have said the Cartesian moment marked the transition from third-person to first-person philosophy, from commentaries to essays.

Catholic Philosopher Benjamin Wiker (whose forerunners, the medieval philosophers, were much taken with third-person commentaries on such authorities as the Bible and Aristotle) was not impressed, and he grouped Descartes with Machiavelli as one of the enablers for the terrible things to come from the pens of Nietzsche, Marx, Darwin, Freud, Kinsey, and even Hitler. (His rogues gallery can be found in *Ten Books that Screwed Up the World: And 5 Others That Didn't Help*.) Far more impressed were British philosophers (and professing Christians along with Descartes) John Locke and George Berkeley, who argued that the foundation for sensible talk was sense experience.

This approach, "empiricism," went off the Christian rails (indeed, the theistic rails) when David Hume "mounted to the cabin" (yes, a reference to Casey Jones). He sowed doubts about not only God and his goodness (vs. Descartes); not only about the difference between primary and secondary qualities, such as, respectively, motion and color (vs. Locke); not only about transubstantiation (cf. Berkeley); but also about causality and the human soul. And, at this point, the skeptical Scot Hume woke the German science enthusiast Immanuel Kant from his "dogmatic slumbers," and Kant constructed a system whereby mechanisms of the mind rigged things so that the Enlightenment could proceed with its confidence in human savvy, while preserving less-certain but still-edifying talk of God and the afterlife. (See the "Strip Map" article on Kant and his successors.)

Undaunted, the empiricists maintained that you had to give epistemic priority to the deliverances of the senses. After all, "This is red" is less susceptible to disconfirmation than "This is Saddam Hussein" (for he had body doubles); which, in turn, is less certain than "Iraq has weapons of mass destruction" (which may have been sent to Syria); which is even less certain than "Iraq will flourish under democracy" (which depends upon a lot of variables, many of which are in play in an artificially constructed

Maps

nation beset with long-standing strife involving Sunni, Shia, Chaldean, Yazidi, Baathist, and Kurdish factions, with some overlap).

The ideal is to build some sort of knowledge edifice on relative certainties, going from solid particulars to summary generalities, from "This hurts" and "This scenery is enjoyable" to "We should put cancer warnings on cigarette packages" and "We need a national park system." Of course, you don't have to be methodical in building up from brute sensations. You can make theoretical leaps to "Gender fluidity is salubrious" or "Bleeding the patient will reduce fever." But whatever big guesses you might make, you still have to submit them to sensory checks and balances. Fly as high as you will, but you still have to come back to the ground of experiential testing.

Doubling down on certainty, they moved from talking about red things to talking about red "sense data," and then to adverbial constructs such as "being appeared to redly," which brings us to our newspapers pictured above. An Austrian philosopher named Ludwig Wittgenstein came to England, where he worked with Bertrand Russell at Cambridge, first as a foundationalist (with a firm structure of foundational meanings and propositions, matching up nicely with the world), and then as an "ordinary language" philosopher. (Thus we talk of the early and late Wittgenstein, with a move from *Tractatus Logico-Philosophicus* to *Philosophical Investigations*.) In this latter mode, he took aim at the foundational status of "redness" and such, arguing that these personal experiences were beyond confirmation. How, for instance, can I be sure I'm using the word "red" consistently? Maybe I called the same color "orange" yesterday. And it does no good to answer, "No, I recall that yesterday I used the word to refer to the same experience." It's like buying a second copy of the same newspaper to see if what the first copy said was true. (Or, in this instance, to see if the weather map is correct: "No way it's 75 degrees in Boston in January! Clerk, here's a dollar. Give me another copy of today's *Tribune*. I have to be sure.")

Wittgenstein argued that it was impossible to sort this out. Since I couldn't be sure of my self-checks, then there was no valid usage rule enforcement, and so, in effect, no rules. But you can't have a ruleless language, in this case a ruleless "private language," so the personal experience foundation was bogus. His answer was to wax sociological rather than personal when it came to valid speech. He started talking about "language games" and "family resemblances" as the way we can extend the meaning of terms. (See the discussion of art as an "open concept" in the Brancusi article.) It

Weather Map Copies

was a much looser enterprise, not so much a matter of certainties as conventionalities. So, "Take *that*, empirical foundationalism!"

(For what it's worth, I devoted part of my dissertation to defending empiricism from the "private language" argument. I argued that metaphor, a respectable part of language, was not rule governed, that there were no exclusive "constitutive rules" for speech, so Wittgenstein's ground for disallowing private language was unreasonable. Be that as it may, there is still abroad the conviction that there has to be a way to get to the bottom of theoretical disputes, and if the bottom is utterly independent of what we can experience, whether in this world or the world to come, then, again, it is "non-sense." We may not have knockdown certainty, and we may not build out theories brick by brick from the sensory ground up, but what you say has to be answerable to what we can conceivably experience.)

As for God, the *sensus divinitatis*, delightful intimations of glory in the resplendent heavens, and gratifying impulses and insights leading to and stemming from regeneration—all can set us on the right track in our thinking, but the track needs to lead us to a "face-to-face" encounter to be fulfilled. Experience early; experience late (what Ian Ramsey calls "eschatological verification"). All part of the empiricist's program.

Discussion Questions:

1. Might the "second newspaper" argument be extended to my claim that I am happy, afraid, puzzled, or envious? Could I be construing as happiness what yesterday I construed as sadness and not know that I'd done it? If so, would behavior be the only way I could legitimately talk about emotions and moods?

2. Wittgenstein was homosexual. His translator and editor, G. E. M. Anscombe, was a devout Catholic, for whom sexual purity groups on major secular campuses are named. While Anscombe was a Thomist (a philosophical "disciple" of Thomas Aquinas), Wittgenstein was not a Christian of any stamp, and his writings reflect it. What business does a Christian have in highlighting the work of an unbeliever?

3. In 1972, New Yorker film critic Pauline Kael said, "I live in a rather special world. I only know one person who voted for Nixon. Where they are I don't know. They're outside my ken. But sometimes when I'm in a theater I can feel them." Is there an analogue to Wittgenstein's

newspaper problem in our tendency to live in an echo chamber, where we confirm our biases by consulting only people who think like us?

4. Is the chance of getting your color judgments wrong so remote that it borders on absurdity to say that I might confuse blue with gray on successive days? Are we so obsessed with absolute certainty at the foundational level that we miss the point that foundations are meant only to provide *relative* certainty, a workable starting point for verification?

5. Jackson Pollock's drip paintings (e.g., *Number 8*) are said to have "alloverness" in that there is no clear point of focus. Rather, each part bears the same value. In contrast, we find paintings like Rembrandt's *The Night Watch*, where, through chiaroscuro (the distinction between light and dark, dramatic) some figures dominate the work. Has Wittgenstein commended a sort of "alloverness" by consigning meaning and truth to the external and shifting world of community perceptions and behavior?

Index of Names

Abbott, Jim, 29
Albright, Alvin, 96
Ali, Muhammed (Cassius Clay), 152
Anaximander, 8
Anaximenes, 8
Anscombe, G.E.M., 32, 201
Anselm, 54, 128
Aquinas, Thomas, 3, 4, 33, 116, 135, 191-192, 201
Aristotle, 3, 42, 57, 78, 79, 116, 119, 133, 134-136, 155
Arnold, Matthew, 96
Asbury, Francis, 33
Augustine, 3, 4, 54, 57, 64, 83, 100, 115, 128
Austin, J.L., 70-72, 75
Ayer, A. J., 4, 167, 169

Bacon, Francis, 52
Baker, John Robert, viii
Beck, Harry, 141
Beethoven, Ludwig von, 100
Behe, Michael, 39
Bell, Clive, 20
Bentham, Jeremy, 64
Berkeley, George, 4, 101, 167, 199
Bernadin, Joseph, 64
Bernini, Gian L., 148
Bierstadt, Albert, 97
Blackmun, Harry, 28
Blackstone, William, 52
Bloom, Allan, 79, 110
Boethius, 57
Bok, Sissela, 124

Bonhoeffer, Dietrich, 181
Borges, Jorge Luis, 117-118
Broome, Arthur, 47
Buckley, William F., 161
Buddha, Gautama, xvi, 147
Bunyan, John, 107
Bush, George W., 11, 44

Cabal, Ted, 128
Cahill, Thomas, 192
Calvin, John, 124
Camus, Albert, 115
Carlin, George, 168
Carey, William, 102
Carroll, Lewis, 117
Carson, Ben, 160
Chakrabarty, Ananda, 101
Chambers, Whittaker, 39
Chesterton, G.K., 10
Chomsky, Noam, 165
Cicero, 48
Cochran, Johnny, 66
Coppenger, Raymond, vii
Coulter, Ann, 36
Crichton, Michael, 132
Cromwell, Oliver, 196

Danto, Arthur, 20
Darrow, Clarence, 60-62
Darwin, Charles, 15, 39, 50, 146, 199
Dembski, William, 39
De Morgan, Augustus, 175
Dennett, Daniel, 4
Derrida, Jacques, 4, 111

Index of Names

Descartes, Rene, 6, 67, 68, 146, 170, 198, 199
Dewey, John, 141
Dickie, George, 20
Dore, Clement, viii
Douglas, William O., 91
Duchamp, Marcel, 20

Eco, Umberto, 174
Eddy, Mary Baker, 83
Einstein, Albert, 92
Empedocles, 8
Engels, Friedrich, 163
Epicurus, 8, 127
Epimenides, 175

Feinberg, John, 85
Fichte, Gottlieb, 146, 183
Fodor, Jerry, 136
Foot, Philippa, 34
Foreman, Amanda, 48
Foucault, Michel, 111
Freud, Sigmund, 169, 199
Fry, Roger, 20, 97

Gaddifi, Muammar, 111
Gage, Phineas, 172
Gardiner, Martin, 176
Gay, Peter, 98
Genet, Jean, 116
Gericault, Theodore, 97
Gödel, Kurt, 176
Gurdjieff, Georgi, 137-138

Hand, Learned, 76-78
Handel, George F., 148
Hegel, G.W.F., 146, 164-165, 183
Helmsley, Leona, 50
Henry, Carl F.H., 192
Hentoff, Nat, 192
Heraclitus, 8
Hiebert, Paul, 177-178
Hitchens, Christopher, 54
Hitler, Adolph, 3, 98, 120, 149, 195
Hobbes, Thomas, 15, 127
Hobson, Theo, 197
Hoffer, Eric, 128

Huckabee, Mike, 82
Hume, David, 4, 38, 42, 83, 97, 182-183, 199
Husserl, Edmund, 115
Huysum, Jan van, 97

Innocent VIII, 48
Isidore of Seville, 152

Jackson, Andrew, 104
James, William, 5, 141, 142, 144
Jefferson, Thomas, 25, 28
John of the Cross, 185
Johnson, Phillip, 37, 38
Jones, E. Michael, 169
Judson, Adoniram and Ann, 102

Kael, Pauline, 201
Kant, Immanuel, 4, 28, 43, 46, 89, 92, 146, 157, 159-161, 182-184
Keble, John, 14
Keller, Helen, 29
Kepler, Johannes, 187
Ketchum, Richard, viii
Kierkegaard, Søren, 13, 115, 179-180
King, Martin Luther, 165
Kinsey, Alfred, 169, 199
Kripke, Saul, 150-151, 153
Kuhn, Thomas, 110, 134, 186-189
Kushner, Harold, 82

Lachs, John, viii
Leary, Timothy, 3
Leibniz, Gottfried, 4, 126-128, 146
Lenin, Vladimir, 163
Leon, Richard, 123
Lewis, C. I., 142
Lewis, C. S., 11, 54, 63, 107
Lewontin, Richard, 37
Liddell, Eric, 89
Lincoln, Abraham, 103
Locke, John, 15, 43, 105, 146, 167, 199
Lukasiewicz, Jan, 178
Luther, Martin, 52
Lyotard, Jean-François, 110

MacDougall, Duncan, 173

Index of Names

MacIntyre, Alasdair, 78
M'Naghten, Daniel, 62
McTaggart, J.M.E, 58
Majors, Alexander, 47
Machiavelli, Niccolo, 199
Mao Zedong, 163
Marcel, Gabriel, 115
Marcy, Oliver, 33
Marshall, John, 103, 105-106
Mather, Cotton, 52
Marx, Groucho, 176
Marx, Karl, 15, 163, 199
Mead, Margaret, 169
Mendel, Gregor, 134
Menninger, Karl, 153
Merleau-Ponty, Maurice, 115
Mill, John Stuart, 4, 23
Milne, A. A., 138
Molina, Luis de, 57
Morris, Errol, 150
Mothersill, Mary, 88
Mubarak, Hosni, 111
Munch, Edvard, 97
Mussolini, Benito, 142-143

Newton, Isaac, 128, 135
Nietzsche, Friedrich, 4, 62-63, 111, 146-147, 183, 195-196, 199
Novak, Michael, 89
Nozick, Robert, 63

O'Hair, Madalyn Murray, 14
O'Reilly, Bill, 36
Ouspensky, P.D., 137

Parmenides, 8
Pascal, Blaise, 4, 54, 161, 180
Paul, 24, 78
Peck, Don, 150
Peirce, Charles S., 128, 141
Picasso, Pablo, 169
Piper, John, 89
Planck, Max, 187
Plantinga, Alvin, 4, 6, 36
Plato, 3, 8, 15, 19, 48, 73, 79, 100, 115, 119, 130, 150, 195
Pollock, Jackson, 202

Popper, Karl, 15, 164
Protagoras, 17
Pythagoras, 8

Rawls, John, 63
Reid, Thomas, 183-184
Reynolds, Joshua, 97
Rice, Luther, 102
Rousseau, Jean-Jacques, 15
Rowe, William, 84
Rubens, Peter P., 148
Ruskin, John, 95-96
Russell, Bertrand, 4, 110, 127, 174-176, 200
Ryan, George, 64

Sartre, Jean-Paul, 113-116, 180
Sayre, Wallace, 97
Schaeffer, Francis, 180, 183, 192
Schlafly, Phyllis, 36
Schopenhauer, Arthur, 146-147, 183
Scott, Dred, 103
Scruton, Roger, 47
Searle, John, 72-73
Shakespeare, William, 68, 174
Siebert, Charles, 48
Singer, Peter, 47
Socrates, 3-4, 19, 62, 90, 100
Sowell, Thomas, 25
Spinoza, Baruch, 47, 138-139, 146, 198
Stalin, Joseph, 149
Stevenson, Robert L., 174
Strauss, Richard, 196
Suarez, Francisco, 64
Swinburne, Richard, 134

Teresa of Avila, 185
Tertullian, 192
Thales, 8
Thatcher, Margaret, 196
Theocritus, 28
Thomson, Judith Jarvis, 188
Tolstoy, Leo, 20, 97

Unamuno, Miguel de, 115

Venn, John, 178

Index of Names

Vitoria, Francisco de, 64
Voltaire, 127

Washington, Denzel, 160
Washington, George, 150, 196
Weitz, Morris, 20
Wesley, John, 33, 52
Whistler, James A. M., 95-96
Whitehead, Alfred North, 19

Wiker, Benjamin, 199
Wilde, Oscar, 116
Willard, Frances, 33
William of Ockham, 173
Wisdom, John, 84
Wittgenstein, Ludwig, 20, 72, 110, 200-201
Wright, Frank Lloyd, 137
Wright, Steven, 117

Index of Scripture

OLD TESTAMENT

Genesis
1:26-28	48-49, 160
7:11-24	85
9:3	48
9:6	49
22:1-19	180

Exodus
20:1-17	15, 53, 147
22:19	165

Leviticus
18:21	165

2 Samuel
12:1-4	122

Nehemiah
2:11-16	73

Psalm
8:4	17
90:4	59
90:10	171

Proverbs
6:6	50
6:10-11	177
14:12	143
21:1	84
22:6	177

Ecclesiastes
3:1-8	123

Isaiah
61:3	143

Jeremiah
8:7	50

Daniel
4:28-33	124

Matthew
7:6	53
13:24-30	24
23:13-15	122

Mark
5:1-20	44, 124

Luke
2:52	11

Acts
16:11-15	124
17:16-34	3, 6

Index of Scripture

Romans
2:14-15	116
8:28	85
9:16-18	124

Galatians
5:22-23	156, 195

Ephesians
2:8-9	181

Philippians
2:12	24
4:6-7	168

Colossians
1:15-20	190
2:8	8

1 Corinthians
5:11	24
13:1-3	143

2 Timothy
3:1-9	164

Titus
1:12	176

Hebrews
4:12	45
11:2	39

James
2:18	143

2 Peter
3:8	59

1 John
2:15	131

Revelation
1:10	147

www.ingramcontent.com/pod-product-compliance
Lightning Source LLC
Chambersburg PA
CBHW070315230426
43663CB00011B/2144